New Casebooks

POETRY

WILLIAM BLAKE Edited by David Punter
CHAUCER Edited by Valerie Allen and Ares Axiotis
COLERIDGE, KEATS AND SHELLEY Edited by Peter J.Kitson
JOHN DONNE Edited by Andrew Mousley
SEAMUS HEANEY Edited by Michael Allen
PHILIP LARKIN Edited by Stephan Regan
PARADISE LOST Edited by William Zunder
DYLAN THOMAS Edited by John Goodby and Chris Wigginton
VICTORIAN WOMEN POETS Edited by Joseph Bristow
WORDSWORTH Edited by John Williams

NOVELS AND PROSE

AUSTEN: *Emma* Edited by David Monaghan
AUSTEN: *Mansfield Park* and *Persuasion* Edited by Judy Simons
AUSTEN: *Sense and Sensibility* and *Pride and Prejudice* Edited by Robert Clark
CHARLOTTE BRONTË: *Jane Eyre* Edited by Heather Glen
CHARLOTTE BRONTË: *Villete* Edited by Pauline Nestor
EMILY BRONTË: *Wuthering Heights* Edited by Patsy Stoneman
ANGELA CARTER Edited by Alison Easton
WILKIE COLLINS Edited by Lyn Pykett
JOSEPH CONRAD Edited by Elaine Jordan
DICKENS: *Bleak House* Edited by Jeremy Tambling
DICKENS: *David Copperfield* and *Hard Times* Edited by John Peck
DICKENS: *Great Expectations* Edited by Roger Sell
ELIOT: *Middlemarch* Edited by John Peck
ELIOT: *The Mill on the Floss* and *Silas Marner* Edited by Nahem Yousaf and Andrew Maunder
E.M. FORSTER Edited by Jeremy Tambling
HARDY: *Jude the Obscure* Edited by Penny Boumelha
HARDY: *The Mayor of Casterbridge* Edited by Julian Wolfreys
HARDY: *Tess of the D'Urbervilles* Edited by Peter Widdowson
JAMES: *Turn of the Screw* and *What Maisie Knew* Edited by Neil Cornwell and Maggie Malone
LAWRENCE: *Sons and Lovers* Edited by Rick Rylance
TONI MORRISON Edited by Linden Peach
GEORGE ORWELL Edited by Byran Loughrey
SHELLY: *Frankenstein* Edited by Fred Botting
STOKER: *Dracula* Edited by Glennis Byron
STERNE: *Tristram Shandy* Edited by Melvyn New
WOOLF: *Mrs Dalloway* and *To the Lighthouse* Edited by Su Reid

DRAMA

BECKETT: *Waiting for Godot* and *Endgame* Edited by Steven Connor
APHRA BEHN Edited by Janet Todd
REVENGE TRAGEDY Edited by Stevie Simkin
SHAKESPEARE: *Antony and Cleopatra* Edited by John Drakakis
SHAKESPEARE: *Hamlet* Edited by Martin Coyle
SHAKESPEARE: *Julius Caesar* Edited by Richard Wilson
SHAKESPEARE: *King Lear* Edited by Kiernan Ryan
SHAKESPEARE: *Macbeth* Edited by Alan Sinfield
SHAKESPEARE: *The Merchant of Venice* Edited by Martin Coyle
SHAKESPEARE: *A Midsummer Night's Dream* Edited by Richard Dutton
SHAKESPEARE: *Much Ado About Nothing* and *The Taming of the Shrew* Edited by Marion Wynne-Davies
SHAKESPEARE: *Romeo and Juliet* Edited by R.S. White
SHAKESPEARE: *The Tempest* Edited by R.S. White

(continued overleaf)

SHAKESPEARE: *Twelth Night* Edited by R.S. White
SHAKESPEARE ON FILM Edited by Robert Shaughnessy
SHAKESPEARE IN PERFORMANCE Edited by Robert Shaughnessy
SHAKESPEARE'S HISTORY PLAYS Edited by Graham Holderness
SHAKESPEARE'S TRAGEDIES Edited by Susan Zimmerman
JOHN WEBSTER: *The Duchess of Malfi* Edited by Dympna Callaghan

GENERAL THEMES

FEMINIST THEATRE AND THEORY Edited by Helene Keyssar
POSTCOLONIAL LITERATURES Edited by Michael Parker and Roger Starkey

New Casebooks Series
Series Standing Order
ISBN 0–333–71702–3 hardcover
ISBN 0–333–69345–0 paperback
(outside North America only)

You can receive future titles in this series as they are published by placing a
standing order. Please contact your bookseller or, in case of difficulty, write to
us at the address below with your name and address, the title of the series and
the ISBN quoted above.

Customer Services Department, Macmillan Distribution Ltd
Houndmills, Basingstoke, Hampshire RG21 6XS, England

New Casebooks

THE MILL ON THE FLOSS
and
SILAS MARNER

GEORGE ELIOT

EDITED BY NAHEM YOUSAF
AND ANDREW MAUNDER

palgrave

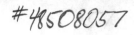

First published 2002 by
PALGRAVE
Houndmills, Basingstoke, Hampshire RG21 6XS and
175 Fifth Avenue, New York, N. Y. 10010
Companies and representatives throughout the world

PALGRAVE is the new global academic imprint of
St. Martin's Press LLC Scholarly and Reference Division and
Palgrave Publishers Ltd (formerly Macmillan Press Ltd).

ISBN 0–333–72804–1 hardback
ISBN 0–333–72805–X paperback

This book is printed on paper suitable for recycling and made from
fully managed and sustained forest sources.

Cataloguing–in–publication data

A catalogue record for this book is available
from the British Library.

A catalogue record for this book is available
from the Library of Congress

10   9   8   7   6   5   4   3   2   1
11   10   09   08   07   06   05   04   03   02

Printed in China

Contents

Acknowledgements

The editor and publishers wish to thank the following for permission to use copyright material:

Terence Dawson, for '"Light enough to trusten by": Structure and Experience in *Silas Marner*', *The Modern Language Review*, 88:1 (1993), 26–45, by permission of the author and the Modern Humanities Research Association; Joshua D. Esty, for 'Nationhood, Adulthood, and the Ruptures of *Bildung*: Arresting Development in *The Mill on the Floss*', *Narrative*, 4:2 (1996), 144–59. Copyright © 1996 by the Ohio State University Press, by permission of Ohio State University Press; Susan Fraiman, for material from *Unbecoming Women: British Women Writers and the Novel of Development* by Susan Fraiman, pp.121–41. Copyright © 1993 Columbia University Press, by permission of Columbia University Press; Mary Jacobus, for material from *Reading Women: Essays in Feminist Criticism* by Mary Jacobus, pp.62–79. Copyright © 1986 Columbia University Press, by permission of Routledge and Columbia University Press; José Angel García Landa, for 'The Chains of Semiosis: Semiotics, Marxism, and the Female Stereotypes in *The Mill on the Floss*', *Papers on Language and Literature*, 27:1 (1991), 41–50. Copyright © 1991 by the Board of Trustees, Southern Illinois University at Edwardsville, by permission of *Papers on Language and Literature*, Southern Illinois University at Edwardsville; J. Hillis Miller, for 'The Two Rhetorics: George Elliot's Bestiary' from *Writing and Reading Differently: Deconstruction and the Teaching of Composition and Literature*, ed. G. Douglas Atkins and Michael L. Johnson (1985), pp.101–14, by permission of University Press of Kansas; Jeff Nunokawa, for 'The Miser's Two Bodies: *Silas Marner* and the Sexual Possibilities of the Commodity', *Victorian Studies*, 36:3 (1993), 273–92, by permission of Indiana University Press; Jim Reilly, for material from

Shadowtime: History and Representation in Hardy, Conrad and George Eliot by Jim Reilly (1993), pp.83–97, by permission of Routledge; Sally Shuttleworth, for material from *George Eliot and Nineteenth-Century Science: The Make-Believe of a Beginning* by Sally Shuttleworth (1984), pp.79–95, by permission of Cambridge University Press.

Every effort has been made to trace the copyright holders but if any have been inadvertently overlooked the publishers will be pleased to make the necessary arrangement at the first opportunity.

General Editors' Preface

The purpose of this series of New Casebooks is to reveal some of the ways in which contemporary criticism has changed our understanding of commonly studied texts and writers and, indeed, of the nature of criticism itself. Central to the series is a concern with modern critical theory and its effect on current approaches to the study of literature. Each New Casebook editor has been asked to select a sequence of essays which will introduce the reader to the new critical approaches to the text or texts being discussed in the volume and also illuminate the rich interchange between critical theory and critical practice that characterises so much current writing about literature.

In this focus on modern critical thinking and practice New Casebooks aim not only to inform but also to stimulate, with volumes seeking to reflect both the controversy and the excitement of current criticism. Because much of this criticism is difficult and often employs an unfamiliar critical language, editors have been asked to give the reader as much help as they feel is appropriate, but without simplifying the essays or the issues they raise. Again, editors have been asked to supply a list of further reading which will enable readers to follow up issues raised by the essays in the volume.

The project of New Casebooks, then, is to bring together in an illuminating way those critics who best illustrate the ways in which contemporary criticism has established new methods of analysing texts and who have reinvigorated the important debate about how we 'read' literature. The hope is, of course, that New Casebooks will not only open up this debate to a wider audience, but will also encourage students to extend their own ideas, and think afresh about their responses to the texts they are studying.

John Peck and Martin Coyle
University of Wales, Cardiff

Introduction

NAHEM YOUSAF and ANDREW MAUNDER

I

The rise, fall and resurgence of George Eliot's literary reputation represents many of the changes and fluctuations in literary taste that have taken place over the last 150 years. In her own day Eliot was widely regarded as an iconic sage, a sibyl, and moral teacher – roles which she herself seemed to take very seriously.[1] Through her work, the English novel was seen to reach new heights of social and philosophical concern. Justin McCarthy described the reading public's adulation of Eliot as 'a kind of cult, a kind of worship'.[2] Yet in the years following her death, attacks on a morality that came to be regarded as quintessentially Victorian rapidly displaced Eliot as a literary idol and she was transformed into a figure of ridicule: 'Pallas with prejudices and a corset', as W. E. Henley labelled her in 1895.[3]

The publication, in 1885, of John Cross's *George Eliot's Life as Related in her Letters and Journals* had intensified this emerging picture of a stern moralist and respectable daughter of middle England who ruled over the realm of English literature as majestically as Queen Victoria did her own Empire.[4] With Cross's careful expurgation of any details of his wife's life that could be regarded as scandalous or simply improper, it became very easy to see Eliot as 'oppressively great',[5] too out of date and too pompous to speak meaningfully to a modern sensibility.[6] Indeed, in 1906, Edmund Gosse referred to her cruelly as a 'ludicrous pythoness'.[7] Later, in 1919, he returned to the subject, remembering her as

1

a large, thickset sibil [sic], dreamy and immobile, whose massive features, somewhat grim when seen in profile, were incongruously bor-
dered by a hat, always in the height of the Paris fashion, which in those
days commonly included an immense ostrich feather; this was George
Eliot. The contrast between the solemnity of the face and the frivolity
of the headgear had something pathetic and provincial about it.[8]

Although one wonders how trustworthy Gosse's recollections are,
his intentions seem clear enough. He sought to make Eliot look
foolish and grotesque, and does so by making fun of her transgression of two fiercely protected boundaries: class and gender.[9] Gosse
thus singles out her bizarre headgear, which he presents as a frivo-
lous attempt on the part of a less than attractive woman to appear *à
la mode*. By emphasising the enormity of Eliot and her hat, Gosse
presents her as vulgar, lacking in subtlety, and obsessed by triviali-
ties. As an intellectual with working-class origins (her father, Robert
Evans, was a land-agent), Gosse's constructed Eliot cannot possibly
have mastered the intricacies of good taste and refinement of dress.
Even when decked out in the height of Parisian fashion, Eliot's
provinciality is, for Gosse, all too evident. Eliot's hat is also, of
course, a covering for what was often viewed as a masculine brain
and Gosse's attack is demonstrative of his inability to accept a
woman of intellect. He is unable to fault her either as a scholar or
an artist and therefore attempts to contain her by deriding her
appearance and depicting her as a social outsider. In contrast, and
although renowned for her own snobbery, Virginia Woolf was able
to appreciate Eliot's achievements as an artist without dwelling on
her class origins and depicting her as a 'counter-jumper'. Woolf
published her important centennial essay 'George Eliot' in the *Times
Literary Supplement* in November 1919, a time when it was all too
clear that Eliot was no longer in favour. Articles in periodicals referring to her work had become few and far between, and those that
existed were often derogatory and condescending. She was, as
Woolf noted, 'one of the butts for youth to laugh at', yet, she
added, 'They do not find what they seek and we cannot wonder'.
Woolf admired Eliot's brilliance and originality, describing
Middlemarch as 'one of the few English novels written for grown-up
people'.[10]

    It is interesting to speculate as to why Eliot was so little regarded
by the beginning of the twentieth century. In a very obvious sense,
the decline and subsequent revival of interest in Eliot's work are
indicative of the kinds of shifts and changes in taste and understand-

ing that Hans Robert Jauss details in his important *Toward an Aesthetics of Reception* (1982). Jauss would argue that the lack of interest in Eliot at the beginning of the twentieth century can be attributed to a change in the 'horizon of expectations' and an 'altered aesthetic norm' that causes 'the audience [to] experience formerly successful works as outmoded and [to] withdraw its appreciation'.[11] Yet, it is also apparent that Eliot was a frustrating figure simply because she was very difficult to pigeonhole. Amongst women writers there was resentment at and envy of what was regarded as Eliot's tendency to hold herself too far above the fray. In particular, her presentation of herself as superior, not so much in what she said but in her bodily movements, was disliked, as were her gestures and assumption that she was different from others. Eliza Lynn Linton, one of many contemporaries for whom the Eliot cult provoked gall coupled with admiration, deemed her fellow novelist (whom Linton had known in the early 1850s as plain Marian Evans) 'artificial, posée, pretentious, real ... interpenetrated head and heel, inside and out, with the sense of her importance as the great novelist and profound thinker of her generation'.[12] For the succeeding generation of 'New Women' writers in the 1880s and 1890s Eliot was seen to fall too short of their radical gestures (just as she did for many feminist critics in the 1970s). Such impatience is exemplified in *The Woman Who Did* (1895), when Grant Allen's Herminia Barton declares in a typically impassioned moment: 'When George Eliot chose to pass her life with Lewes on terms of equal freedom, she defied the man-made law – but still, there was his wife to prevent the possibility of a legalised union. As soon as Lewes was dead, George Eliot showed she had no principle involved, by marrying another man.'[13] Elsewhere, the belittling of Eliot's physical appearance combined with the sense of her as what Jane Gallop would term a 'phallic mother', whose influence must be shaken off, lay behind a good many reactions.[14] At the same time, Eliot's lifestyle (in spite of her best efforts, referring to G. H. Lewes as her 'husband' and styling herself 'Mrs Lewes'), intellect, and work were simply too unconventional to allow her to be slotted in with the other mid-Victorians. This difficulty in categorising Eliot is perhaps why Virginia Woolf felt she was such an 'attractive character' and why she was enthusiastic about her work.

In spite of Woolf's admiration, it was F. R. Leavis in the journal *Scrutiny*, and later in *The Great Tradition* (1947), who made the most passionate response to Eliot's novels and, convinced of their relevance to contemporary society, began the project of rehabilitating Eliot. For Leavis and the Scrutiny group, writing in the aftermath of World War II and searching for literary works that could be used to resist what they saw as the debilitating influence of modern commercial and media culture, Eliot was a peculiarly fortifying and wholesome writer whose novels embodied the possibility of a moral art, 'significant in terms of that human awareness they promote; awareness of the possibilities of life'.[15] Although it is now fashionable to disparage Leavis, a critic whose readings of Eliot are based on a narrow and 'literary' analysis of British society, his views were extremely influential in the development of the study of English literature in British universities, especially in the 1950s and 1960s. Since then, however, the celebration of Eliot as a mainstay of liberal individualism, whose strengths were her social and psychological realism and her skill in creating character, has gradually been broken up and a multiplicity of readings of her work have come into play. New interpretations have resulted from a range of twentieth-century critical developments: the resurgence of Marxist criticism as a mode of intellectual inquiry; deconstruction, taking its cue from the work of the French philosopher Jacques Derrida; and a revived interest in the intellectual contexts of Eliot's fiction. Biblical hermeneutics, positivism, and science have formed the basis for studies by, for example, Elinor Shaffer, Gillian Beer and Sally Shuttleworth.[16] The emergence, in the 1970s, of a generation of feminist critics, who lauded Eliot's unconventional lifestyle, while lamenting the novelist's apparent reluctance to take a more stridently feminist position in her writings, has also added to the number of critical positions.

Notwithstanding the lengthy spell in which Eliot all but vanished from the literary canon, her novels can only be considered superb creative achievements. Her first work of fiction, 'The Sad Fortunes of the Reverend Amos Barton', was initially published in *Blackwood's Magazine* in 1857 and reappeared in 1858 as one of the three stories comprising *Scenes of Clerical Life* (1858). The younger Eliot was a prolific writer: *Adam Bede* followed in 1859 and then *The Mill on the Floss* (1860), *Silas Marner* (1861), *Romola* (1863), *Felix Holt: The Radical* (1866), *Middlemarch* (1871–2) and *Daniel Deronda* (1876). In addition, Eliot's diverse output included novellas (*The Lifted Veil* [1859] and *Brother Jacob* [1864]), and poetry (*The Spanish Gypsy* [1861], *Armgart* [1871] and *The Legend of Jubal and Other Poems* [1874]). Before she transformed herself into 'George Eliot', Marian (Mary Ann) Evans penned numerous essays and reviews, mostly for John Chapman's radical *Westminster Review*, a quarterly periodical set up in 1824 by Jeremy Bentham and James Mill to support political reform. The extraordinary nature of her position – an unmarried woman pursuing an independent career in a free-thinking man's world of London in 1852 – should not be underestimated. Serving as assistant editor on the *Westminster* from 1851 to 1854, Eliot also wrote for the magazine, producing not only reviews, but also several now well-known critiques of novel-writing and realism, including 'The Natural History of German Life' and 'Silly Novels by Lady Novelists'. Having taught herself German, she had also translated important works of philosophy and theology, notably David Frederick Strauss's *The Life of Jesus, Critically Examined* (1846) and Ludwig Feurbach's *The Essence of Christianity* (1854). After the death of her partner George Henry Lewes in November 1878, Eliot distracted herself by preparing his great work of psychology, *The Problems of Life and Mind*, for publication, assembling and redrafting the text from Lewes's notes. Eliot's final published work, a series of disturbing essays, *The Impressions of Theophrastus Such* (1879), records her bleak vision of the modern world and imagines an even bleaker future constructed in its likeness. The diversity of these achievements is a reminder that Eliot is a figure who cannot be conveniently classified with a single label.

Like the list of Eliot's works given above, the essays reprinted in this *New Casebook* serve as a reminder of the dimensions of Eliot's achievements and the complex and often open-ended questions her work elicits. That there has always been and still remains a difficulty in 'pinning' down Eliot owes much to the confusion that her roles as realist, scientist and sage provoke. It also has a great deal to do with the immense complexity and scale of her work. As Elizabeth Ermarth rightly points out: 'The counterbalancing dip of one interpretation against another is basic to her message, which is far more capacious and consistent than any of the lesser messages she is seen either to support or to fall short of.'[17] The capaciousness that Ermarth identifies is formulated in many ways in the criticism offered here. The pieces selected exemplify the tensions between Eliot's unorthodox life and her often reactionary portrayals of women's experience; the schism within a writer with a nostalgic longing for the past, but who was also geared firmly towards the future, and a writer caught between the clashing forces of provincial respectability and the wrench of an emotional turmoil stemming from her fundamental unconventionality.

The essays included in this volume were written between 1981 and 1996. By its very nature, any anthology of criticism dealing with such rich and multivalent works can only offer a slice of the many different types of essay elicited by the texts. This collection is no exception, and the various structuralist, psychoanalytic, deconstructive or feminist readings of *The Mill on the Floss* and *Silas Marner* offered here are intended to whet the reader's appetite. The articles in this new anthology are also designed to complement the essays featured in the original Casebook edited by R. P. Draper (1977) by demonstrating some of the ways in which George Eliot has fared over time with developments in critical theory. In particular, by examining the two collections alongside one another, one can see the progression from the emotive responses of the novels' early readers to a less impassioned, more academic stance that is assumed once Eliot's place in the canon has been secured. Like Eliot, the sensitive critic can often feel caught between two worlds; one of nostalgia for a reader-response steeped in sheer enthusiasm, and one of impatience for the onward march of critical progress.

II

The Mill on the Floss has been since its first publication in 1860 a novel that has provoked strong and mixed emotions. Some of its earliest reviewers hailed it as a work which 'awes us with a glimpse into the deepest questions, and the most tremendous realities of life, questions and realities about our temptations, our sins, and our destiny'.[18] 'We feel the throbbing of her heart at each new sensation', as Richard Holt Hutton wrote in *The Spectator*.[19] John Ruskin was rather less lyrical in his praise, declaiming that 'Tom is a clumsy lout' and the rest of the characters are simply the 'sweepings out of a Pentonville omnibus … personages picked up from behind the counter and out of the gutter'.[20] Yet, no less a representative of middle-class morality than Queen Victoria was to express her 'great admiration' for the novel.[21] And 60 years later, the young Simone de Beauvoir found in *The Mill on the Floss* an expression of her own sense of frustration as a young woman living in a narrow, rigid society, faced with the dilemma of needing to find self-fulfilment, but expected to live for others. Maggie Tulliver's story seemed, she wrote, to 'translate my exile into words':

I saw my own isolation not as a proof of infamy, but as a sign of my uniqueness. I couldn't see myself dying of solitude. Through the heroine I identified myself with the author: one day other adolescents would bathe with their tears a novel in which I would tell my own sad story ... Maggie Tulliver, like myself, was torn between others and her self: I recognised myself in her. She too was dark, loved nature, and books and life, was too headstrong to be able to observe the conventions of respectable surroundings; and yet she was very sensitive to the criticism of a brother she adored.[22]

De Beauvoir's passionate response was shared by Marcel Proust, who admitted having been moved to 'weep' uncontrollably when he read and re-read Maggie's story.[23] In addition, D. H. Lawrence claimed Maggie as his favourite heroine and 'adored' *The Mill on the Floss*,[24] while in 1979 A. S. Byatt stressed the affective qualities of this complex novel, highlighting 'the problems of custom, development, sexuality, intellectual stunting, real and imaginary duty, which we have been made to see and live'.[25] Undoubtedly, it is this capacity of the characters to soar between the plains of 'keenest joy and keenest sorrow', as Eliot herself put it,[26] that has enabled readers to identify with *The Mill's* protagonists from 1860 to the present day. Even when it was transferred from the printed page to the screen, the rather ponderous 1997 BBC film of *The Mill on the Floss* made the *Guardian's* Stuart Jeffries want to 'read George Eliot's novel, to leave the shallows behind and dive into the depths of this very British tragedy'.[27] Eliot's storytelling exhibits a timeless, transcendent appeal that aligns her tales with a strong sense of national selfhood.

Feminism, deconstruction, psychoanalysis and the deeply held interest in the relation between literature and other forms of discourse underlie the readings and re-readings of *The Mill on the Floss* discussed in this section. In the first essay, Susan Fraiman explores some of the early reactions to the novel and to Eliot's ambiguous stance on the 'Woman Question', before focusing on some of the problems that Maggie Tulliver has presented to critics. In the essay's opening section, she usefully charts developments in feminist scholarship about Eliot since the 1970s, in order to situate her own work within what she describes as a 'doubled view of women as agents as well as victims' (p. 34). She places *The Mill on the Floss* in the tradition of the novel of development, or *Bildungsroman*. How, asks Fraiman, can there be a female *Bildungsroman* when a woman's life which may seem able to go anywhere, will inevitably need to return to the starting post, to the values of family and home? Whilst the journey of the male involves travelling onward and upwards through the world, eventually reaching psychological and financial autonomy, the route of a woman's life is more likely to be circular rather than linear, involuted rather than progressive. The limitations placed on women, ranging from social prescriptions for feminine behaviour to restraints on female mobility, are difficult to jettison. However, such social baggage can also represent desirable and necessary ties of love and bonds of social connection as crucial forms of attachment that complicate and impinge upon any attempt to deviate from the norm. In her discussion of Maggie and Tom Tulliver, Fraiman stresses the conflicts between these possibilities of growth, which a new emphasis on the idea of individuality might offer women (via forms of education and learning, for example) and what was considered the proper structure of a woman's life: a life, that is, without incident, plot or development. As Fraiman argues: 'If Tom indicates the work's nominal status as *Bildungsroman*, Maggie's problem – and the problematic of the novel – is her inability to enter the designated mode' (p. 39). Brimming with energetic potential though she may seem, the aspirations of Maggie Tulliver come to naught.

Eliot certainly offers a challenge to the conventions of the *Bildungsroman* in the early pages of *The Mill on the Floss*, when Maggie is notable for an active impulse that leads her out into the public world. While for Tom an encounter with the gypsies would have proven to be little more than a boyish scrape, Maggie herself feels threatened and it is here that the limitations of the female world are demarcated. The juxtaposition of Maggie's thwarted energy with the rather dull passivity of her cousin Lucy emphasises just how convention has curtailed Maggie's aspirations toward self-fulfilment and development. Maggie lacks her brother's 'easy mobility', and as they become adults she and her cousin Lucy 'are ushered into a diminishing space', their vitality suppressed (p. 42). Ultimately, Eliot is unable to resolve the tensions between the oppressive demands of society and her heroine's own spiritual growth and is forced to satisfy the demand for narrative closure in a catastrophic flood of self-sacrifice and oblivion.

Fraiman's essay presents not so much a new approach to Eliot as a woman writer, as an attempt to locate the kinds of narrative discontinuities feminist criticism has uncovered within the *Bildung* tradition. In her resistance of the role of passive heroine and the brief period in which she frustratingly embraces it whole-heartedly, Fraiman suggests that Maggie with a kind of colonial intent, as it were, is attempting to appropriate her brother's *Bildung* narrative. As a result of her entrapment within the domestic sphere, her thwarted attempts at participation are peppered with gothic prison motifs, as Maggie escapes one prison of convention only to tumble into another. Such a tracing of narrative complexities in *The Mill on the Floss* may not lead to revolutionary retheorising but it does lead to a solid interpretation of form, character and event which is all too frequently shunted by critics to one side. If Fraiman's essay has a weakness, it is a tendency (shared with many twentieth-century critics) to reaffirm her own values in discussions of Eliot's fiction, notably a faith and endorsement of individualism.[28] In terms of Eliot criticism generally, it is a tendency which manifests itself most obviously in feminist searches for role models of self-fulfilment and strong images of women in 'a literature of their own' (to use Elaine Showalter's evocative phrase).[29] What is most important and valuable about Fraiman's essay is her recognition that the privileging of gender as a total category by which to understand Eliot can sometimes be inadequate. Yet she recognises, too, that women have been formed – as has feminism itself – by those vertical histories of power, ambition and mobility, by the very discourses of individualism that Eliot interrogates.

If many feminist critics view women's writing as a process of writing against the authority of a hegemonic discourse, J. Hillis Miller (essay 2) undertakes another kind of radical reading which points to the basic indeterminacy of all literary discourse. Hillis Miller has written extensively on Eliot, who, he suggests, in writing *Middlemarch* produced the 'English masterpiece' of realistic fiction.[30] The essay on *The Mill on the Floss* reprinted here was first published in 1985. As a poststructuralist in the American tradition, Miller is engaged in the task of 'deconstructing' the text. 'Deconstruction' is often referred to as 'reading against the grain' or reading the text against itself, with the purpose of 'knowing the text as it cannot know itself'.[31] One way of describing this would be to say that such readings seek to uncover the unconscious rather than the conscious dimensions of the text, all the things that its overt textuality glosses over. Barbara Johnson has defined deconstruction as 'the careful teasing out of warring forces of signification within the text'.[32] Miller, himself, however, reads against the grain of deconstruction and argues that all meanings are embedded in the text, which deconstructs itself. Miller's argument answers the charge that deconstruction is 'nihilism or the denial of meaning in literary texts'; rather, it is an attempt to show 'that language is figurative through and through, all the way down to the bottom, so to speak' (p.70).

Just as Fraiman makes a case for a dual reading of *The Mill on the Floss*, so Hillis Miller points to the importance of a number of often-incompatible readings, which stem from the cultural conditions under which the text was produced. The importance of ideological and social context to Miller's project is outlined in his introduction to his book *Victorian Subjects* (1991).[33] Each author is interpellated, brought into being by pre-existing reigning ideologies, but is never simply their subaltern. The essay included here, 'The Two Rhetorics: George Eliot's Bestiary', posits the ways in which Victorian subjects were not merely subjected to social, historical, and ideological forces, but actually reworked and transformed them. Miller's version of deconstruction, then, attempts to capture the multiplicity of Victorian experiences embedded within the text, while registering that the reader will bring her/his own historical context to bear on her/his interpretations. By employing a close reading of a passage from chapter 14, focusing on Tom Tulliver's school experiences at the hands of Mr Stelling, Miller posits that 'good readers have always been deconstructionists' (p. 57). According to Miller, this passage manifests a type of textual self-awareness by the way in which it 'rises from height to height by a continual process of capping itself or going one better'. The passage 'constantly deconstructs itself' in order to register the fundamental instability of all language (p. 62). To put it another way, 'the deconstructive movement of this passage is constituted by the proffering and withdrawing of one metaphorical formulation after another'. Moreover, the excerpt not only gives 'oblique hints to the reader about how to read the novel', but hints at the dangers lurking in the pedagogy of grammar and composition, the type of rules and regulations (grounded in male authority) which are responsible for Maggie's state of frustration (p. 61). According to Miller, Eliot's text revels in the anarchy that is posed by its realisation that it cannot say what it truly means. Instead of being challenged by this prospect (as one would suspect the rigidly ordered Mr Stelling and the patriarchal world-order he represents would be), the sign-manipulating omniscient narrator delights in the jouissance. Metaphor is piled on top of metaphor to demonstrate the linguistic predicament, and perhaps also to subtly undermine Tom Tulliver's all too rigid assertions of what is right and wrong. Such studies of the text's rhetoric of doubleness and equivocation reveal how this kind of deconstructive criticism may prove productive in helping students deal with or divide the rhetorical potentialities of the texts they read.

In *The Second Sex* Simone de Beauvoir wrote that 'one is not born a woman one becomes one'. De Beauvoir's point behind her much-quoted comment was that '"woman" is a cultural construction rather than a biological one'. As Ruth Robbins notes, the reason why this remark is so important is that it highlights the fact that 'the ideas about sex roles which any given society may have come to regard as natural are not really so and given that they are not natural, they may even be changed'.[34] De Beauvoir's insight is a useful starting point for discussion of the third essay included in this volume, José Landa's 'The Chains of Semiosis: Semiotics, Marxism and the Female Stereotypes in *The Mill on the Floss*'. Like Miller's, this essay takes language as its central concern. Landa's interest, however, is in the way in which literature can act as a code-giver, offering the reader examples by which s/he should behave. The nineteenth-century novel is no exception, telling its readers how to live and in doing so forming the culture in which it is read. But the novel is also born out of a specific culture.

Taking up the argument where Miller left off, Landa considers the work of the Marxist linguistic theorist V. N. Voloshinov as a way of examining how all representations or theories are governed and shaped by ideology by their very nature as (unreliable) semiotic constructions. As Landa observes, '[t]hat a semiotic chain is endless does not mean that it is cut off from the world. Instead it means that the world is a semiotic construct', a construct in which meaning is never fixed since it will be adjusted by each new interpreter. In other words, the literary work is in a constant state of flux as each new reader brings her/his context to bear upon it. Landa's argument continues (p. 75):

> A writer is working in two contexts. The first is the institution of literature, consisting of works by writers of other nations or other ages, models, plots, character types, and narrative strategies. The second is his experience of social life at large. A writer – for example, George Eliot – may derive her semiotic materials from any of the 'real life'

contexts she is involved in, such as the discourse on/of woman in
Victorian England.

Taking up the issues of gender representation and female self-
representation, Landa reads *The Mill on the Floss* as a 'liberating
fiction' centring on Eliot's conscious dramatisation and undermining of the different kinds of representation of women available to
mid-nineteenth-century writers. In particular, he focuses upon the
various conflicts of gender within the text, most notably in the
perpetuation and subtle undermining of the fictional stereotypes
of the blonde, blue-eyed heroine (who is conformist and desirable) and the dark heroine (who is neither of these things). Such
binary oppositions in which one element is privileged over the
other are, as Dale Spender has pointed out, 'fundamental premises
in an order based on the supremacy of one group over another'.[35]
Landa identifies the arbitrariness of such categories and divisions
and draws attention to how the perpetuation of such traits as a
desirable norm functions on an ideological level to reinforce the
power base of a dominant group. Thus, according to Landa,
although Eliot makes use of these stereotypes in the novel (in the
characters of Maggie Tulliver and her cousin Lucy), her aim is to
expose the way in which these stereotypes are used as a form of
female education/indoctrination within bourgeois society. They
represent, as Landa notes, 'a whole catalogue of activities,
hearsays, admonitions, and attitudes of the child towards her own
body, which is supposed to become the emblem of her successful
socialisation into female difference ...' (p. 76). Eliot shows the
process of Maggie's acculturation – her family's attempts to make
her act as sign rather than subject – and her own refusal to fit into
the stereotype.

Of course, by announcing the dark-haired Maggie's refusal to fit
in or her inability to do so, Eliot exploits the very stereotype she
condemns, caught up as she is in a vicious creative circle imposed
upon her literary tradition. Yet Landa suggests that Maggie is a self-
aware character who resists attempts to read her according to convention and who as 'an intertextual heroine' (p. 77) seeks to
explode the stereotypes that attempt to contain her. Eliot's characters negotiate and react against a set of ideologies that are
simultaneously constructs and very real for the characters whose
movements are curtailed by them. It is in this sense that the novel
can be read as 'a direct attack on the subject positions available to

nineteenth-century women' (p. 81). Of course, readers who remember Maggie's death might say that Eliot herself cannot think beyond the restraints of a patriarchal culture. In 1820s St Ogg's, the dark, rebellious woman cannot be vindicated, nor can the apparently 'fallen' woman be slotted back into society. Landa demonstrates that, in fact, Maggie reveals all the qualities espoused by the mid-Victorian bourgeoisie which had rejected Eliot herself. However, because of her gender, the individual growth and self-examination she manifests pose a threat to the order of things. The self-scrutinising, self-improving woman will not be content to accept her socially imposed role as homemaker and threatens to disrupt male hegemony by venturing out into the world and behaving autonomously. Constrained herself by the ideologies of realist fiction, Eliot cannot envisage any existence wherein her independent, free-spirited heroine will be anything other than an outcast. She is therefore compelled by the marketplace demand for narrative closure to drown Maggie. Thus, as a result of her position within a patriarchal culture, Eliot ultimately reveals her own internalisation of the social conventions against which she seeks to rebel, thereby revealing the strength and rigidity of the ideological power structure.

As is perhaps becoming apparent, many of the essays included in this volume refer to, or are informed by, a feminist perspective (the obvious exception being Hillis Miller's chapter on *The Mill on the Floss*). The essays highlight the plurality of feminist criticism, which seldom seeks to be prescriptive. Some, like Peggy Johnstone (essay 6), deploy a psychoanalytic model to discover a repressed feminism beneath the surface of *The Mill*. Others, like Landa, detect hidden meanings beneath a patriarchal surface, or find subversive reworkings and parodies of patriarchal literary conventions. The influence of a further strand is also apparent in Mary Jacobus's 'Men of Maxims and *The Mill on the Floss*' (essay 4). Jacobus's work, along with that of Nancy K. Miller, can be said to exemplify the poststructuralist direction of a good deal of feminist criticism.[36] While Susan Fraiman studies the relationship between Eliot and genre, Mary Jacobus is interested in the question of language, but from a feminist perspective. Following Luce Irigaray, she poses the question: How is it possible for a woman to express her otherness or difference through a discourse that is both phallocentric and the expression of the dominant culture in which she is an inexpressible 'other'? *The Mill on the Floss* is chosen by Jacobus as a work which will permit 'putting the question of our social organisation of gender', and as a feminist, Jacobus says that she aims to be 'at once transgressive and liberating, since what [feminist criticism] brings to light is the hidden or unspoken ideological premise of criticism itself'. According to Jacobus 'what pleases the feminist critic most ... is to light on a text that seems to do her arguing, or some of it, for her – especially a text whose story is the same as hers' (p. 87). Indeed, she highlights the propensity (noted above) of a number of 1970s feminists who grafted their own struggles onto nineteenth-century protagonists and thus identifies a more subjective, personal relationship between the feminist critic and the text. In her reading of *The Mill on the Floss*, Jacobus analyses what she takes to be Eliot's implicit criticism of the language of the dominant culture, 'the maxims that pass for the truth of human experience' (to quote Nancy Miller).[37] This makes itself felt in various forms in the novel but most obviously in the scenes surrounding Tom's education at the hands of Mr Stelling. In Jacobus's reading of this scene, Maggie's covert unlawful learning of Latin provides access to an elitist education and language from which women are excluded. As Jacobus sees it, such 'lapses' on Maggie's part can be read as the *aporia* that reveal what is unique to women's writing. They are directed against the system that creates them, raising the question of women's access to power and knowledge and how notions of the feminine are determined by (male) discourse. Jacobus's move from a subtle analysis of the text to the larger theoretical debate via Luce Irigaray has deservedly made this a very influential essay in feminist criticism, with its pressing questioning of how women can disentangle themselves alive from the concepts that bind them. Jacobus notes that both Irigaray – for whom 'the price paid by the woman writer for attempting to describe the claims of women, within an order prescribed by the masculine' may ultimately be death – and George Eliot 'kill off the woman engulfed by masculine logic and language ...'. Thus, in Jacobus's terms, gender constructions and the misery that they produce can only be erased through death. Whilst she lives Maggie is doomed to be constantly interpreted and signified upon by a male-dominated order that cannot think metaphorically and can only view her conduct as 'wrong-doing and absurdity' (p. 88).

The next extract (essay 5) in this volume is from Joshua Esty's 'Nationhood, Adulthood, and the Ruptures of *Bildung*: Arresting Development in *The Mill on the Floss*'. Esty's essay is a pertinent example of the way in which critics have engaged with Eliot partly because of their own curiosity as to the instability of meanings, signs and metaphors and also because of her centrality within the history of nineteenth-century fears and ideas. Like Fraiman, Esty is interested in the obstructions to Maggie Tulliver's growth and development, but whereas Fraiman is interested in the *Bildungsroman* as a generic structure in which women sit uneasily, Esty focuses on the larger historical forces preventing their full participation. In part, Esty's essay can be read as belonging to a long tradition of Eliot criticism which has sought to investigate her relationship with history and the establishment of a myth of rural England. It is worth reminding ourselves that when they were first published all Eliot's early works – *Adam Bede*, *The Mill on the Floss*, *Silas Marner* – were cherished by some readers for their evocation of a stable, pre-industrial, rural world. One of the reasons behind *Adam Bede*'s popularity was that it could be read as a pastoral idyll of *Gemeinschaft* or community, to use the typology of Ferdinand Tönnies, which displaced the tensions of 1859 by projecting an idealised world of 1799.[38] Thus, for example, Frances Taylor, writing in the *Dublin Review*, exhibited nostalgia for the time Eliot depicted so evocatively, when 'war kept the population under, and men were thankful to stay in their own homes, and die in the place in which they had been born'.[39] This idealisation was no doubt the result of the social and political upheaval ensuing from the large-scale industrialisation of the mid-Victorian period, which saw the mass migration of labourers from the country to the city as agriculture gave way to the factory. In 1801 less than 20 per cent of the British population lived in cities, by 1851 more than 50 per cent had become city dwellers, while by 1901 more than 77 per cent of the people lived in urban concentrations. With a society in literal and social flux, one can hardly be surprised at such nostalgia for a more static way of life.

Yet, the idealised communities which Eliot might appear to promote are not without their instabilities. Eliot shows a society in transition from *Gemeinschaft* (the old communal values of a feudal economy) to *Gessellschaft* (a society governed by the cash nexus relations of an industrial economy) which is deeply unsettling to her protagonists who are essentially communal dwellers. In the essay included here, Esty argues that *The Mill on the Floss* resists the readings of historical and psychical contiguity that some readers have associated with Eliot. In the novel, modernisation is a lethal force, killing off characters and social traditions and 'arresting the development of Maggie and Tom Tulliver' (p. 106). A crucial event is the change in irrigation technology, an innovation which alters the lives of the Tullivers for the worse, and which can also be read as representative of the technological developments of the Industrial Revolution. As Esty points out, 'By describing drastic changes (not smooth transitions), the text implicitly casts doubt on recuperative, organic versions of English history, wherein the land and the folk remain mystically constant despite the complete re–organisation of their economy' (p. 102). Instead, as Esty has rightly noted, 'The economic transformations that Eliot documents leave Maggie stranded in the historical gap between old St Ogg's and modern industrial England' (pp. 106–7).

As well as showing us Eliot trying to make sense of the rapid, but disruptive, process of social change which she regards as both tragic and necessary, Esty also suggests that *The Mill* can be read as an interrogation of national identity, a process which is never complete. Any sense of a continuity of identity is disrupted by supplementary, competing or radically alternative versions of Englishness, from both the past and the present within which its characters are helpless. Optimistic assertions of England's cohesion are impossible to sustain in the aftermath of the industrial revolution; in Esty's words: 'The modern economy of industry and empire has forced England to develop into something quite different from what romantic nationalism would identify as its essential core' (p. 106). In this sense Esty's reading once again cuts into the construction of Eliot as the novelist of England and quintessential Englishness, a representation Josephine McDonagh has laid at the door of John Cross,[40] although, as Chris Baldick has shown, many later critics continued this trend, particularly in the period surrounding World War I.[41] Later, F. R. Leavis was also partly responsible, emphasising the value of Eliot's representation of a 'rooted community' and 'the atmospheric richness of the past seen through home tradition and the associations of [her] childhood.' [42]

Leavis's comment is also a telling reminder that one of the most common consequences of confusion in the interpretation of Eliot's work has been the persistence of a tendency to read the novels directly as autobiographies. The parallels between Eliot's own life and *The Mill on the Floss* have undoubtedly made it a compelling work, both for the inquisitive reader and for critics concerned with Eliot's literary creativity. In *George Eliot and the Politics of National Inheritance* (1994), Bernard Semmel reads *The Mill* as a very personal, nostalgic novel about the conflict between different generations and the 'failure of the young to rate sufficiently the bonds that join them to their parents ...'.[43] Kerry McSweeny has likewise called it Eliot's 'most autobiographical novel', and detects a wistful tone in the book, especially in the early sections where the setting is 'unmistakably the Warwickshire of [Eliot's] childhood'.[44] In many ways this stance is a critical throwback to that adopted by George Eliot's contemporary reviewers who offloaded their censure of what they regarded as her infamous relationship with the married G. H. Lewes onto the erring women in her fiction. In 1885, the *London Quarterly Review*, true to its Methodist sympathies, described Maggie Tulliver as a sign of Eliot's 'unquiet conscience', noting that 'the figure of the woman under a social ban recurs rather frequently in George Eliot's vigorous representation of English life'.[45] Dissatisfaction with Cross's *Life* prompted Margaret Oliphant to suggest that we can only recover the details of Eliot's early years that Cross omitted by reading the story of Maggie Tulliver's childhood. Although Oliphant hesitated in accepting the novel as 'an actual picture of the scenes that surround the child of genius',[46] many twentieth-century critics have not been so reluctant. Indeed, as some of the essays included here demonstrate, as a critical habit this Maggie/Eliot conflation has proved remarkably persistent. In reading Eliot's fiction it is often assumed without much discussion that the narrator is the author, or that a particular character is a 'mouthpiece' for Eliot or that s/he is a psychological slip on Eliot's part. The limitations of some of these kinds of readings become increasingly evident as the extent of Eliot's achievements is grasped more fully.

Peggy Johnstone's 'Narcissistic Rage in *The Mill on the Floss*' (essay 6) walks this critical tightrope. The essay is traditional in its concern for Eliot's life, but modern in its application of psychoanalytic principles, presenting us with a carefully detailed case study of Maggie Tulliver. Johnstone suggests that Maggie's aggressive actions in childhood, followed by feelings of guilt and desire for reparation, reflect her 'chronic and disproportionate anger in response to any incident perceived as a narcissistic injury' (p. 124). When she reaches adulthood these actions and feelings of low self-esteem prevent her from disentangling herself from her old patterns of behaviour and develop into a 'misuse of sexual power' in her relationships with men. Maggie's cruelty to Philip and then Stephen comes about as a 'cyclical reaction to her underlying narcissistic rage against her family and society ...' (p. 133). Yet for Johnstone the apparently confessional nature of the novel also reveals a good deal about George Eliot herself. Johnstone is not concerned solely with the author's memories of her childhood home at Gryff, but focuses also on the parallels in the patterns of both Maggie and her creator's relationships with other men as they are written out in the novel. Johnstone believes that the mature Eliot projects the idealised self-image of her youth onto Maggie. It is Eliot's 'failure to separate her own life from her heroine's [which] results in a work of art flawed by decreasing control over the narrative as the novel approaches its deus ex machina ending' (p. 139). Johnstone's reading offers perhaps the most challenging analysis of the relationship between text and author's life in the *Mill on the Floss*, and certainly one very different from those in the first *Casebook*.

III

'There is a multiple typicality about the case of *Silas Marner*', wrote Q. D. Leavis in 1967 and, indeed, Leavis's response to the novel has continued to ring true.[47] On the one hand, critics hold up the novel as another contribution to realism. Thus Joseph Wiesenfarth has written that its action is 'best seen as one of demythologising: of divesting men, their actions, and institutions of mythological or legendary attributes'.[48] On the other hand, Robert Dunham has viewed the novel as 'essentially a Romantic statement' centring on Eliot's allegiance to the Wordsworthian child.[49] Like *Adam Bede* it deals in an apparently realistic manner with rural life but it has often been seen as a fairy tale.[50] When it was widely studied in schools (as it was for much of the twentieth century), *Silas Marner* tended to be taught as a simple Christian moral fable in which good triumphs over bad and moral order is restored at the end. Yet as Ken Newton has argued, it is surely significant that *Silas Marner* was written soon after Darwin's *Origin of Species* was published in 1859. The world that the novel's characters have to confront is 'Darwinian in basis; that is, a world in which there is no evidence of a divine or providential world order, a world in which events are the product of chance, circumstance and accident.'[51] This was the second time Eliot was to fictionalise the concerns of Darwin's book. *The Mill on the Floss* is also studded with Darwinian metaphors referring to the successful or otherwise attempts by the Tullivers and their counterparts to adapt to a changing environment. In both novels, Eliot evinces her interest in the unseen laws of nature which underlie the process Darwin was to call 'inheritance and the complex action of natural selection, entailing extinction and divergence of character'.[52] Characteristically, she also adopts a carefully considered position which is very much her own.

When it was first published in 1861, *Silas Marner* restored Eliot's moral standing with readers who had shuddered at *The Mill on the Floss*. The novel's successful blending of realism and romance, the historical and the legendary, its combination of humour and pathos made it an instant hit – 8000 copies were sold in the first year.[53] E. S. Dallas praised its charm and truth to life, lauding the way in which the characters were 'ennobled and beautified' by their 'wonderful' sense of 'sympathy' with each other's problems.[54] Eliot's publisher, John Blackwood, told her: 'You paint so naturally that in your hands the veriest earthworms become most interesting perfect studies in facts'.[55] It was fortunate, too, that, unlike *The Mill on the Floss*, the novel's story provided less opportunity for snide comments about sexual error. None of the critics invoked the vision of the author as a strong-minded woman of dubious morals.

While we can no longer resort to a simple amalgamation of the life and the work to dismiss Eliot's work as involuntary self-revelation rather than deliberate self–diagnosis, twentieth-century critics of *Silas Marner*, as of *The Mill on the Floss*, find such biographical approaches difficult to avoid. Thus in '"Light enough to trusten by": Structure and Experience in *Silas Marner*' (essay 7), one of the ways in which Terence Dawson reads Eliot's novel is as an example of 'spiritual autobiography'. The novel becomes an expression of a 'woman's psychological concerns' (p. 145) and in Dawson's reading it is Nancy Lammeter, a character often relegated to the critical sidelines, who takes centre stage alongside the novel's eponymous hero. Drawing on the patterns suggested by structuralism and the (unfashionable) patterns of Jungian psychoanalysis, Dawson suggests that it is Nancy above all other characters who functions as a 'carrier of an aspect of her [Eliot's] unconscious personality' (p. 158). Dawson displays the need to find a remorseful or dissatisfied Marian Evans lurking in the text and argues that *Silas Marner*, even more than *The Mill on the Floss*, is a work haunted by Eliot's personal ghosts. In this discussion of the novel the events of the narrative can be read as symptoms; they are at one and the same time real within the narrative and metaphoric of a psychic structure. Thus according to

Dawson, a close study of the novel reveals a strong desire on Eliot's part to find imaginary solutions not only to social but also to personal dilemmas. *Silas Marner* 'is about Nancy's relationship with Godfrey, which has been made difficult as a result of an over-attachment to her father, and a corresponding tendency to suspect the worth of any other man' (p. 158). Nancy's story, which, like that of Silas, is characterised by isolation, was, Dawson suggests, particularly relevant to Eliot at the time of the novel's writing. She was herself living a life of ostracism, shunned by respectable society. Dawson is cautious enough to point out that Eliot does not equal Nancy (or indeed Silas) any more than Godfrey equals G. H. Lewes, but believes that the process of writing the novel was undeniably therapeutic.

While Dawson finds a good deal of milage in psychoanalytic and textual readings, other critics adopt a socio-political approach to *Silas Marner*. This is notably so in the case of Jeff Nunokawa (essay 8) who, building on the work of Michel Foucault, links commodity exchange to decadent bodies. In 'The Miser's Two Bodies: *Silas Marner* and the Sexual Possibilities of the Commodity', Nunokawa draws together three different strands of thought about *Silas Marner*, each of which has been the focus of recent criticism but they have not been generally synthesised together. The first is the investigation of illicit sexuality; the second the exploration of the themes of property and commodification; and the third is Eliot's stance as 'an unblinking monitor of proper conduct' (p. 168). Thus whereas Dawson's essay in this volume suggests that Silas's exile is representative of his author's own social exile, Nunokawa posits that Silas's isolation is a mixture of both the personal and the economic. He interrogates the novel's apparently obsessive flagging of family values to provide a complexly argued account of the novel's fear of illicit sexual contact and Victorian anxieties about the kinds of alienation caused by money and capital. Silas Marner is strange, a kind of 'spinning insect', an 'emigrant ... from town into the country'. He is one of those 'pallid undersized men, who by the side of the brawny country-folk, looked like the remnants of a disinherited race' and one of 'those scattered linen-weavers-emigrants from the towns into the country – who were to the last regarded as aliens by their rustic neighbours.'[56] But Nunokawa also suggests that Eliot's account of this 'pallid undersized man' reads 'like a case study of the solitary practices and enervating consequences of masturbation imagined by nineteenth-century sexology, the consequences of which range from bodily debilitation to homosexuality (p. 165). Although other critics have noticed and analysed the ways in which Eliot fixates on what happens when relationships between characters exceed expected bounds of behaviour (one thinks of the relationship between Maggie and Stephen in *The Mill on the Floss*, and Hetty Sorel and Arthur Donnithorne in *Adam Bede*), they have not located its origins and the anxiety it produces with Nunokawa's precision.

The crux of Nunokawa's argument is that by hoarding his gold and living alone, Silas is guilty of a form of economic masturbation, whereby his wealth alone gives him pleasure without being put to the use for which it was intended, i.e. expenditure. This conflation of the economically productive body with the sexual body is one that Foucault traced to the beginning of the seventeenth century when sexuality began to be regulated according to a set of economic criteria which were inextricably bound to the body's (re)productivity. Sexual acts which did not produce new labourers or consumers (such as masturbation, or same-sex relationships) were labelled 'deviant' and criminalised. According to Nunakowa, 'The appearance of impropriety that clings to the miser's fondlings is an affront to the rules of proper bodily conduct, or more precisely, of proper bodily contact ...' (p. 166). Nunakowa argues that it is only with the arrival of Eppie and the proper domesticity she represents that the miser can return to more normative relations of social exchange. To follow this argument to its logical conclusion we must realise that Eppie's arrival transforms Silas, not simply as a character and a social being, but also as a consumer. By becoming a family unit, Silas learns the value of the gold he has lost and comes to understand that it cannot be productive through being hoarded, but that it must enter into circulation and be used to purchase.

Nunokawa has developed this argument in his book *The Afterlife of Property* in which he suggests links between Eliot and Dickens – another nineteenth-century novelist who, in novels such as *Dombey and Son* (1846–8) and *Little Dorrit* (1855–7) connects commodity exchange to decadent bodies. Nunokawa also argues that in Eliot's *Daniel Deronda*, Gwendolen Harleth has good reason to linger in the marriage market, for this state of commodification is better than being bought either as a physical or a psychic property, and the state of dread and powerlessness her role as a 'secured' woman entails. Significantly, Nunakowa notes how *Silas Marner* is slightly different in its focus since it suggests that perversion can just as easily be attached to withdrawal from the marketplace as to activity in it.

The notion that the hoarding of money should be associated with abstraction, perversion and the loss of physical sensation, is a theme continued in the third extract on *Silas Marner*, Jim Reilly's 'A report of unknown objects': *Silas Marner*' (essay 9) which comes from his 1993 study, *Shadowtime: History and Representation in Conrad, Hardy and George Eliot*. Reilly's approach to the novel (his announcement, for example, that in *Silas Marner* Eliot is 'evidently engaging with a contemporary construction of identity in its new, bourgeois form' [p. 189]) signals an allegiance to historicist approaches to literary texts. His work represents a growing trend within literary studies to situate literature within history once more, but a history understood not in the simplistic manner of 'Background' but instead as 'cultural text, which is the matrix or master code that the literary text both depends on and modifies'.[57] Although this kind of work was initially associated most frequently with the study of the English Renaissance, the transitional state of nineteenth-century society which Eliot represents, together with her own interest in historical and scientific debate, offers a good deal of potential for this method of approach. Catherine Gallagher's book, *The Industrial Reformation of English Fiction* (1985), was influential in that it helped set a precedent for viewing Eliot's fiction from the perspective of its wider social, economic and political contexts. Gallagher relates both the politics and the realism of *Felix Holt* (1866) to the question of representation in literature and debates about political representation involving such writers as John Bright and Matthew Arnold.[58] Reilly himself argues that 'history' as it is represented in Eliot and later novelists such as Thomas Hardy and Joseph Conrad is merely a 'gigantic tale', to use Conrad's phrase, of world dimensions which, as Reilly has observed, 'might well be a big lie'.[59] This last remark may suggest that Reilly's aim is to get at a truer history, underrepresented or misrepresented by Victorian novelists – the type of ideological constructs that both Esty and Landa attempt to unravel in their essays on *The Mill on the Floss*. In fact, history is only that which is written and it is the manner in which it is recorded, whether in the form of a diary, newspaper, novel, or poem, that is important. What Reilly, like Gallagher, is interested in is the extent to which Eliot's fiction can be said to have been shaped by social structures and ideological sources, given the conflict in the nineteenth century between the declining older land-owning class and the developing commercial industrial bourgeoisie. In *Silas Marner*, as in *The Mill on the Floss*, Eliot quite clearly draws attention to her characters' positions within this changing social structure and the impingement of society on the development of the individual.

One frequently seen way of starting New Historicist critique is the quoting of another textual source which offers a brief snapshot of what the critic wants to highlight about the main text she is discussing.[60] Thus Reilly opens his essay with an extract from Karl Marx's *Economic and Philosophical Manuscripts* of 1844 in which Marx argues that the 'sense of having' has insidiously replaced the physical and intellectual senses. Reilly's essay also begins with a discussion of Dickens's *Dombey and Son*, in which the cold, money-obsessed Mr Dombey initially misses his opportunity for redemption through a relationship with his loving daughter. The point of these extracts is to allow Reilly to introduce ideas of alienation, acquisition and greed, versus more natural human relations, and the issue of whether *Silas Marner*, too, interrogates the question of 'whether it is not now natural to be unnatural?' (p.189). This manner of opening the discussion offers a useful way of pointing out that histories, whatever we know of one text or event, are depicted differently by any number of texts. *Silas Marner* takes part in a contest between competing ideologies and Eliot's role in this conception should be seen in relation to such contemporary texts as those of Dickens, and Marx, or Samuel Smiles's *Self Help* (1859) and Ruskin's *The Stones of Venice* (1851). Read alongside these (con)texts, Eliot's novels begin to take on new dimensions, emerging as records of social crisis and ensuing social conflicts. It is the transitional and embattled nature of nineteenth-century society that interests Reilly and in particular the concept of the individual subject.

According to New Historicist thought, the 'individual' is not inherently unique or complete but is produced as an effect of the social order.[61] One immediate discursive context for *Silas Marner* is the urgency with which mid-nineteenth-century writers debated the figure of the alienated commodified worker. In *Capital*, Karl Marx argues that commodities are inherently contradictory 'sensuous things which are social' and objects which have only 'the semblance of objectivity'.[62] The much-quoted result of this contradiction is commodity fetishism, the forms of which continue to resist analysis. Reilly's main thesis, therefore, is that in fictional terms the world of *Silas Marner* is an early expression of themes that would be taken up by later novelists. Henry James, in works such as *The*

Golden Bowl (1904), is a notable example. Yet *Silas Marner* is also very much a product of its own time, 1861. Eliot utilises the fears of alienation and the commodified worker of Marx's analysis in a way which, according to Reilly, is 'strikingly congruent', and he places extracts from Eliot's romance alongside extracts from Marx in order to illustrate this. In Reilly's compelling discussion of *Vergegenstandlichung* ('objectification', 'commodification') Marx's text is thus used to establish the grounds of the analysis. The alliance is not, one should stress, without potential problems. If one wanted to point out a weakness in Reilly's approach it would be possible to argue that Eliot's representation of the dehumanising consequences of commodity production is more primarily meaningful in the context of her historicist humanism. Marx, on the other hand, is proposing a radical deconstruction of the appearance of value in which 'humanity' is a result of the mode of production of value, an effect and not an end in itself.

The acknowledgement of Eliot's place within the history of nineteenth-century ideas has been one of the most positive developments in recent criticism, even if it has meant that critics have perhaps spent too much time trying to link Eliot to Comtism and many other 'isms' to the extent it becomes a heavily academic pursuit. Nonetheless, what is certainly important is the acceptance that the Eliot as revealed in Gordon Haight's and Rosemary Ashton's important biographies is not so much the 'dull' (Margaret Oliphant's description) kept woman, as an important intellectual and literary figure, part of a dynamic network of prominent scientists, philosophers, artists and writers. The relationships to Eliot's thought of philosophical and social theories of figures such as David Friederich Strauss, Ludwig Feurbach, Auguste Comte, and Herbert Spencer, to say nothing of the work of G. H. Lewes, have been incisively established.[63]

The final essay in the current collection is taken from Sally Shuttleworth's *George Eliot and Nineteenth-Century Science* (1984). This is a study that underlined a good deal of what had already been noted but not fully explored, that is the extent of George Eliot's scientific interests and how she integrated them into her writing. Obviously science makes a claim to knowing and controlling the world in a certain way, and to be accepted as a scientist one must speak, write and act in a 'scientific' manner, that is, within the discourse of science. What Shuttleworth argues is that Eliot's knowledge of science was 'unmatched by any of her peers' and she stresses the communality of the beliefs she shared with nineteenth-century philosophers such as Comte, Spencer and Lewes. Most notable of all these beliefs is the one that 'science could provide the foundations for a system of ethical conduct'. Shuttleworth also tries to show how 'scientific ideas and theories of method affected not only the social vision but also the narrative structure and fictional methodology'.[64]

In the extract reprinted here, Shuttleworth argues that the Raveloe community of Silas Marner is used by Eliot to explore 'the various historical routes of man's behaviour' and 'to offer, in accordance with Comtean theory, a full account of the ways in which the characters evolved through interaction with their surrounding social medium' (p. 208). However, what Shuttleworth is at pains to point out is that Eliot's engagement with these ideas is far from passive or reflective (a charge brought against her by early twentieth-century critics such as Leslie Stephen). Thus, as Shuttleworth sees it, Eliot actively 'challenges dominant assumptions of social and psychological community', particularly in her presentation of the novel's eponymous hero. Eliot's 'analysis' of her hero's growing alienation 'inverts organicist theories of historical development' (p. 211). Silas, after all, evokes hostility, not altruism, from his Raveloe neighbours, while he himself is thrown into isolation and egoism.

The world of Silas Marner which Shuttleworth reads is also heavily influenced (naturally enough perhaps) by G. H. Lewes, himself an influential figure in the development of a physiologically based psychology, alongside Alexander Bain and Herbert Spencer. For Shuttleworth, the novel reveals Eliot adopting Lewes's theories as a means of making her characters' behaviour scientifically plausible. However, Eliot is not dealing simply with a question of descriptive accuracy but rather a way of shifting between different levels of analysis, 'combining intricate psychological analysis with wider social and moral conclusions' (p. 214). Thus, Silas's move to 'full consciousness' is not only a psychological state ('an integrated sense of self based on continuous memory'), but also an awareness and acceptance of social life (p. 213). According to Shuttleworth, Eliot also uses physiology to reinforce the moral structure of the tale; Silas's isolation is made to appear not as a product of social relations but as an accident of personal circumstances to be resolved on an individual level.

The diverse critical reactions to the novel show no sign of abating. The essays in this section reveal that a number of very different Silas Marner exist and co-exist. The four essays included suggest once again that such different constructions of Eliot are the result of productions of cultural politics, of positions being constantly formed and held, challenged and subverted but also of Eliot's own complexity as a writer. This same complexity means, of course, that the directions in which criticism might go are numerous. For example, if early twenty-first century critics are not as obviously concerned with the poetics of the novels as they might have been 30 years ago, they are more alert to their involvement in the creation of social discourse and to the anxieties that fiction may manipulate or conceal. They are beginning to be conscious, too, of the economic milieu in which Eliot's novels were produced.[65] The recognition that Eliot's writing was a form of labour, that publishing is a business and that the shape of her novels was equally marked by these material facts is a growing area of interest. Finally, as the works of non-canonical women novelists of the nineteenth century are rediscovered, Eliot's hard won and much cherished status as a 'high culture' novelist, as well as her surprising envy of the mass readership enjoyed by Ellen Wood, Dinah Craik and Mary Braddon, are also providing new contexts for thinking about her fiction and its importance.[66]

NOTES

1. See F. H. Myers' obituary of Eliot in the *Century* magazine: 'Taking as her text the three words which have been used so often as the inspiring trumpet-calls of men, – the words, God, Immortality, Duty, – [she] pronounced with terrible earnestness, how inconceivable was the first, how unbelievable the second, and yet how peremptory and absolute the third. [...] her grave majestic countenance turned toward me like a sibyl's in the gloom.' Cited in Gordon Haight, *George Eliot: A Biography* (Oxford, 1968), p. 464.

2. Justin McCarthy, *Reminiscences* (London, 1899), Vol. II, p. 310. For a more recent examination of the power of the George Eliot myth, her acolytes and the financial benefits she gained by its perpetuation, see Leah Price, 'George Eliot and the Production of Consumers', *Novel*, 30:2 (1997), 145–70.

3. Cited in Gordon S. Haight (ed.), *A Century of George Eliot Criticism* (Boston, 1965), p. 162.

4. John Cross, *George Eliot's Life as Related in her Letters and Journals*, 3 Vols (Edinburgh, 1885).

5. Eliza Lynn Linton, 'George Eliot', in *Women Novelists of Queen Victoria's Reign*, ed. Margaret Oliphant et al. (London, 1897), p. 64.

6. See: F. Joseph Jacobs, *Literary Studies* (London, 1895): '[T]he reputation of George Eliot is undergoing a kind of eclipse in this last decade of the nineteenth century. It is becoming safe to indulge in cheap sneers at the ineffectiveness of her heroes, at the want of *élan*' (p. xxi). George Saintsbury, *Corrected Impressions* (London, 1895), likewise noted that by 1895 she had passed out of 'contemporary appreciation' (p. 172).

7. Cited in Haight, *A Century of George Eliot Criticism*, p. 162.

8. Edmund Gosse, *Aspects and Impressions* (London, 1922), p. 1.

9. See, for example, Kristen Brady, *George Eliot* (London, 1992), pp. 4–12.

10. Virginia Woolf, 'George Eliot', in *Collected Essays* (London, 1966), Vol. I, p. 196.

11. Hans Robert Jauss, *Toward an Aesthetics of Reception* (Minnesota,1982), p. 27. On the changing categories by which fiction is evaluated, see also Jane Tompkins, *Sensational Designs: The Cultural Work Of American Fiction* (Oxford, 1985). The classification of fiction is dependent upon the 'changing currents of social life', currents which affect the perceptual frames and horizon of expectations through which critics read and evaluate texts (p. 192).

12. Cited in Deirdre David, *Intellectual Woman and Victorian Patriarchy: Harriet Martineau, Elizabeth Barrett Browning, George Eliot* (London, 1987), p. 171.

13. Grant Allen, *The Woman Who Did* (Oxford, 1995), p. 45. For further discussion of the apparent decline of Eliot's critical reputation, see Elaine Showalter, *Sexual Anarchy: Gender and Culture at the Fin de Siècle* (London, 1992), ch. 4, and J. Russell Perkin, *A Reception History of George Eliot's Fiction* (London, 1990), ch. 4.

14. To designate the female figure 'who wields the phallic tools of the symbolic order, of language and culture ... ' Jim Reilly in *Shadowtime: History and Representation in Conrad, Hardy and George Eliot* (London, 1993), uses Jane Gallop's term 'phallic mother' (p. 89). See, also, Jane Gallop, *The Daughter's Seduction* (Ithaca, NY, 1982), pp. 77–8.

15. F. R. Leavis, *The Great Tradition: George Eliot, Henry James, Joseph Conrad* (Harmondsworth, 1962), p. 10.

16. Elinor Shaffer, *Kubla Kahn and the Fall of Jerusalem: The Mythological School in Biblical Criticism and Secular Literature 1770–1880* (Cambridge, 1975); Gillian Beer, *Darwin's Plots: Evolutionary Narrative in George Eliot and Nineteenth Century Fiction* (London, 1983); Sally Shuttleworth, *George Eliot and Nineteenth Century Science* (London, 1984).

17. Elizabeth Ermarth, *George Eliot* (Boston, 1985), p. 139.

18. From an unsigned review, *Guardian*, 25 April 1860, in David Carroll (ed.), *The Critical Heritage* (London, 1971), p. 115.

19. From an unsigned review, *Spectator*, 7 April 1860, in Carroll, *George Eliot: The Critical Heritage*, p. 112.

20. John Ruskin, 'Fiction Foul and Fair', *Nineteenth Century*, October 1881, in Carroll, *George Eliot: The Critical Heritage*, p. 167.

21. In Eliot's *Journal*, 22 November 1860, in R. A. Draper (ed.), *The Mill on the Floss and Silas Marner: A Casebook* (London, 1977), p. 35.

22. Simone de Beauvoir, *Memoirs of a Dutiful Daughter*, trans. James Kirkup (Harmondsworth, 1963), p. 140.

23. Cited in Draper, *Casebook*, p. 17.

24. Jessie Chambers, *D. H. Lawrence: A Personal Record* (London, 1965), pp. 17–18.

25. A.S. Byatt, 'Introduction', *The Mill on the Floss* (Harmondsworth, 1979), p. 7.

26. George Eliot, *The Mill on the Floss*, ed. Byatt, p. 657.

27. Stuart Jeffries, 'Channel Surfing: So much Floss', *Guardian*, 4 January 1997, p. 7.

28. Examples of earlier feminist impatience with George Eliot are given in Zelda Austen's article, 'Why Feminists are Angry with George Eliot', *College English*, 37 (1976), 549–61.

29. Elaine Showalter, *A Literature of Their Own: Women Novelists from Brontë to Lessing* (Princeton, NJ, 1977).

30. J. Hillis Miller, 'Narrative and History', *ELH*, 41 (1974), 462.

31. These are Terry Eagleton's definitions. For a usefully succinct discussion of deconstruction, see Peter Barry, *Beginning Theory* (Manchester, 1996), pp. 70–1.

32. Barbara Johnson, *The Critical Difference: Essays in the Contemporary Rhetoric of Reading* (Baltimore, MD, 1980), p. 5. For other examples of deconstruction in action, see G. Douglas Atkin, *Reading Deconstruction/Deconstructive Reading* (Lexington, MA, 1983).

33. J. Hillis Miller, *Victorian Subjects* (London, 1991).

34. Simone de Beauvoir, *The Second Sex* (1949), trans H. M. Parshley (London, 1972), p. 1; Ruth Robbins, '"Snowed Up": Feminist Approaches', in Julian Wolfreys and William Baker (eds), *Literary Theories* (London, 1996), p. 118.

35. Cited in Catherine Belsey and Jane Moore (eds), *The Feminist Reader: Essays in Gender and the Politics of Literary Criticism* (London, 1997), p. 46.

36. Nancy K. Miller, 'Emphasis Added: Plots and Plausibilities in Women's Fiction', *PMLA*, 96 (1981), 36–48. See *Perkin A Reception History of George Eliot's Fiction*.

37. Miller, ibid., p. 37.

38. In *George Eliot and Community* (Berkley, CA, 1984), Suzanne Graver discusses Eliot's novels in relation to the typology of Ferdinand Tönnies. In Tönnies' formulation, society could be divided into two types: *Gemeinschaft* or 'local, organic, agricultural communities that are modelled on the family and rooted in the traditional or the sacred'; and *Gesellschaft* or 'urban, heterogeneous, industrial societies that are culturally sophisticated and shaped by the rational pursuit of self-interest in a capitalistic and secular environment' (p. 14).

39. Frances Taylor, 'Adam Bede', *Dublin Review*, 47 (1859), 34.

40. Josephine McDonagh, *George Eliot* (Plymouth, 1997), pp. 5–6.

41. Chris Baldick, *The Social Mission of English Criticism 1848–1932* (Oxford, 1983), pp. 87–108.

42. F. R. Leavis, 'Re-evaluations (XV): George Eliot (I)', *Scrutiny, 13* (Autum–Winter 1945), in Stuart Hutchinson (ed.), *George Eliot: Critical Assessments* (London, 1996), Vol. 2, p. 151.

43. Bernard Semmel, *George Eliot and the Politics of National Inheritance* (London, 1994), p. 11. In 'Industrial Culture and the Victorian Novel' Joseph Childers also stresses Eliot's 'quiet but insistent nostalgia' (in Deirdre David [ed.], *Cambridge Companion to the Victorian Novel* [Cambridge, 2001] p.91).

44. Kerry McSweeny, *George Eliot* (London, 1991), p. 88.

45. From an unsigned review, *'George Eliot's Life'*, *London Quarterly Review*, 64 (April–July 1885), 208–9, in Teresa Mangum, 'George Eliot and the Journalists: Making the Mistress Moral', in *Victorian Scandals*, ed. Kristen Garrigan (Ohio, 1992), p. 175. Eliza Lynn Linton was likewise in no doubt that 'in the sensitive, turbulent, loving nature of Maggie Tulliver Marian Evans painted herself' ('George Eliot', in *Women Novelists of Queen Victoria's Reign*, p. 72).

46. Margaret Oliphant, review in, *Edinburgh Review*, 161 (Jan.–June 1885), 519, in Mangum, 'George Eliot and the Journalists', p. 174.

47. Q. D. Leavis, 'Introduction', *Silas Marner* (Harmondsworth, 1967), p. 41.

48. Joseph Wiesenfarth, 'Demythologizing *Silas Marner*', *ELH*, 37 (1970), in *Critical Assessments*, ed. Hutchinson, Vol. 3, p. 180.

49. Robert Dunham, 'Silas Marner and the Wordsworthian Child', *Studies in English Literature*, 16 (1976), in *Critical Assessments*, ed. Hutchinson, Vol. 3, p. 196.

50. In 1897, Eliza Lynn Linton suggested that the novel could best be understood by taking this 'beautiful unreality ... out of the ranks of human history and placing it in those of fairy tale and romance' ('George Eliot', in *Women Novelists of Queen Victoria's Reign*, p. 83).

51. Ken Newton, 'Victorian Values and Silas Marner', in *Varieties of Victorianism*, ed. Gary Day (London, 1998), p. 113.

52. Charles Darwin, *The Origin of Species* (1859), in Rosemary Ashton, *George Eliot: A Life* (London, 1996), p. 238.

53. Cited in Ashton, *George Eliot*, p. 252.

54. E. S. Dallas, 'Silas Marner', *The Times*, 29 April 1861, p. 12, in Carroll, *Critical Heritage*, p. 179.

55. John Blackwood to George Eliot, 19 February 1861, in Ashton, *George Eliot*, p. 253.

56. George Eliot, *Silas Marner*, ed. Q. D. Leavis, p. 51.

57. Robert Scholes, *Textual Power: Literary Theory and the Teaching of English* (London, 1985), p. 33.

58. Catherine Gallagher, *The Industrial Reformation of English Fiction: Social Discourse and Narrative Form, 1832–1867* (Chicago, 1985).

59. Jim Reilly, *Shadowtime: History and Representation in Hardy, Conrad and George Eliot*, p. 136.

60. For a useful overview of New Historicist methodologies see: John Brannigan, 'A New Historicist Reading of "Snowed Up"', in Wolfreys and Baker, *Literary Theories*, pp. 157–76.

61. Ibid., p. 166.

62. Karl Marx, *Capital* (New York, 1965), p. 167.

63. See, for example, David Maria Hesse, *George Eliot and Auguste Comte* (London, 1996); Nancy L. Paxton, *George Eliot and Herbert Spencer* (Princeton, NJ, 1991).

64. Sally Shuttleworth, *George Eliot and Nineteenth Century Science*, p.ix; p. 11; p. x.

65. See K. McCormack, 'George Eliot's First Fiction: Targeting *Blackwood's*', *The Bibliotheck*, 21 (1996), 69–80.

66. See, for example, Nicola Thompson, 'Responding to the woman question; rereading non-canonical Victorian women novelists', in *Victorian Women Writers and the Woman Question*, ed. Nicola Thompson (Cambridge, 1999), pp. 9–10.

1

The Mill on the Floss, the Critics, and the Bildungsroman

SUSAN FRAIMAN

I

Critics of *The Mill on the Floss*, no less than Maggie herself, have been troubled by the questionable appeal of Stephen Guest. Alongside the more famous debate between those who favour the pictorial charms of *Adam Bede* and those who prefer the philosophical challenges of *Middlemarch*, readers of Eliot have continued to ask: Is the handsome heir to Guest and Co. really, as Leslie Stephen would have it, 'a mere hair-dresser's block'? F. R. Leavis's contribution in *The Great Tradition* (1948) was arguably not only to recuperate the later novels and Eliot's reputation in general but also to raise the stakes in discussions of Maggie's lover by claiming that Eliot herself, identifying with her heroine, 'shares to the full the sense of Stephen's irresistibleness'.[1] Eliot's own blind weakness for Stephen constitutes, according to Leavis, a lapse from 'the impersonality of genius' into an embarrassing mode of 'personal need'.[2] Gordon Haight, on the other hand, in his 1961 introduction to the Riverside Edition, spent several pages defending Stephen. Noting Eliot's interest in the theory of evolution, he characterised Philip and Stephen as rivals in a Darwinian process of sexual selection and observed that 'in simple biological terms Stephen is a better mate'.[3]

As Haight's formulation implies, the continual question of Stephen is in many ways the question of finding a mate for Maggie.[4] A similar phrasing of Maggie's dilemma – and the dilemma of *The Mill on the Floss* – as a matter of heterosexual options was implicit, I think, in John Hagan's careful 1972 overview of Eliot criticism. Hagan sorted Eliot critics into two opposing camps: those who value Maggie's self-denial, associated with her loyalty to Tom and her father (Bernard J. Paris, Reva Stump, George Levine) and those who value her self-assertion, associated with her attraction to Stephen and Philip (William R. Steinhoff and Jerome Thale). Resuming Hagan's metacritical project some twenty years later, I would say that his reading not only codified but was itself the culmination of that pre-1970s critical strand tending to cast *The Mill on the Floss*'s narrative alternatives in terms of competing male claims.[5]

Yet there were also critics of the fifties and sixties who, rather than judge the sufficiency of this man or that to satisfy Maggie, interpreted her fate in ways that exceeded such a framework. In his 1968 book on the early novels, U. C. Knoepflmacher paused over the 'enlightened', pro-Stephen view (that Maggie should just have gone with the flow) only to moot the controversy altogether by asserting that 'Stephen is merely a convenient device'.[6] Arguing that 'Maggie is condemned, regardless of her choice',[7] he speculated on the relation between her downfall and issues of gender identity.[8] Barbara Hardy's reading of Maggie, though written nine years earlier, went further still to circumvent the Stephen–Tom continuum. The tragedies of Eliot's heroines begin, she proposed, in their disabilities as women, particularly their lack of education.[9] Since Hardy and Knoepflmacher, the emergence in the seventies of feminist criticism – an intervention that will be one of this chapter's recurrent concerns – has produced a wealth of elaborations on these early gender analyses of Maggie's plight. Whereas Hagan saw both of Maggie's male-defined objects as 'good', her tragedy arising from their incompatibility,[10] feminist critics have in general insisted that both goals available to Maggie are 'bad'; variations on the same catastrophe, the endings implied by lover and by brother may each, in and of itself, entail Maggie's self-denial. Though Stephen and Tom still have their partisans, critics of many feminist stripes have taken for granted the overdetermination of Maggie's doom, reshaping the critical debate accordingly. If they agree on Maggie's inevitable defeat (and its comment on conditions for Victorian women), they are divided about whether she goes to her destiny kicking or quiescent.

In the context of an early seventies feminism concerned to expose and protest female victimisation, one strain of readings stressed Maggie's systematic disempowerment and resignation to her plight. Elizabeth Ermarth, in 'Maggie Tulliver's Long Suicide' (1974), suggested that Maggie internalises 'crippling norms' and 'grows up fatally weak'.[11] Three years later, in *A Literature of Their Own*, Elaine Showalter concurred, calling Maggie a 'heroine of renunciation' in contrast to the rebellious Jane Eyre.[12] Another early feminist critic, in an impulse again typical of the seventies, gave this reading for female self-sacrifice a different political twist. Patricia Spacks also identified Maggie with what seem to be choices against herself but explained that, in terms of Eliot's distinctly 'female' Victorian morality, the acceptance of worldly defeat may constitute a spiritual victory.[13] Marianne Hirsch's more recent consideration of *The Mill on the Floss* as a female *Bildungsroman* is arguably in this tradition as well. Like Ermarth and Showalter, Hirsch laments Maggie's disadvantage in the social sphere; like Spacks, however, she is also interested in tracing another, compensatory path of spiritual success. Once again, by shifting into a recuperated 'female' register (in this case a developmental model valuing inner over outer growth, return to origins over separation from family), Hirsch is tempted to redeem Maggie's fate. What looks like a disastrous *Bildung* by male standards may actually look something like success within a renovated paradigm.[14] Of course this kind of revision is crucial, and Hirsch makes an appealing case. Yet to conclude that Maggie's untimely death completes what is 'nevertheless a development of a total individual, spiritual, moral, intellectual, emotional, even sexual'[15] is to downplay what Hirsch admits is the continual difficulty of Maggie's story and to ignore the anger and resistance packed around this difficulty. Focusing either on failure or on a redefined success, the ground-breaking readings I have outlined above seem limited, finally, by their inattention to *The Mill on the Floss*'s portion of radical discontent. Here Nina Auerbach's depiction of Maggie's 'demonism' provides a valuable antidote. In 'The Power of Hunger: Demonism and Maggie Tulliver',[16] Auerbach catalogued not Maggie's weakness but rather her power to terrorise: Maggie kills rabbits, spills wine, crushes cake, mutilates dolls, drops books, dashes card houses, and hangs on Tom in 'a strangling fashion'. This forceful rendition of the gothic extremity present in *The Mill on the Floss* strikes me as a necessary corrective to more palliating versions. Oddly, however, Auerbach's essay links Maggie to witches, pagan goddesses, vampires, and other types of the monstrous female without examining the social meaning and operation of these types, and the result is almost to reify Maggie-the-witch as evil.[17] Only by placing Maggie's witchery in the context of 'St Ogg's' circa 1825 can seemingly simple and arbitrary evil be recognised as systematic defiance and, moreover, a key site of protest in Eliot's text.

Just as feminist scholarship in general needs to maintain a doubled view of women as agents as well as victims, it seems to me the most useful responses to *The Mill on the Floss* combine the two perspectives I have described. As the 1970s gave way to the 1980s, feminist critics began to explore the complex tension between resignation and defiance in Eliot's work. They did this in part by looking less at Maggie as a character and more at authorial strategies: George Eliot's manipulation of 'masculine' plots and discourse. Sandra Gilbert and Susan Gubar, Nancy Miller and Mary Jacobus[18] to take three prominent examples, all decline to romanticise Maggie's fate but look elsewhere in the text for struggle and ire. My own argument proceeds from these, and specifically from the view that the thwarting of Maggie's *Bildung* can coexist with oppositional effects. I want to reaccent the way Maggie is dominated at every turn – denying, however, that all disobedience is curbed or that subordination can be rescued for a new ethical scheme. Sharing the interest of many of the studies above in *The Mill on the Floss* as a fiction of female development, I would situate the text's polemic in precisely the story of Maggie's embattled formation, which both invokes and, I believe, finally distances itself from the *Bildungsroman* based on Goethe's *Wilhelm Meister*. [...] I want to move from the perception that Maggie has trouble growing up to argue that George Eliot's text takes on and has trouble with Goethe's version of growing up, in a way that begins to call it into question. Inquiring into the uncomfortable fit between the conventional *Bildungsroman* and *The Mill on the Floss*, I will eventually be asking not only what this says about the novel but also what it might further reveal about the generic category. [...] I will be resuming that genealogy of the genre with a few of those critics subsequent to Susanne Howe, exploring somewhat further the ideological implications of her legacy. Extending the investment throughout this book in feminist interventions into literary studies, I will be, more specifically, returning to the early 1970s in order to situate some popular notions about the *Bildungsroman* in relation to the dawning of American feminist criticism. Finally, I will be offering an alternative way of reading for formation, insisting less on the progress of an alienated individual than on her or his constitution by manifold social relationships – once again, attending less to the single-minded development of one character than to the tangle of conflicting notions about development and the duelling narratives that result.

For if the novel as a genre is notoriously about the individual in society – according to Ian Watt's history, arising alongside and enabled by Cartesian, capitalist, and Calvinist conceptions of the individual – then the *Bildungsroman*, as Dilthey and Howe among others have defined it, brings this deep structure of the novel to the surface. Or if, as Fredric Jameson rephrases Watt's account, the nineteenth-century novel does not reflect individual selves born of new philosophies and practices but rather works itself to produce a 'mirage' of isolate subjectivity,[19] then the classic *Bildungsroman* would seem to do this work especially well. Thus Hartmut Steinecke, referring narrowly to those German novels in the wake of Goethe's *Wilhelm Meister's Apprenticeship* (1795), called the *Bildungsroman* the 'individual novel' as opposed to the social novel.[20] It will be recalled that when Jerome Buckley extended the term to a British tradition from *David Copperfield* to *A Portrait of the Artist as a Young Man*, he too emphasised the special, artistic child set off from 'his' inimical environment. David Miles's contention that the *Bildungsroman* since Goethe has become increasingly psychological (as the picaresque hero begins to look in his heart and write) suggests, indeed, a heightening of this genre's preoccupation with the solitary, ever more introverted self. These views of the *Bildungsroman* are structured by and structure assumptions not only about the (male) protagonist's autonomy but also about his progressive movement through the world. A crude picture of the genre shows an especially rugged or especially sensitive young man, at leisure to mull over some life choices, not so much connected to people or the landscape as encountering or passing through them as 'options' or 'experiences' en route to a better place. Travel, I have said, is key, for though the story pulls toward settling the youth – its telos is repose – what it actually recounts is his relentless advance.[21]

Several qualifications of this traditional mapping of the genre are in order. Goethe's optimism notwithstanding, few of his successors' novels progress toward happy, assimilative endings. But if the *Bildungsroman* is less hopeful and less integrative than *Wilhelm Meister* (it does not always, as Hegel claimed, bring its hero to embrace bourgeois society),[22] it still generally assumes that some kind of movement is possible. This movement is not necessarily a literal journeying, say, from country to city; it may involve mental travel to a higher moral or emotional ground. It may bring the hero to terms or to blows with society. Often, as Buckley and Miles agree, it brings him to art. But in all cases it takes for granted that the *Bildungsheld* has room to manoeuvre and somewhere to go. Finally, I would note that these two imperatives – individualism and mobility – are closely related. Their coincidence is explicit in Buckley's account, the hero journeying to the city in order to separate from his family. Of course all development narratives, including the classic German text, can be seen to strain against the composite model I have recounted. But it is fair to say that *The Mill on the Floss*, while alluding to the model (one that, unlike my other novelists, Eliot knew intimately), also resists it with special vehemence.[23] In their introduction to *The Voyage In*, Elizabeth Abel, Marianne Hirsch, and Elizabeth Langland point out the insufficiency of the *Bildungsroman*, as it is usually construed, to describe works by women and featuring female protagonists. Yet this volume is mostly interested in identifying 'distinctively female versions of the *Bildungsroman*';[24] as in Hirsch's essay on *The Mill on the Floss* (anthologised there), its emphasis is on recuperating an exclusively female form. My own, by contrast, is on Eliot's engagement and struggle with the dominant paradigm. I read *The Mill on the Floss* less as a wholly alternative structure than as an ironisation and interrogation of the old.[25] My primary purpose is to locate the continual collisions between gender and received genre in *The Mill on the Floss*, to examine the stress points, blockages, and jammings, because these seem to me the infuriated places productive of critique.

II

The isolating mobility of the *Bildungsroman* 'proper' is strongly evoked by the adventures of Tom Tulliver. As Judith Lowder Newton has remarked, 'Tom is already in motion when we first encounter him'.[26] He is first seen bowling along in a gig, which soon deposits him into the arms of an eager family. His first words, spoken 'with masculine reticence as to the tender emotions', suggest a kind of anticonversation: 'Hallo! Yap – what! are you there?' (p. 30). To whom, we might ask, is this actually addressed? Is 'hallo!' meant for Yap (the dog) or simply shouted out into the void? Is 'what!' a cry of recognition or, as the last phrase implies, a question? And again, is this recognition-immediately-doubted still directed to Yap? or has Tom suddenly noticed Maggie and Mrs Tulliver? Perhaps he intends a metaphysical 'you' – as if to ask, 'Is there anyone listening?' Possibly the subject of this fragment is really 'yap', or language estranged from intelligibility. More than a boy's amusing shyness, displacing his real love for sister and mother onto dog, the speech conveys an almost existential doubt about whether an interlocutor exists and whether meaningful exchange can occur. This is not an uncertainty shared by the text as a whole; indeed, I will ultimately be arguing that *The Mill on the Floss* encourages its readers both formally and thematically to see characters in interlocutory terms. What Tom's stammering hello suggests, rather, is the difficulty of dialogue for him. The subsequent action reiterates this difficulty. When Maggie grabs her brother around the neck, Tom absents himself by looking and travelling in his mind's eye 'towards the croft and the lambs and the river, where he promised himself that he would begin to fish the first thing to-morrow morning' (p. 30). In fact, Tom hardly ever allows Maggie (or any Other) to be *present* to him until their penultimate crisis, face to face in the flood. Only then does he utter a genuine cry of recognition – 'Magsie!' (p. 455) – finally controverting the elided recognition above, in which 'Yap' followed by a dash seems to indicate the place where Maggie and a chance at connection are suppressed.

Tom's desire for autonomy and its relation to mobility are illustrated time and again. He maintains (the illusion of) his freedom from extended kin ties by absconding whenever the uncles and aunts appear (p. 40). And the one time Tom decides to risk their visit for the sake of 'the pudden', he braces his ego by asserting his independence of Maggie in the famous jam puff scene (pp. 41–3). Here Tom's studied division of the pastry into 'mine' and 'yours', the resolute descent of his 'hovering knife', seems to figure the severing from Maggie that this scene literally accomplishes. Carefully orchestrated to find fault with his sister whether she gives him more or less puff, it ends like so many of their encounters with Tom running off in anger. It is also an example of how Tom's resisted family ties are mediated by food, by Uncle Deane's peppermints and Mrs Tulliver's cakes and puddens, as if hearkening back to a pre-oedipal feeding. The violent bisection of the puff attempts to undo the children's earlier communion over cake, when Maggie 'put out her mouth for the cake and bit a piece: and then Tom bit a piece, just for company, and they ate together and rubbed each other's cheeks and brows and noses together' (pp. 35–6).

When Tom abandons Maggie, he typically turns to Lucy, Luke, or Bob Jakin, 'an inferior, who could always be treated with authority' (p. 43), not to console but rather to consolidate his separateness. Anxious to lead Lucy, fire Luke, or patronise Bob, Tom defends his solitary state by demonstrating his (gender and class) superiority. This will, of course, be accomplished more lastingly by the genteel education and apprenticeship in trade that, seemingly mismatched, together raise him farther above Maggie, Bob, and even his own father. As in most *Bildungsromane*, the mobility underwriting Tom's sovereignty is finally *social* mobility. But what distinguishes *The Mill on the Floss* from *Wilhelm Meister, David Copperfield*, and even Ann Murry's *Mentoria* is its repudiation of precisely this story of self-advancement – its critical if not satirical view of Tom's lonely climb from averted adolescent to competitive businessman, its evident concern to dramatise the moral and narrative deficiency of Tom's story. This deficiency is especially clear at the trajectory's highest point, the moment of 'arrival' that should bring semantic and formal satisfaction. For when Tom's laborious apprenticeship is at last completed by an offer to join his uncle's firm, it is still not enough. He also wants to recover and manage the mill, both to avenge his father and because, as he explains, 'I want to have plenty of work. There's nothing else I care about much'. Here the narrator remarks, 'There was something rather sad in that speech from a young man of three-and-twenty' (p. 348). Uncle Deane assures Tom he will one day have a wife to care about, but Tom's interest in Lucy never goes anywhere. For the male protagonist, marriage is not a goal so much as a reward for having reached his goal; it symbolises his gratification. But unlike Dickens's social-climbing Pip, Tom never manages to reframe his great expectations, does not reroute his course in time for a chance at romantic 'happiness', and he reaches a moral turning point only moments before his death. By killing instead of wedding Tom, Eliot's text refuses, narratively, to validate his formation and to invest it with significant content.[27]

Of course, *The Mill on the Floss* undercuts Tom's *Bildungsroman* principally by shoving it off to the side, unwilling to make it the centre or norm. Jerome Buckley and Charlotte Goodman have tried to conserve Tom's primacy by arguing that *The Mill on the Floss* is a 'double' *Bildungsroman*. Buckley cites George Eliot's own statement to publisher John Blackwood, describing her novel as 'the history of two closely related lives'. Though readers may prefer Maggie, Buckley says, 'we must not ignore the declared duality of purpose'.[28] Goodman also asserts that *The Mill on the Floss* places 'virtually equal emphasis on both a male and a female protagonist'.[29] This seems to me a somewhat misleading claim. Whatever Eliot's professed intention, from the very first moment one's attention, like the narrator's, is devoted to Maggie. Readers enter the Tulliver household because Maggie leads them there, and it is her interior life, more lovingly detailed than Tom's, that catches them up and carries them through. She refigures, in short, enough of Wilhelm or Pip to be recognisable in some conventional sense as the character whose formation ought to be primarily at issue. But though Maggie may be the more conspicuous protagonist, it is equally true that any comfortable centrality is thrown off by Tom. Her narrative deposes but does not, however, wholly displace his. Nor are the two balanced in some stable symmetry or amiable doubleness. They tend, rather, to pull each other off balance, to conflict with and contest one another.

Perhaps the tension is a generic one. Taking Fredric Jameson's point that 'genre theory must always in one way or another project a model of the coexistence or tension between several generic modes or strands',[30] one may provisionally regard the distance between brother and sister as the space between genres. If Tom indicates the work's nominal status as *Bildungsroman*, Maggie's problem and the problematic of the novel – is her inability to enter the designated mode. The novel is structured by her vain attempts to participate in the genre I have attributed to Tom and by her inevitable lapses back into another, something resembling the gothic and recalling *Evelina*; in spite of her aspirations to *Bildung*, Maggie is continually returned to a place of terror, re-enclosed in a familiar prison.[31] In Jameson's reading of Manzoni's *I Promessi Sposi*, the separation of lovers occasions a very similar tension, splitting the work into

> two very distinct narrative lines which can be read as two different generic modes. The plight of Lucia, for instance, gives [Manzoni] the material for a Gothic novel, in which the feminine victim eludes one trap only to fall into a more agonising one ... Meanwhile, Renzo wanders through the *grosse Welt* of history and of the displacement of vast armed populations ... His own episodic experiences, formally something like a *roman d'aventures* ... thus provide a quite different narrative register from that, inward and psychologising, of the Lucia narrative.[32]

Jameson describes but does not take notice of the evident gender specificity of these two registers. As in *The Mill on the Floss*, Manzoni's female character is seized by an agonising, claustrophobic circularity, while the male adventures his way through a more spacious landscape. Insisting on the manifestly gendered aspect of these divergent plot lines is the first step toward making sense of such a seeming generic discontinuity and its organisation of *The Mill on the Floss*.

I would argue that, although Tom's is the coveted mode, the elusiveness of this mode for Maggie serves to call it into question. The problem it poses for her makes the form itself finally problematic. In a sense, her continual tugging at the *Bildungsroman* works eventually to loosen its moorings. Furthermore, the rivalry between sibling narratives has a decentring effect that puts *The Mill on the Floss* itself at odds with the usual novel of formation. Buckley and Goodman are right to notice that Eliot's *Bildungsheld* is, if not doubled, then at least decentred. What they fail to appreciate is how this decentring contests the very terms of the *Bildungsroman*, to which a single, central character has been seen as fundamental.[33] Not only Tom's particular story, but the genre as a whole and its implied values are unsettled by this configuration. Apparently the centred subject was not so thoroughly or enthusiastically constructed by the nineteenth-century novel as Jameson implies. The critique he locates in our current period of late capitalism[34] may have antecedents in the work of women such as George Eliot for whom, from the start, the centred subject wavered suspiciously like a mirage.[35]

Maggie's wishes to learn Latin and earn money by plain sewing typify her futile efforts to make Tom's *Bildung* her own. Among these efforts, her flight to the gypsies is particularly revealing, and its disappointed outcome is key to my argument. This episode *begins* as a rejection of Tom and his middle-class values, as Maggie recklessly embraces the whole string of overlapping pejoratives marking her as 'bad': darkness/dirtiness/demonism/gypsyness. In this sense, joining the gypsies is continuous with pushing 'little pink-and-white Lucy into the cow-trodden mud' (p. 91) and urging the fair-skinned Tom to 'stain his face brown' (p. 94). Repudiating the 'clean' and 'fair' while asserting the disreputable, reviling genteel sensibilities (much as the blackened Lucy does when she appears in aunt Pullet's parlour), it represents a strategy of impenitence. Yet claiming a nomadic people, like the act of running away itself, also expresses Maggie's longing for Tom's easy mobility. And though she begins in opposition to Tom, Maggie soon comes to imagine her relation to the gypsies in Tom's own condescending terms. She tells herself they will 'pay her much respect on account of her superior knowledge' (p. 94). At the camp, the once defiantly messy girl begins to wish her gypsy friends were less dirty and plans to introduce washing basins along with books (p. 97). Having briefly challenged bourgeois notions of dirty and clean, Maggie now reverts to the old valuations. But the moral agenda Maggie brings to the gypsies is less about feminine virtue reflected in aunt Pullet's glossy floors than it is about teaching, improving, and 'civilising'. Her eagerness to explain who Columbus was – 'a very wonderful man, who found out half the world' (p. 98) – makes explicit the colonial mission Maggie has assigned herself, and it is an eminently masculine one.[36] In fact, this second phase of Maggie's venture is a kind of cross-dressing as Columbus. Her running away to the gypsies is, the narrator remarks, a larger-scale version of what Tom would have done under similar circumstances (p. 93). Likewise, the Columbian dream of crossing oceans to rule a 'barbarian' nation is a larger-scale version and logical extension of Tom's more modest capitalist career. Here then is Maggie's bid to generate a *Bildungsroman* for herself and even to beat Tom at his own genre.

Maggie's conquesting *Bildungsroman* takes, however, a sudden gothic swerve, leading her through terror back to where she began. By the time a gypsy escorts her home, 'no nightmare had ever seemed to her more horrible. ... Not Leonore, in that preternatural midnight excursion with her phantom lover, was more terrified than poor Maggie' (p. 102). And Maggie's 'rescue' by her father only returns her to the constraining community she so desperately fled in the first place; her wanderings produce not escape but reimprisonment, and in this they anticipate her later flight with that phantom lover, Stephen Guest. Yet if the colonial version of the *Bildungsroman* proves inaccessible to Maggie, her disenchantment does make this story-type somewhat less appealing. On the one hand, Eliot's text is itself complicit with the tale of thieves and primitives in need of reform. On the other, however, Maggie's foolish misconceptions about the gypsies, her laughable arrogance about schooling and governing them, also lampoon this particular narrative of self-definition through domination, including Tom's domestic variety.

Ousted from the footloose 'male' mode, Maggie lapses back into the claustrophobic 'female' mode – the gothic register associated with aunt Pullet in the chapter immediately before Maggie departs for gypsydom. This scene, the unveiling of aunt Pullet's new bonnet, offers not only (what the bonnet implies) a peek at female sexuality, but also an ominous glimpse of the usual plotting of female destiny. The drawn-out solemnity of the disclosure, reverently witnessed by Mrs Tulliver and the two fearful girls, makes it indeed a kind of ritual initiation into the ways of womanhood.[37] It is marked off as such by the perilous climb up polished stairs, Maggie and Lucy trailing after the older women, leaving Tom behind (p. 79). Needless to say, this is not the steady march to masculine selfhood, but a slippery anti-expedition to femaleness, which threatens to be crippling. Once upstairs, in search of the touted bonnet, aunt Pullet leads her sister and nieces through a Chinese puzzle of locked rooms and wardrobes. Far from an invigorating mobility, this is an approach to greater and greater stillness, passing by 'the corpses of furniture in white shrouds' (p. 80) in a movement away from movement. Even the unshrouded furniture postures its passivity, legs in the air. Think of Paul Morel, striding at the end of *Sons and Lovers* 'towards the faintly humming, glowing town'; by contrast, Maggie is led inward to compartments of increasing darkness and disuse. Think of *The Prelude*, its ecstatic protagonist looking out from Alpine heights, or David Copperfield more quietly stirred by his view of a Swiss valley; here Eliot depicts the plumbing of a house for its dimmest and narrowest perspective.

So Maggie and Lucy, excluded from a boy's roving, self-enlarging genre, are ushered into a diminishing space. Adult femininity, here as in a gothic novel, seems to require live burial in the smallest closets of a large house. More terrible still, however, is the banality of the object finally uncovered: 'The sight of the bonnet at last was an anticlimax to Maggie, who would have preferred something more strikingly preternatural' (p. 80). What aunt Pullet reveals is the trick of female destiny, that there is no rabbit in the hat – only the hat. Aunt Pullet's bonnet is ineluctably ordinary, non-magical, empty. Like Jane Austen in *Northanger Abbey*, Eliot seems to revise the gothic in anticipation of Freud's perception that the scariest place and worst villain are not only the most remote, but also the most familiar. In these domesticated gothic novels, the cruellest torments are the boredom and triviality of a woman's routine; the tightest bonds – could they be the strings of her bonnet? There is also a sense in which the bonnet refers to the fashionable Dodson female herself. Turning 'slowly around, like a draper's lay-figure', (p. 81), aunt Pullet seems indeed a shell of clothing with very little inside. Like her clothes, she is primarily ornamental, signifying her husband's wealth and taste. And in this objectification aunt Pullet resembles her favourite sister, Bessie, who falls apart when she loses her things. 'Elizabeth Dodson' is literally written into her table-cloths, so that when these are dispersed she herself is hopelessly scattered. Maggie, in short, quite correctly intuits that there is 'some painful mystery about her aunt's bonnet' (p. 82). Though uncomprehending, she is not too young to catch the allusion of this head-gear to the claustrophobia, inconsequentiality, and desperate consumerism of Victorian women's lives.

In all the ways I have described, the bonnet scene suggests a gothicised formation in keeping with the long suicide view of Maggie's fate and in stark contrast to Tom's aggressive forays into the world. Yet, while marking Maggie's exclusion from the masculinised *Bildungsroman*, it may also communicate a restless desire for it and ultimately, I would argue once again, serve to criticise by parodying the official genre. Take, for example, this musing on the bonnet by the two sisters:

> 'Ah', [aunt Pullet] said at last, 'I may never wear it twice, sister; who knows?'
> 'Don't talk o' that, sister', answered Mrs Tulliver. 'I hope you'll have your health this summer.'
> 'Ah! But there may come a death in the family, as there did soon after I had my green satin bonnet. Cousin Abbot may go, and we can't think o' wearing crape less nor half a year for him.'
>
> (p. 81)

Aunt Pullet's moan seems at first, to us and Mrs Tulliver, like a woeful and even wishful prediction of her own death. Yet as it turns out, Aunt Pullet is not thinking about herself at all, but about some other family member – preferably cousin Abbott. Remembering cousin Abbott's wealth, one realises that aunt Pullet's fantasy, far from suicidal, is in fact distinctly homicidal. Judging by the lethal effect of her previous, green satin bonnet, she is optimistic about her new one. 'Cousin Abbott may go', she says hopefully. So aunt Pullet in the last analysis stands for more than female victimisation and more than resignation to a gothic fate; here she reveals an inflated and enjoyed sense of power over others reminiscent of Tom, and even her hypochondria is really a form of competitiveness akin to his. Aunt Pullet takes a quantitative approach to illness, enumerating the various medicines she ingests, hoarding up her physic-bottles, and calculating the shelves they fill. She measures her status in the community in numbers of visits to the doctor. In the same sad, self-dramatising vein, aunt Pullet competes in quantities of tears: poor Bessy 'couldn't cry so much as her sister Pullet did, and had often felt her deficiency at funerals' (p. 82). The desire to surpass extends to clothes as well. According to a sartorial logic by which more is again assumed to be better, aunt Pullet's shoulders are wide as a doorway, her sleeves balloonlike, her bonnet 'architectural' (p. 51). Naturally, hers is 'the best bonnet at Garum Church, let the next best be whose it would' (p. 81).

Thus while aunt Pullet likes to think of herself as wasting away she also contrives to take up as much space as possible, at least in the terms available to her. If she cannot participate directly in Tom's economic rivalries or physical aggressions, still she finds comparable ways to push herself forward in order, like him, to tyrannise the rest. Aunt Pullet simply expresses her ambitions in acceptably female terms, challenging everyone else to be sicker or more over-dressed than she. The story she stages for Maggie is not only a gothic foil to the *Bildungsroman*; it is also an aping, humiliated rendition of it. Yet I would argue that aunt Pullet's efforts in the direction of a *Bildungsroman* do not legitimate so much as travesty the genre. The impulse she shares with Tom to scramble into selfhood over and beyond other people is shown to be petty, illogical, and even self-destructive. Like Maggie in her attempt to colonise the gypsies, aunt Pullet engages and then manages to caricature the *Bildungsroman*. Her futile pursuit of this mode defamiliarises and eventually mocks it, so that envy slides into critique.

III

Having looked at *The Mill on the Floss* in relation to the *Bildungsroman*, I turn now to the generic category itself, especially as schematised and popularised by Jerome Buckley's *Season of Youth: The Bildungsroman from Dickens to Golding*. Published in 1974, *Season of Youth* was the first book-length study of the English *Bildungsroman* since Susanne Howe's initial mapping of the German genre onto English terrain in 1930 (Hans Wagner's 1951 book, in German, excepted).[38] Buckley's focus on canonical novels and his highly excerptable formulation have, moreover, made the book influential perhaps beyond its merits; its interest for me lies less in its scholarly than in its ideological significance as a text invariably cited in subsequent teaching and writing about the English genre. According to Buckley, this form originated with Wordsworth, who in *The Prelude* 'first gave prolonged and serious attention to each stage of the imagination, to boyhood, maturity, and the darker space between'.[39] Though different in tone, Buckley continues, Byron's *Don Juan* 'likewise follows a young man in his progress from boyhood to the threshold of a poised maturity'.[40] Carlyle's 1824 translation of *Wilhelm Meister* provided the first novelistic model, and the genre developed from there through such major works as *David Copperfield* and *Sons and Lovers*. As noted earlier, Buckley stresses the form's autobiographical cast, arguing that the English *Bildungsroman* is therefore typically a *Künstlerroman*: 'what Joyce's title promises, *A Portrait of the Artist as a Young Man*'.[41]

It would be easy enough to take Buckley to task for continually equating 'youth' with 'boyhood', but the editors of *The Voyage In* have already sufficiently shown that Buckley's phases of development (formal education, leaving home, making one's way in the city, etc.) are inapplicable to most female protagonists.[42] My concern here is with some of the other implications of the approach I take Buckley to represent and what they meant in the particular social context of 1974. Buckley comments on 'the awkwardness of the German term [*Bildungsroman*] as applied to English literature';[43] yet, like late 1960s essays by Tennyson and Jost, his book holds onto the clumsy foreignism and what I have already shown to be its considerable ideological baggage. What, one might wonder, was at stake in privileging the German denomination at this particular moment? Like all generic categories, the *Bildungsroman* is bound up with a process of canon formation, called upon to identify a tradition of texts. Jeffrey Sammons observes that the early twentieth-century delineation of the *Bildungsroman* by Dilthey 'placed Goethe and Romanticism firmly at the core of the [German] canon'.[44] The concept worked then to foreground a certain thematics – Goethe's 'scheme of the salvation of the striving individual in an ultimately benign universe'[45] – and also to define and promote a distinctively German literature at a time of surging nationalist sentiment. Thomas Mann among others, Sammons explains, was instrumental in setting up 'the inherent German tradition of the *Bildungsroman* as a defence against the infiltration of the social and political novel'.[46] Sammons argues that the *Bildungsroman* is thus a 'phantom genre', more responsive to modern ideological needs than to any objective body of texts.

What canon was being asserted, what infiltration defended against in the early 1970s? The canon represented by *Season of Youth* is, not coincidentally, also derived from the Romantics and again includes Goethe. [...] Buckley's emphasis on 'portrait of the artist' novels seems to indicate that what he and others get from Romanticism and bring to the examination of later works is primarily an infatuation with alienated genius; their *Bildungsheld* is by definition a child whose lyric tendencies are at odds with a prosaic community. Clearly, Buckley not only invoked the emphatic individualism of the *Bildungsroman* described earlier in this chapter but also helped to construct it along these lines. He makes passing mention, in relation to the American 1930s, of 'the Studs Lonigan trilogy of James T. Farrell with its new insistence on the social and economic determinants of character'.[47] For the most part, however, the protagonist's constitution by social and economic factors is precisely what Buckley's canon and approach function to obscure. His conclusion – that the *Bildungsheld* from Wilhelm Meister to Stephen Dedalus 'brings his own inner resources of sensitivity to confront a hostile and insensitive environment'[48] – reveals the book's attraction to heroes developing not in, but in spite of their social contexts, not shaped by cultural pressures so much as bravely withstanding and transcending them. Favouring works that dramatise a triumph of the artistic temperament, its paradigm can better explain David Copperfield's successful literary/moral apprenticeship than the bridling of Emma Woodhouse's imagination by marriage. Preferring firm, independent protagonists, stable and unequivocally central, it can only make sense of *The Mill on the Floss* by hitching Maggie's moral stamina to Tom's commercial success, as if sister and brother were the inseparable halves of a single, battle worthy character. Accordingly, in a chapter on later novels, *Season* chooses Woolf's *Jacob's Room* (though troubled by its elusive hero) over the more diffuse *To the Lighthouse*, which Buckley says 'turned away from the content as well as the form of the Bildungsroman'.[49] And finally, it happily leaves Woolf altogether for the Angry Young Men of the fifties, in whose 'fictions reappear many motifs of the conventional Bildungsroman'.[50]

To the Lighthouse is a revealing example of the kind of text that fails to register as a novel of development within the schema crystallised by *Season of Youth*. For Lily Briscoe, its putative *Bildungsheld*, is never permitted to dominate the narrative, which continues to shift away from her even as she approaches her climactic vision.[51] Lily and her vision are always inextricable from the social relationships that define the woman artist – from parent figures Mr and Mrs Ramsay or from Mr Tansley, figure for the male critic. In formal terms, moreover, Lily is quite literally displaced from the centre of the text by the spectre of 'Time Passing': Prue Ramsay, done in by childbirth; Andrew Ramsay blown up in France; Mrs Ramsay, wearied to death by marriage and maternity; Mrs McNab and Mrs Bast, scrubbing against the forces of decay. And perhaps this is not Lily's story after all, so much as an array of rival fictions about gendered development variously represented by Lily, Minta, Prue, Andrew, James, Cam, and the Ramsay parents themselves. Yet the effect of Buckley's canon was to ward off the infiltration of just such texts in which history and society, not the masterful individual, are central; texts in which development is not one, clear thing, but many, unsure, contested and changing things. I want to argue that it did this at precisely the moment when feminist criticism was beginning to discover new works and reread old ones with Woolf's contextual and polyphonic model very much in mind.

So my point is not to offer the easy poststructuralist critique of Buckley's modernist view of the 'self' as stable, integrated, etc., but to look at this view in relation to articles such as 'Maggie Tulliver's Long Suicide' by Elizabeth Ermarth, which also appeared in 1974. This was the year the twentieth-century women's movement began to rock the academy. In literary criticism, Mary Ellmann's precocious *Thinking about Women* (1968) had already been around for six years, Kate Millett's *Sexual Politics* (1970) for four. The previous year had seen, for example, the publication of Carolyn Heilbrun's *Toward a Recognition of Androgyny* and, in *Ms.* Magazine, Adrienne Rich's 'Jane Eyre: The Temptations of a Motherless Woman'. Clearly the storm of feminist criticism that broke in the following years – with Patricia Spacks's *The Female Imagination* in 1975, Ellen Moers's *Literary Women* in 1976, Elaine Showalter's *A Literature of Their Own* in 1977, and Barbara Smith's 'Toward a Black Feminist Criticism', also in 1977[52] – was visible on the horizon in 1974. Not that Buckley consciously sought to head off feminist criticism when he refused to look at Maggie Tulliver or George Eliot in relation to their sexist societies, or when he failed to see that development itself, especially for girls, may be a controversial plot; the effect of doing so was nevertheless to man the barricades that were already under attack by feminist scholars.

To this mixed metaphorical account I would add a further observation about David Miles's 'The Picaro's Journey to the

Confessional: The Changing Image of the Hero in the German Bildungsroman', also published in 1974. [...] Miles argues that the *Bildungsroman* becomes progressively more introspective, reaching its logical culmination in Rainer Maria Rilke's *Die Aufzeichnungen des Malte Laurids Brigge* (1910), which takes the form of a confessional journal.[53] Even more than Buckley, Miles articulated a privatised notion of the *Bildungsroman*, to the point of suggesting that development takes place wholly in the twentieth-century hero's head. Construing the genre as a form of self-address, Miles forecloses on more dialogic narratives that might, for example, take the form of letters rather than journals. To consider, say, epistolary novels from *Evelina* to Alice Walker's *The Color Purple* might be to think of a young woman's formation as a process of exchange, an ongoing debate, a social relationship. The problem, therefore, goes beyond the fact that fictions of development such as *Evelina, To the Lighthouse*, and *The Color Purple* go unrecognised by the precepts of a Buckley or Miles. By neglecting these works one also neglects their invitation to reconceive identity in terms of interlocutory structures.

Unlike Sammons, I am not saying that the *Bildungsroman* is a 'phantom' genre as opposed to 'the actual German [or British] novel of the nineteenth century'.[54] For while Sammons claims to see genres as 'instrumental, not ontological',[55] he remains implicitly attached to the notion of an 'actual', flesh and blood genre in some objective sense. If genres are simply pragmatic constructs then they are all phantoms, defined in the service of some explanation (and ideology) or another, and I would like to conclude this chapter and book by recurring to my own feminist phantom: the different way of reading for formation that I hope has haunted the preceding pages, that I have wanted, in relation to women writers, to conjure into being. I have been arguing that Maggie and *The Mill on the Floss* regard Tom's individualistic *Bildungsroman* with some desire, but that its difficulty for Maggie estranges and ironises it. This theme – Maggie's inability to enter the story of self-culture, her stubbornly relational mode – points further to the formal tendency of Eliot's novel, and of novels in general, to establish character interactively. The very structuring of the work as a series of colloquies, intimacies, disputes, suggests not a lone figure pushing past a painted backdrop, but a girl hedged in, defined at every point, by a specific cultural conversation. She is formed as a girl only in opposition to her brother's stubborn boyness (and vice versa), just as Bob's

class identity emerges from the scuffle with his overpowering play-
mate, and Maggie's class and race from her condescending contact
with the gypsies. Above and beyond its critique of the traditional
Bildungsroman, The Mill on the Floss may, in its very dialogic form,
offer to reformulate development as a matter of social context and
conflict.[56]

Maggie's development, then, in the crucible of sibling conflict, consists of a series of transactions in the context of dominative male-
female, among many other, social relations. But *The Mill on the Floss* is
more than its struggles between brother and sister. It is also [...] a competition of narratives, referring less to the apprenticeship of a central
figure than to a drama of dissonant ideas about just what formation is
or should be. In rephrasing the genre, I have been recommending a
shift away from character altogether – and especially from that Ur-
character, Wilhelm Meister – and a turning of critical attention to
those discourses of development at war in a given text. I have guessed
that this approach might shed particular light on conduct materials and
novels by women, whose representations of female formation are so
typically beset by contradiction. I hope I have shown that when the
ideology of *Bildung* is driven up against ideologies of femininity urging
self-effacement one result may be precisely the splintering and counter-
pointing of narratives [...] in Burney, Austen, and Brontë, and that
appear with particular explicitness in *The Mill on the Floss*.

To recapitulate briefly, in relation to Eliot, these divergent narratives are succinctly invoked early in the novel in the episode of the
dead rabbits. Maggie's neglect has killed Tom's pets, and now she
nervously offers to pay for them. But Tom doesn't want *her* money,
as he explains: 'I always have half-sovereigns and sovereigns for my
Christmas boxes, because I shall be a man, and you only have five-
shilling pieces, because you're only a girl' (p. 32). Here in a phrase –
'I shall be a man' – is just that tale of individual agency and growth
associated with wealth played out, to its discredit, by Tom. And
here in the figure of 'only a girl' with little money and no future
tense is the embittered, gothic story of repetition and diminution
recognisable as Maggie's destiny. Revising an earlier precept, I am
now proposing that the disjunction between these be thought of not
as the space between genres but as the space within a genre for confusion, complaint, critique, and possibly compensation regarding
issues of female development.

Eliot's controversial ending provides a final image of the relationship between Tom's conventional narrative of formation and

Maggie's counternarrative. The moment when brother and sister are pulled beneath the waves in a dying embrace has been variously interpreted as androgynous reunion, incestuous orgasm, the climax of a long suicide or perhaps sororicide, and also as authorial revenge. Wishing neither to redeem Maggie's fate nor to discount Tom's, I suggest their simultaneous deaths mark a moment when their narratives collide for the last time, and now Tom's upward-bound *Bildungsroman* is fatally assimilated to Maggie's downward spiral. Little to celebrate except the negation of a story that, failing to work for Maggie, is finally discarded altogether. And yet – if self-centred *Bildung* is traumatically abandoned here, nevertheless assert this conclusive grappling may be the inescapable relatedness of circumstances and subjectivities.

From Susan Fraiman, *Unbecoming Women: British Women Writers and the Novel of Development* (New York, 1993), pp. 121–41.

NOTES

[This excerpt, taken from Susan Fraiman's book *Unbecoming Women: British Women Writers and the Novel of Development*, is the first of several essays in this volume which focus very specifically on feminist interpretations of Eliot's novels. In her full-length study Fraiman, in addition to offering a reading of Eliot's *The Mill on the Floss*, considers novels by Fanny Burney, Jane Austen and Charlotte Brontë. The essay reproduced here is in many ways representative of Fraiman's thesis and her interest in the way in which the heroine's progress towards selfhood in the western *Bildungsroman* or 'novel of development' is often obstructed by the burdens of femininity which society imposes upon her. These burdens can include moral and social prescriptions for female decorum to more physical inhibitions and restraints on mobility. All quotations in the essay are taken from *The Mill on the Floss* (Boston, 1961). Eds]

1. F. R. Leavis, *The Great Tradition* (New York, 1960), p. 44.

2. Ibid., p. 32.

3. George Eliot, *The Mill on the Floss*, ed. Gordon S. Haight (Boston, 1961), p. xiii. All further references are contained in the text.

4. Haight concludes that Eliot, while accepting Darwin's theory, refused to celebrate a process of selection based on biological criteria alone, to the exclusion of moral factors – thus Maggie's ultimate rejection of Stephen (p. xix). Yet Haight's interpretive schema remains an evolutionary one, invested in the procreative couple. It is tempting, I might

add, to see the accumulation of critical language around Stephen, the repeated assigning and analysing of desire including Eliot's own, as an attempt to gain control over the spectre of female sexuality raised by Maggie's elopement.

5. See John Hagan, 'A Reinterpretation of *The Mill on the Floss'*, *PMLA*, 87:1 (1972), 53–63. Hagan sums up Maggie's quandary as an impossible choice among men: 'Had she gone on to love and marry Philip against her father's and Tom's wishes' or 'had she run away and married Stephen' she would, in either case, have betrayed someone's trust (p. 54). Hagan argues, I should note, that readers are meant to value Maggie's loyalty to her earliest ties and duties, not Tom per se – in fact Hagan blames Tom for making family loyalty and erotic love mutually exclusive for Maggie. Underlining the concept of 'division' between 'the large-souled woman ... and the narrow-souled father and brother' (p. 62), he could be said to anticipate feminist discussions of 'difference' in George Eliot.

6. U. C. Knoepflmacher, *George Eliot's Early Novels: The Limits of Realism* (Berkeley, CA, 1968), p. 214.

7. Ibid., p. 213.

8. The problem of Maggie's destiny might have been solved, Knoepflmacher points out, had she been either a man or, like her mother, a less gifted woman. But he undercuts the feminist implications of this perception by agreeing with Mr Tulliver that Maggie's female intelligence was a genetic fluke; her frustration and eventual sacrifice are therefore the result less of character or social conditions than of 'hereditary caprice' (ibid., p. 213). For Knoepflmacher, this makes her story unsuccessful as 'tragedy'.

9. Barbara Hardy, *The Novels of George Eliot: A Study in Form* (New York, 1959), pp. 47–53.

10. Hagan, 'A Reinterpretation of *The Mill on the Floss'*, p. 57.

11. Elizabeth Ermarth, 'Maggie Tulliver's Long Suicide', *Studies in English Literature*, 14:9 (1974), 587.

12. Elaine Showalter, *A Literature of Their Own: British Women Novelists from Brontë to Lessing* (Princeton, NJ, 1977), p. 112.

13. Patricia Spacks, *The Female Imagination* (New York, 1975), pp. 44–6. Spacks's appropriation of conventionally feminine values for feminist purposes is a strategy descended from Eliot's time to our own. It is especially characteristic of 'cultural feminism', emergent in the 1970s and exemplified by such diverse figures as Adrienne Rich, Carol Gilligan and Hélène Cixous.

14. Marianne Hirsch, *The Mother/Daughter Plot: Narrative, Psychoanalysis, Feminism* (Bloomington, IN, 1989), p. 37.

15. Ibid.

16. See Nina Auerbach, 'The Power of Hunger: Demonism and Maggie Tulliver', *Nineteenth-Century Fiction*, 30:2 (1975), 150–71.

17. In *Woman and the Demon: The Life of a Victorian Myth* (Cambridge, 1982), by contrast, Nina Auerbach goes on to read through the Victorian myth of the feminised demon to a fantasy of empowered womanhood. But the 1975 essay lacks the historical analysis that distinguishes her later book, and in this it resembles still another strain of seventies work – of which Kate Millet's *Sexual Politics* (New York, 1970) is the most notable example. Calling attention in important ways to misogynist characterisations of women, particularly in writing by men, this approach tended initially to produce lists of 'virgins' and 'bitches' without considering how such categories function in a specific context.

18. Sandra Gilbert and Susan Gubar, *The Madwoman in the Attic: The Woman Writer and the Nineteenth-Century Literary Imagination* (New Haven, CT, 1979); Nancy Miller, 'Emphasis Added: Plots and Plausibilities in Women's Fiction', *PMLA*, 96:1 (1981), 36–48; and Mary Jacobus, *Reading Women: Essays in Feminist Criticism* (New York, 1986), pp. 62–79 [reprinted in this volume, essay 4 – Eds].

19. Fredric Jameson, *The Political Unconscious: Narrative as a Socially Symbolic Act* (Ithaca, NY, 1981), p. 153.

20. This observation by Hartmut Steinecke in *Romantheorie and Romankritik in Deutschland* (Stuttgart, 1975), I, p. 27 is cited by Jeffrey L. Sammons in 'The Mystery of the Missing *Bildungsroman*, or: What Happened to Wilhelm Meister's Legacy?', *Genre*, 14:2 (1981), 232–3. As I discuss later, Sammons offers a very suggestive metacommentary on the popularisation of the *Bildungsroman* as a critical category in the early twentieth century. I take my lead from Sammons as well as Jameson in speculating about more recent uses of the term and their implied political agenda. Here I want also to note Georg Lukács's dissenting view, at least about *Wilhelm Meister* itself. In *The Theory of the Novel* (Cambridge, MA, 1971), Lukács stresses that Wilhelm is representative not unique, that Goethe's novel is not about individual development so much as 'common destinies and life-formations' (p. 135). It is the 'modern' novel of education that has, to his regret, become a merely 'private memoir of how a certain person succeeded in coming to terms with his world' (p. 137).

21. Franco Moretti phrases this as a tension between 'dynamism and limits, restlessness and the "sense of an ending"' (p. 6). Though weakened by a disregard for gender differences, Moretti's recent book on the *Bildungsroman* makes an important case for the genre's *'intrinsically contradictory'* nature (p. 6). While for me this makes it the locus of struggle and dissent, Moretti sees it as implicitly conservative, an attempt to gain consent to the contradictions of modern bourgeois culture. We differ on Eliot as well, for Moretti does not consider *The*

Mill on the Floss, and his discussions of *Middlemarch, Felix Holt*, and *Daniel Deronda* all privilege the stories of male destiny. What we share, however, is an interest in the *Bildungsroman* as the 'symbolic form' of a particular time and place (p. 5), thus an attention to its ideological components. See Franco Moretti, *The Way of the World* (London, 1987).

22. See Hegel's *Vorlesungen uber die Aesthetik*, in *Werke in zwanzig Banden* (Frankfurt, 1970), p. 220, a reference called to my attention by David Miles. See David H. Miles, 'The Picaro's Journey to the Confessional: The Changing Image of the Hero in the German *Bildungsroman*', *PMLA*, 89:5 (1974), 980–92.

23. Eliot wrote about *Wilhelm Meister* for the *Leader* ('The Morality of *Wilhelm Meister*', 21 July 1855), and George Lewes was no less than Goethe's biographer.

24. Elizabeth Abel, Marianne Hirsch and Elizabeth Langland (eds), *The Voyage In: Fictions of Female Development* (Hanover, NH, 1983), p. 5.

25. In her work on gender and genre, Celeste Schenck has suggested that female interventions into masculinised genres involve both deconstruction and reconstruction. In these terms, I associate Eliot primarily with the first project – in Schenck's words, speaking here of the elegy), 'the deliberate undoing of generic conventions ... the despoiling of generic purity by recourse to attenuated, incomplete, even parodic renderings' (p. 23). See Celeste M. Schenck, 'Feminism and Deconstruction: Reconstructing the Elegy', *Tulsa Studies in Women's Literature*, 5:1 (1986), 13–27.

26. Judith Lowder Newton, *Women, Power, and Subversion: Social Strategies in British Fiction* (New York, 1985), p. 139.

27. Since I am making feminist criticism's usual assumptions about the gender specificity of George Eliot's text, let me briefly extend this comparison of *The Mill on the Floss* to *Great Expectations*. Dickens's novel, one might easily observe, similarly invokes a conventional version of *Bildung* only to debunk it. Nevertheless, Pip's story of ties broken and money made, although criticised, is still taken more seriously and made more central than Tom's; however wrong-headed, it always dominates the text and finally proves redeemable, even therapeutic, in a way Tom's never is. It is also worth noting that Estella, quite like Maggie, is a girl whose story of expectations is appropriated by a boy – Magwitch is, after all, her father. Yet Estella's inability to have a *Bildung* of her own is not an issue for *Great Expectations*. I will be arguing that Maggie's comparable exclusion from the male *Bildungsroman* (denying her Pip's chance to live out, if only to reject, this plot) is by contrast a major issue for *The Mill on the Floss*. In short,

Eliot's distance from the normative genre seems to me more dramatic than Dickens's, her stake in critique more profound.

28. Jerome Hamilton Buckley, *Season of Youth: The Bildungsroman from Dickens to Golding* (Cambridge, 1974), p. 97.

29. Charlotte Goodman, 'The Lost Brother, the Twin: Women Novelists and the Male-Female Double *Bildungsroman*', *Novel*, 17:1 (1983), 30.

30. Jameson, *The Political Unconscious*, p. 141.

31. As I have mentioned, Auerbach is also intrigued by the gothic elements of Eliot's novel, which she agrees are embodied by Maggie. She makes the helpful biographical observation that 'just before beginning *The Mill on the Floss* [Eliot] turned from the rather overinsistent naturalism of *Scenes of Clerical Life* and *Adam Bede* to write "The Lifted Veil", a short story in which gothic fantasies run wild'. See Auerbach, 'The Power of Hunger: Demonism and Maggie Tulliver', p. 235. But whereas Auerbach discusses Maggie as a type of the gothic uncanny (witch, vampire, lamia), I am interested in the unluckily gothic orbit of Maggie's narrative, its downward, drowning spiral. Judith Wilt is another critic in pursuit of 'ghosts of the gothic' in Eliot. Wilt identifies Maggie's fatal relation to Tom, their inevitable double death, as evidence of a distinctly gothic 'machine' (whose operation she explores in 'The Lifted Veil', *Romola*, *Middlemarch*, and *Daniel Deronda*): the murderous marriage. See Judith Wilt, *Ghosts of the Gothic: Austen, Eliot and Lawrence* (Princeton, NJ, 1980), pp. 187, 195. I disagree somewhat in arguing that Maggie's plot *as opposed to* Tom's is controlled by a gothic logic of repeated imprisonment, though in the very last pages this logic subsumes Tom as well.

32. Jameson, *The Political Unconscious*, p. 143.

33. It is true that Goodman sets out to redefine the genre in relation to the male-female pair in novels – Emily Brontë, George Eliot, Willa Cather, Jean Stafford, and Joyce Carol Oates. But her mapping posits an initial 'prelapsarian' unity, followed by separation and ending with a return to 'androgynous wholeness'. Her mythification of *The Mill on the Floss* still pulls toward the formation of a single, 'whole' individual, thereby neutralising what I see as the critical struggle between Maggie's narrative and Tom's. See Goodman, 'The Lost Brother, the Twin', pp. 30–1.

34. Jameson, *The Political Unconscious*, pp. 124–5.

35. Virtually all of Eliot's novels, in spite of their titles, are similarly decentred. *Adam Bede* is parcelled out among Adam, Hetty, and Dinah; Book 1 of *Romola* focuses on Tito; *Felix Holt* is divided between Felix and Mrs Transome, as *Middlemarch* is between Dorothea and Lydgate; and the right to the title of *Daniel Deronda* is notoriously contested by Gwendolen Harleth. Austen's *Sense and Sensibility, Mansfield Park,*

and Charlotte Brontë's *Shirley* happen also to feature duelling protagonists. Sandra A. Zagarell explores a related diffuseness in what she calls 'narratives of community'. This genre is dominated by women writers and includes nineteenth-century novels by Elizabeth Gaskell, Eliot, Harriet Beecher Stowe and Sarah Orne Jewett. Jonathan Arac has also commented on the decentredness of *The Mill on the Floss*. His sense of two patterns at work in Eliot's novel – one suggesting harmony, unity, stability, while the other (associated with the figure of 'hyperbole') suggests excess, incoherence, and instability – is similar to my sense of the book's generic dialectic. Though Arac does not see these patterns as gendered, he does at one point tie hyperbolic speech to Maggie, in so far as her language and desires exceed masculine norms. See Jonathan Arac, 'Rhetoric and Realism in Nineteenth-Century Fiction: Hyperbole in *The Mill on the Floss*', *ELH*, 46:4 (1979), 680.

36 Newton makes the similar point that 'Maggie's notion of life among the gypsies is essentially a fantasy of power and significance – and a rather "masculine" fantasy at that'. I want to elaborate on this and also on her remark that Maggie's 'sojourn among the gypsies ends, predictably enough, in confirmation not of her power but of her powerlessness'. See Newton, *Women, Power, and Subversion*, p. 144; pp. 144–5.

37. It was a student of mine, Carolyn Price, who first called my attention to the importance of this scene as a rite of female initiation. In a highly provocative reading, Price stressed the sexual subtext of the manifold cloaking and mystification of the obviously symbolic bonnet. The incident, she argued, introduces the two girls both to the shrouding of female sexuality and, in Aunt Pullet's flirtatious modelling of her hat, to the forms of sexual displacement.

38. For notable early essays on the English genre, see G. B. Tennyson, 'The *Bildungsroman* in Nineteenth-Century English Literature', in Rosario P. Armato and John M. Spalek (eds), *Medieval Epic to the 'Epic Theater' of Brecht* (Los Angeles, 1968), pp. 135–46; François Jost, 'La Tradition du *Bildungsroman*', *Comparative Literature*, 21:2 (1969), 97–115.

39. Buckley, *Season of Youth*, p. 2.

40. Ibid., p. 7.

41. Ibid., p. 14.

42. Ibid., pp. 7–9.

43. Ibid., p. vii.

44. Sammons, 'The Mystery of the Missing *Bildungsroman*, or: What Happened to Wilhelm Meister's Legacy?', p. 240.

45. Ibid., p. 241.

46. Ibid.

47. Buckley, *Season of Youth*, p. 265.

48. Ibid., p. 282.

49. Ibid., p. 265.

50. Ibid., p. 267.

51. Lily's relatively advanced age might seem to disqualify her altogether from a genre conventionally associated with youth. But as the editors of *The Voyage In* have argued, attention to female protagonists suggests a different pattern. Observing that often 'fiction shows women developing later in life', they include in their collection essays on such late bloomers as Emma Bovary, Edna Pontellier, and Mrs Dalloway. See Abel, Hirsch and Langland (eds), *The Voyage In*, p. 7.

52. Patricia Spacks, *The Female Imagination* (New York, 1975); Ellen Moers, *Literary Women* (New York, 1976); Elaine Showalter, *A Literature of Their Own: British Women Novelists from Brontë to Lessing* (Princeton, NJ, 1977); Barbara Smith, 'Toward a Black Feminist Criticism', *Conditions: Two*, 1:2 (1977).

53. Abel et al. observe in reference to Miles that fictions of female development seem to move in the opposite direction, 'from introspection to activity', culminating today in worldly texts such as Erica Jong's *The Adventures of Fanny Hackabout-Jones*. Clearly Miles's schema both assumes and assures the exclusion of works such as Jong's. See Abel, Hirsch and Langland (eds), *The Voyage In*, p. 13.

54. Sammons, 'The Mystery of the Missing *Bildungsroman*, or: What Happened to Wilhelm Meister's Legacy?', p. 238.

55. Ibid., p. 230.

56. Like the editors of *The Voyage In*, I would draw on feminist object-relations theorists such as Nancy Chodorow to question the possibility and desirability of 'autonomy' as a developmental goal. I want to stress, however, that formation is relational in a socio-economic as well as psychological sense, to a degree that may ultimately be more Marxist than psychoanalytic. My view of the novel as dialogic is obviously indebted to Bakhtin and implies not simply conversation but a roar of antagonistic social voices: male and female, dominant and labouring classes, white and 'gypsy'. Like Bakhtin, I want to build on the Marxist perception that, as Jameson puts it, 'classes must always be apprehended relationally' – and I would add that the same goes for genders.

2

The Two Rhetorics:
George Eliot's Bestiary

J. HILLIS MILLER

In an essay published in 1983, 'Composition and Decomposition: Deconstruction and the Teaching of Writing',[1] I argued that all good readers as well as all good writers have always been 'deconstructionists'. Deconstruction was defined as presupposing a methodical awareness of the disruptive power that figures of speech exert over the plain construable 'grammatical' sense of language, on the one hand, and over the apparent rigour of logical argumentation on the other. I concluded from this that rhetoric in the sense of knowledge of the intricacies of tropes should be taught in courses in composition, along with grammar and rhetoric in the sense of persuasion. Knowledge of figures of speech should also be taught in courses in reading. In the process of arguing that more attention should be given in courses both in reading and in writing to knowledge of figures of speech and their disruptive power, I discussed briefly (as examples of the way the great writers are all 'deconstructionists' before the fact) a passage from Plato and one from George Eliot. I propose here to analyse those passages in more detail in an attempt to identify their deconstructive rigour. It should be remembered that 'deconstruction' is not something that the reader does to a text; it is something that the text does to itself. The text then does something to the reader as she or he is led to recognise the possibility of two or more rigorously defensible, equally justifiable, but logically incompatible readings of the text in question.

The passage from Plato comes from the *Phaedrus*. Plato's rejection in the *Gorgias* and in the *Phaedrus* of empty skill in writing well still has force. It is not enough to learn to write correctly and forcefully about any subject at all, taking any side of an argument, as a gifted lawyer can get the man on trial freed or condemned depending on which side has hired him. Writing well is not writing well unless it is guided by all of those ethical, political, and even metaphysical considerations that cannot be excluded from the teaching of writing. Such considerations involve true knowledge both of the human soul and of language. Here rhetoric as reading or as the knowledge of tropes comes in even for Plato. Plato's discussion of rhetoric in the *Phaedrus* contains a programme for both kinds of rhetoric – rhetoric as writing and rhetoric as reading. The latter, too, must be guided by a knowledge of truth and conducted in the name of truth. Here is the crucial passage in the *Phaedrus*:

> Socrates So contending with words is a practice found not only in lawsuits and public harangues but, it seems, wherever men speak we find this single art, if indeed it is an art, which enables people to make out everything to be like everything else, within the limits of possible comparison, and to expose the corresponding attempts of others who disguise what they are doing.
>
> Phaedrus How so, pray?
>
> Socrates I think that will become clear if we put the following question. Are we misled when the difference between two things is wide, or narrow?
>
> Phaedrus When it is narrow.
>
> Socrates Well then, if you shift your ground little by little, you are more likely to pass undetected from so-and-so to its opposite than if you do so at one bound.
>
> Phaedrus Of course.
>
> Socrates It follows that anyone who intends to mislead another, without being misled himself, must discern precisely the degree of resemblance and dissimilarity between this and that.
>
> Phaedrus Yes, that is essential.
>
> Socrates Then if he does not know the truth about a given thing, how is he going to discern the degree of resemblance between that unknown thing and other things?
>
> Phaedrus It will be impossible.
>
> Socrates Well now, when people hold beliefs contrary to fact, and are misled, it is plain that the error has crept into their minds through the suggestion of some similarity or other.
>
> Phaedrus That certainly does happen.
>
> Socrates But can anyone possibly master the art of using similarities for the purpose of bringing people round, and leading them away

from the truth about this or that to the opposite of the truth, or again can anyone possibly avoid this happening to himself, unless he has knowledge of what the thing in question really is?
Phaedrus No, never.[2]

Rhetoric as reading, as the knowledge of tropes, is here defined as the only means of protection against the powers of rhetoric as writing, as illicit persuasion, as well as the essential means of composition for those who write successfully. A mastery of the truth about things and a mastery of the various forms of similitude turn out to be the two things that are needed by the rhetorician, both in his guise as writer and in his guise as reader. For Plato, too, reading and writing are intrinsically connected.

But what of Plato himself? What happens if we apply to Plato's discourse the method of reading that he himself advises? It is readily observable that Plato's own argument (or that of Socrates) proceeds by just that persuasion by means of similitude against which he warns – for example, when Socrates expresses his condemnation of rhetoric in the *Gorgias* in what he calls 'the language of geometricians': 'Sophistic is to legislation what beautification is to gymnastics, and rhetoric to justice what cookery is to medicine.' A moment before, Socrates has condemned cookery and beautification as being mere semblances of medicine and gymnastics respectively: 'Cookery then, as I say, is a form of flattery that corresponds to medicine, and in the same way gymnastics is personated by beautification, a mischievous, deceitful, mean, and ignoble activity, which cheats us by shapes and colours, by smoothing and draping, thereby causing people to take on an alien charm to the neglect of the natural beauty produced by exercise' (*Gorgias*, 465b, p. 247). By the remorseless logic of the language of geometricians, then, if we condemn cookery and beautification, we must also condemn rhetoric and its brother in false similitude, sophistry. The language of geometricians, however, it is easy to see, is nothing but a somewhat misleading name for that reasoning by similitude which Socrates condemns in the *Phaedrus*.

A is to B as C is to D: this is just the paradigmatic form of a proportional metaphor as Aristotle gives it in the section on metaphor in the *Poetics*. The ship is to the sea as the plough is to the waves, and therefore we say that the ship ploughs the waves. The basic resources of rhetorical argumentative persuasion are, in Aristotle's *Rhetoric*, said to be the example and the enthymeme. An example is a synecdoche – part used for the whole and then applied to another part – with all the problems appropriate to that trope; and the enthymeme is defined as an incomplete syllogism – that is, once more, argument by similitude or trope, since a syllogism is a formally stated proportional metaphor.[3]

It is all very well for Plato to have Socrates claim that he is dividing things according to their essential nature, as a good butcher cleaves a carcass at the joints – for example, in the distinction between body and soul on which the comparison of cookery to rhetoric depends – but Socrates' argument proceeds as much by similitude as by division. Plato's 'dear gorgeous nonsense', as Coleridge called it, is primarily a brilliant gift for arguing by means of similitudes or tropes – for example, in the famous condemnation of writing in comparison with speaking at the end of the *Phaedrus*. Writing is like the stupid farmer who sows his seeds in a barren garden of Adonis, while speaking is like the farmer who sows his seeds in suitable soil, that is, in the souls of living men (276b–7a, pp. 521–2). The wise reader will remember this by-no-means-innocent metaphor of farming when I come in a moment to discuss the passage from George Eliot's *The Mill on the Floss*. In the *Gorgias*, Callicles responds to a metaphor from shoemaking proposed by Socrates, followed by another use of the figure of the farmer who sows seed, by saying in exasperation, 'By heaven, you literally never stop talking about cobblers and fullers and cooks and doctors, as if we were discussing them' (490e, p. 273). That is to say, Plato never stops talking non-literally, not least in personifying himself as Socrates, and the result is that readers of Plato need most of all a skill in interpreting arguments based on tropes.

Plato's writings, too, both in what he says about rhetoric and in how he says it, provide an example of the inextricable interinvolvement of the two kinds of rhetoric and of the impossibility of having one without the other. He also provides another example of the way in which the act of reading can uncover directions for reading the text at hand in such a way as to undermine or deconstruct the apparent affirmations of that text, if the reader is cannily attentive to the play of tropes in the text. This is just what Plato tells us to be, along with learning to use tropes cannily in our own compositions. The text warns against the argument by tropes on which the text itself depends. To put this in another way, all discourse about rhetoric, for example Plato's *Gorgias*, or a modern textbook of freshman composition, is itself an example of rhetoric and demands to be read as such, if we are not to be bamboozled by its enthymemes. This is another argument for the necessity of teaching reading along with writing.

As an exemplification of what might be meant by a 'deconstructive' or rhetorical reading or of a reading as such, along with a demonstration of the truth of my claim that all good readers have always been deconstructionists, I shall discuss a wonderfully penetrating and witty passage from George Eliot's *The Mill on the Floss*. The passage reads itself, or gives the reader directions for how to read it. It is not only a text to be read but also a lesson in how to read. Any careful reader of *The Mill on the Floss* is likely to notice this passage. It has not failed to elicit comment.[4] The passage gives oblique hints to the reader about how to read the novel itself, as well as hints about some dangers lurking in the pedagogy of grammar and composition. The passage has to do with poor Tom Tulliver's sufferings at school in the hands of Mr Stelling. It might have as title 'The Beaver, the Camel, and the Shrewmouse':

> Mr. Broderip's amiable beaver, as that charming naturalist tells us, busied himself as earnestly in constructing a dam, in a room up three pair of stairs in London, as if he had been laying his foundation in a stream or lake in Upper Canada. ... With the same unerring instinct Mr. Stelling set to work at his natural method of instilling the Eton Grammar and Euclid into the mind of Tom Tulliver. ...
>
> [Mr. Stelling] very soon set down poor Tom as a thoroughly stupid lad; for though by hard labour he could get particular declensions into his brain, anything so abstract as the relation between cases and terminations could by no means get such a lodgment there as to enable him to recognise a chance genitive or dative. ... Mr. Stelling concluded that Tom's brain being peculiarly impervious to etymology and demonstrations, was peculiarly in need of being ploughed and harrowed by these patent implements: it was his favourite metaphor, that the classics and geometry constituted that culture of the mind which prepared it for the reception of any subsequent crop. I say nothing against Mr. Stelling's theory: if we are to have one regimen for all minds, his seems to me as good as any other. I only know it turned out as uncomfortably for Tom Tulliver as if he had been plied with cheese in order to remedy a gastric weakness which prevented him from digesting it. It is astonishing what a different result one gets by changing the metaphor! Once call the brain an intellectual stomach, and one's ingenious conception of the classics and geometry as ploughs and harrows seems to settle nothing. But then it is open to some one else to follow great authorities, and call the mind a sheet of white paper or a mirror, in which case one's

knowledge of the digestive process becomes quite irrelevant. It was doubtless an ingenious idea to call the camel the ship of the desert, but it would hardly lead one far in training that useful beast. O Aristotle! if you had had the advantage of being 'the freshest modern' instead of the greatest ancient, would you not have mingled your praise of metaphorical speech, as a sign of high intelligence, with a lamentation that intelligence so rarely shows itself in speech without metaphor – that we can so seldom declare what a thing is, except by saying it is something else?...

At present, in relation to this demand that he should learn Latin declensions and conjugations, Tom was in a state of as blank unimaginativeness concerning the cause and tendency of his sufferings, as if he had been an innocent shrewmouse imprisoned in the split trunk of an ash-tree in order to cure lameness in cattle.[5]

This admirable passage rises from height to height by a continual process of capping itself or going itself one better, which is to say it constantly deconstructs itself. The passage speaks of the activity of reading, manifests a model of that activity, and invites us to read it according to the method it employs. In all these ways it is a fine example of the form of reading that I am calling 'deconstructive' or of reading as such. Though good reading does not occur as often as one might expect or hope, it is by no means confined to any one historical period and may appear at any time, perhaps most often in those, like George Eliot, who are also good writers, masters of composition. The deconstructive movement of this passage is constituted by the proffering and withdrawing of one metaphorical formulation after another. Each metaphor is dismantled as soon as it is proposed, though the sad necessity of using metaphors is at the same time affirmed. No doubt, most teachers of English grammar and composition, like teachers of Latin, have experienced Mr Stelling's exasperation at the obduracy and denseness of their students' inability to remember the rules of grammar and idiom when they try to write or to grasp syntactical concepts, while at the same time they speak with fluency and force, just as Tom Tulliver 'was in a state bordering on idiocy with regard to the demonstration that two given triangles must be equal – though he could discern with great promptitude and certainty the fact that they *were* equal' (p. 215). Though Tom cannot learn Latin grammar, he uses English with devastating cruelty towards his sister.

It might seem that George Eliot is placing in opposition the use of literal language and the abuse of metaphorical language and that she is counselling the former in a way that recalls the late-seventeenth-

and eighteenth-century tradition alluded to in her Lockean figure of
the mind as a sheet of white paper. In fact, the passage demonstrates
that 'rarely' or 'seldom' seems to be 'never'. The only weapon
against a metaphor is another metaphor, along with an awareness of
our linguistic predicament in not being able – or in being so seldom
able that 'rarely' is 'almost never' – to declare what a thing is, except
by saying it is something else. Mr Stelling's problem is not that he
uses the metaphor of ploughing and harrowing for his teaching of
Euclid and the Eton Grammar, but that he takes his metaphor literally, has no awareness of its limitation, and uses it as the excuse for
a brutally inappropriate mode of instruction in Tom's case. Mr
Stelling teaches 'with that uniformity of method and independence
of circumstances, which distinguishes the actions of animals understood to be under the immediate teaching of nature', such as that
beaver who builds a dam 'up three pair of stairs in London' in
sublime indifference to the absence of water (p. 213). The beaver,
like Mr Stelling, is a literalist of the imagination. To take a
metaphor literally is the aboriginal, universal, linguistic error, for as
George Eliot says in an often-quoted passage in *Middlemarch*, 'We
all of us, grave or light, get our thoughts entangled in Metaphors,
and act fatally on the strength of them'.[6]

The escape from this entanglement in the net of a metaphor
(another metaphor!) is not a substitution of literal language for misleading figure, but is the replacement of one metaphor by another.
The second metaphor may neutralise the first or cancel out its distortions. This is a cure of metaphor by metaphor, a version of
homeopathy. So George Eliot replaces the metaphor of ploughing
and harrowing with a metaphor of eating. Forcing geometry and
Latin grammar on Tom is like curing an inability to digest cheese
with doses of cheese, or, the reader might reflect, like curing the
disaster bought on by carrying the metaphorical basis in a pedagogical theory into practice by the application of another theoretical
metaphor, replacing one kind of cheese with another kind of cheese.
It is at this point that the narrator draws herself (himself?) up and
makes the exclamation about how astonishing it is what a different
result one gets by changing the metaphor.

To the other figures here must be added irony and prosopopoeia,
irony as the pervasive tone of the narration and personification as
the trope whereby the ironic discrepancy between narrator and
character is given a name and a personality in the putative story-
teller, 'George Eliot'. That narrator pretends to have made Mr

Stelling's mistake, or the beaver's mistake – namely, to have used a metaphor without reflection – and then to have been surprised by the results into having a metalinguistic insight into the role of metaphor in pedagogical theory. But of course the narrator, who has been aware of this all along, is manipulating the metaphors in full deliberate awareness. He only pretends to be astonished. The sentence is ironic in the strict sense that it says the opposite of what it means, or rather that it says both things at once. It is astonishing and not astonishing, and the reader is challenged to ally himself with one side or the other, though at the same time he is put in a double bind. If he is not astonished, he may be putting himself unwittingly in the same camp as the beaver and Mr Stelling, since another way to define a literalist is to say that he is incapable of being astonished by the workings of language. If the reader is astonished, then he is admitting that until a moment ago at least, he was a linguistic innocent, lagging behind the all-knowing narrator, who only ironically pretends to be astonished by something that he or she has known all along.

The digestive metaphor is then followed by two more traditional metaphors for the mind – the Lockean one of the white sheet of paper, and the figure of the mirror, which has had such a long history in expressions of 'realism' in the novel: for example, in Georg Lukács or in George Eliot herself in the celebrated chapter 17 of *Adam Bede*, the *locus classicus* for the theory of realism in Victorian fiction.

The next metaphor, that of the camel as the ship of the desert, seems to be irrelevant or non-functional, not part of the chain, no more than a textbook example of metaphor.[7] It allows the bringing in of Aristotle and the opposition of the ancients who naïvely praised metaphor, on the one hand, and the moderns, such as Locke, who lament its presence in language and try (unsuccessfully) to expunge it, on the other. Aristotle, by the way, did not, strictly speaking, 'praise ... metaphorical speech as a sign of high intelligence', as George Eliot says. Aristotle said a 'command of metaphor' was the 'mark of genius', 'the greatest thing by far', in a poet, the one thing that 'cannot be imparted by another'.[8] A command of metaphor is for Aristotle not so much a sign of intelligence as an intuitive gift, 'an eye for resemblances' (1495a, p. 87). The poet does not rationally think out metaphors. They just come to him in a flash, or they fall under his eye. In any case, the figure of a camel as a ship accomplishes three moves simultaneously in the intricate sequence of George Eliot's thought in the passage as a whole.

First move: the image of the camel more or less completes the repertoire of examples of metaphor that makes the passage not only a miniature treatise on metaphor but also, unostentatiously, an anthology, bouquet, herbarium, or bestiary of the basic metaphors in our tradition – that is, coming down from the Bible and from the Greeks. No choice of examples is innocent, and it is no accident that metaphors of farming and sowing (for example, in Plato's *Phaedrus* or in Christ's parable of the sower, with the sun lurking somewhere as the source of germination); metaphors of specular reflection, the play of light, of images, of reflection, and of seeing; metaphors of eating, of writing on that blank sheet of paper, and of journeying from here to there (that is, of transport, whether by camel back or on ship board) – all tend to reappear whenever someone, from Aristotle on down to the freshest modern teacher of composition, pulls an example of metaphor out of his pedagogical hat. These remain the basic metaphors still today, and though he will not necessarily have the poet's instinctive command of them, a good reader can learn to thread his way from one to another in their interchangeability and begin to master them as a deliberate reader if not as a writer. If the ship ploughing the waves mixes the agricultural with the nautical region of figure, the sowing of seed, for both Plato and Jesus, is at the same time a form of writing, a dissemination of the word. And does not the assimilation of learning to eating appear in that extraordinary image of Ezekiel eating the scroll, as well as in Hegel's interpretation of the Last Supper in *The Spirit of Christianity*, not to speak of the Communion service itself, in which the communicants eat the *Logos*, and of a strange passage in George Eliot's own *Middlemarch*?[9]

Second move: the camel as ship of the desert is not just an example of metaphor. It is a metaphor of metaphor; that is, of transfer or transport from one place to another. This is not only what the word *metaphor* means etymologically but also what metaphor does. It effects a transfer. If George Puttenham's far-fetched Renaissance name for metalepsis is the 'Far-fetcher', he elsewhere calls metaphor the 'Figure of Transport'.[10] Metaphor gets the writer or reader from here to there in his argument, whether by that 'smooth gradation or gentle transition, to some other kindred quality', of which Wordsworth speaks in the 'Essays upon Epitaphs',[11] following the Socrates of the *Phaedrus* on 'shifting your ground little by little', or by the sudden leap over a vacant place in the argument, of which George Meredith writes: 'It is the excelling merit of similes and metaphors to spring us to vault over gaps and thickets and dreary places.'[12] Pedagogy is metaphor. It takes the mind of the student and transforms it, transfers it, translates it, ferries it from here to there. A method of teaching, such as Mr Stelling's, is as much a means of transportation as is a camel or a ship. My own 'passages' from Plato and Eliot are synecdoches, parts taken from large wholes and used as figurative means of passage from one place to another in my argument.

Third move: the sentence about the camel brings into the open the asymmetrical juxtaposition between the opposition of literal and figurative language, on the one hand, and the opposition of theory and practice, on the other. The reader may be inclined to think that these are parallel, but this probably depends on a confusion of mind. One thinks of literal language as the clear non-figurative expression of ideas or concepts: for example, the 'abstract' concepts of grammar, such as the relation between cases and determinations in the genitive and the dative, which Tom Tulliver has as much trouble learning as a modern student of English composition has in learning the rules of English grammar. At the same time, one thinks of literal language as the act of non-figurative nomination, calling a spade a spade and a camel a camel, not a ship. We tend to think of figure as applied at either end of the scale – from abstract to concrete – as an additional ornament making the literal expression 'clearer', more 'vivid', or more 'forceful'. As George Eliot's sentence makes clear, however, the trouble with theory is not that it is abstract or conceptual but that it is always based on metaphor – that is, it commits what Alfred North Whitehead calls 'the fallacy of misplaced concreteness'.

If it is true that original thinking is most often started by a metaphor, as both Whitehead himself and such literary theorists as William Empson and Kenneth Burke aver in different ways, it is also the case that each metaphorically based theory, such as the alternative pedagogical theories that George Eliot sketches out, has its own built-in fallacious bias and leads to its own special form of catastrophe in the classroom. If a camel is not a ship, the brain is neither a field to plough nor a stomach nor a sheet of paper nor a mirror, though each of these metaphors could, and has, generated ponderous, solemn, and intellectually cogent theories of teaching. Neither theory nor literal meaning, if there is such a thing (which there is not), will help you with that camel. As soon as you try to tell someone how to manage a camel, you fall into theory – that is, into some metaphorical scheme or other. The opposition between theory and practice is not that between metaphorical and literal language, but is that between language, which is always figurative through and through, and no language – silent doing. If the praxis in question is the act of writing, the habit of writing well, it can be seen that there are going to be problems in teaching it, more problems even than in teaching someone how to drive a camel or to make a chair. That the terms for the parts of a chair are examples of those basic personifying catachreses, whereby we humanise the world and project arms and legs where there are none, may cause little trouble as the apprentice learns from watching the master cabinetmaker at work, but it might cause much trouble to someone who is writing about chairs.

After what has been said so far, the function of the final animal in George Eliot's bestiary, the shrewmouse – the vehicle for the last metaphor in the segment that I have excised from her narrative – is clear enough. Having seemingly aligned herself with those fresh moderns who would opt for an antiseptic 'speech without metaphor', George Eliot, far from speaking without metaphors herself, goes on to present the most ostentatious and elaborate of all the metaphors in this sequence – ostentatious in the sense that the literal elaboration of the vehicle of the metaphor, a bit of Warwickshire agricultural folklore, seems far to exceed its parabolic application to Tom's suffering: 'Tom was in a state of as blank unimaginativeness concerning the cause and tendency of his sufferings, as if he had been an innocent shrewmouse imprisoned in the split trunk of an ash-tree in order to cure lameness in cattle.' This not only demonstrates once more that 'we can ... seldom declare what a thing is, except by saying it is something else'. It also shows that the only cure for metaphor is not literal language but another metaphor that so calls attention to itself that no one could miss that it is a metaphor or take it as innocently 'dead'. If literal language is possible, it is likely, paradoxically, to occur in the elaboration of the vehicle of the figure, as in this case or as in the parables of Jesus in the Gospels. It is possible to speak literally about shrewmice in Warwickshire or about the details of farming, fishing, and household care in first-century Palestine, but this literal speech almost always turns out, by a kind of fatality intrinsic to language, to be the means of speaking parabolically or allegorically about something else. The most figurative language, it would follow, is the language that appears to be the most literal. The good reader is one who, like George Eliot, brings this sad fact into the open, as a secret writing in sympathetic ink beneath the writing on the surface is brought out by the application of heat or the right chemicals. Bringing it into the open, alas, is not an escape from it or a 'cure' for it.

From where does my metaphor of 'cure' come? Is it my own licit or illicit addition, the reader's licence? No, it is of course already there as one of the places of passage in the quotation from George Eliot. I have said that the shrewmouse is the last animal in George Eliot's bestiary and that the literal details of the shrewmouse's suffering exceed its figurative application. Obviously, neither of these is the case. The last animals are those lame cattle, and they function to make the figure of the shrewmouse, at a second remove, a figure for the failure of teaching to cure lameness in the sense of linguistic incapacity – for example, an inability to write clear and concise English prose. Mr Stelling's pedagogy, based as it is on the magic literalisation of a metaphor, is as much a piece of superstition as is the countryman's beliefs about shrewmice and cattle. Which of us twentieth-century teachers can be sure that our method is not another such blind belief in an unread metaphor?

In any case, the reader at the end of my sequence from *The Mill on the Floss* remains as trapped as ever within the linguistic situation of not being able to say what a thing is, except by saying it is something else. Tom is imprisoned within the obstinate rigours of Mr Stelling's pedagogy, rigours that result from the literal application of a metaphor. His situation makes him like a poor innocent imprisoned shrewmouse. The melancholy wisdom of this passage affirms that the reader or writer of any sort – you or I – is imprisoned as much as Tom, Mr Stelling, or the shrewmouse within the linguistic predicament that the passage both analyses and exemplifies. The most that one can hope for is some clarification of the predicament, not escape from it into the free light of day.

In 'Composition and Decomposition' I concluded my brief discussion of the passages from Plato and George Eliot with the claim that both teachers and students of rhetoric as persuasion or as composition must aim to become as good readers as Plato, George Eliot, or Jacques Derrida, as wise in the ways of tropes, or else they will not learn to be good teachers or practitioners of writing either. 'Good courses in rhetoric as reading', I concluded, 'must always accompany programmes in composition, not only in preparation for reading Shakespeare, Milton, Wordsworth, and Wallace Stevens, but as an essential accompaniment to courses in writing.' I draw now another, perhaps more radical or disturbing, conclusion. If the medieval trivium of grammar, logic, and rhetoric is indeed a place in which the pathways of those three disciplines come together or cross, as the etymology of *trivium* suggests (*tri-viae*, 'three roads'), it may be that rhetoric is not so much the climax of a progressive mastery of language both for reading and for writing as it is the place in which the impossibility of mastery is definitively encountered. The road called 'rhetoric' is always marked 'impassable' or 'under construction; pass at your own risk' or, as it is succinctly put on signs in England, 'road up!'

Paul de Man certainly thought this was the case with rhetoric as the wrestling with tropes. In an interview with Robert Moynihan, in answer to a question about irony, de Man asserted that 'the claim of control, yes, when it is made, can always be shown to be unwarranted – one can show that the claim of control is a mistake, that there are elements in the text that are not controlled, that it is always possible to read the text against the overt claim of control'.[13] And in another essay, 'Semiology and Rhetoric', discussing Archie Bunker's question 'What's the difference?' de Man asserts: 'The grammatical model of the question becomes rhetorical not when we have, on the one hand, a literal meaning and on the other hand a figural meaning, but when it is impossible to decide by grammatical or other linguistic devices which of the two meanings (that can be entirely incompatible) prevails. Rhetoric radically suspends logic and opens up vertiginous possibilities of referential aberration. ... I would not hesitate to equate the rhetorical, figural potential of language with literature itself.'[14]

Certain notorious quarrels among literary critics or between philosophers and literary critics or among philosophers occupy the polemical field of humanistic study today. I am thinking, for example, of interchanges between Jacques Derrida and John Searle or between Paul de Man and Raymond Geuss or between me and Meyer Abrams, or of attacks on 'deconstruction' in the name of history and straightforward referential language by Gerald Graff, Frank Lentricchia, and others.[15] The issues at stake in these various quarrels are complex, but it may be possible to understand them better by seeing them as disagreements about the proper relation among the three branches of the ancient trivium. A critic such as Meyer Abrams wants to make grammar, what he calls 'construing' of the plain sense of a poem or a novel, the basis for literary study

to which the study of the 'perfidious' language of tropes by deconstructionists might be added as an extra frill for a few specialists in
advanced courses. Analytical philosophers or logicians (with a few
honourable exceptions such as Wittgenstein and Austin) tend to
minimise the effect that figures of speech might have on their enter-
prise, or to believe that logic might, so to speak, reduce, encompass,
or master rhetoric. Such logicians or analysts tend to be violently
and unreasonably hostile to a philosopher of rhetoric such as
Jacques Derrida and even to deny him the name of philosopher (for
is not philosophy purely a matter of logical reasoning?)

The claim of 'deconstruction', by now patiently (and reasonably)
demonstrated with a wide variety of philosophical and literary texts
and patiently (and reasonably) argued in 'theoretical' statements, is
that language is figurative through and through, all the way down to
the bottom, so to speak, and that rhetoric in the sense of tropes
inhibits or prevents both the mastery of the plain sense of texts,
which is promised by grammar, and the mastery of reasoning, which
is promised by logic. 'Rhetoric radically suspends logic and opens
up vertiginous possibilities of referential aberration.' If this is the
case (and it is), rhetoric is not so much the imperial queen of the
trivium and of basic studies in humanities generally, as it is the odd
man out, the jack of spades or the wild card, who suspends the
game or at any rate causes much trouble in playing it. This is not an
argument against the kind of study of rhetoric that I have tried to
define and exemplify in this essay. Far from it. Though the truth
about language may be a dark and troubling one, it is better to know
that truth than to fool oneself or others, since language is an edge
tool, and much harm may be done by even the most amiable and
well-meaning of mistaken assumptions about it, as the sad story of
Mr Stelling demonstrates.

From *Writing and Reading Differently: Deconstruction and the
Teaching of Composition and Literature*, ed. G. Douglas Atkins and
Michael L. Johnson (Lawrence, KS, 1985), pp. 101–14.

NOTES

[J. Hillis Miller, often associated with the Yale School of Criticism, has
written widely on Eliot, drawing attention to linguistic structures and contradictions in Eliot's novels, and the ideological assumptions that inform
them. In this radical essay, which first appeared in the collection *Writing*

and Reading Differently (1985), Miller takes a single passage from *The Mill on the Floss* (Tom Tulliver's suffering in school at the hands of Mr Stelling) as a way of showing how a text deconstructs itself. 'The passage speaks of the activity of reading, manifests a model of that activity, and invites us to read it according to the method it employs.' The passage, with its abundance of metaphorical structures, not only serves to demonstrate George Eliot's skilful and playful use of language (thus acting as an object lesson for students of composition) but reveals her 'awareness of our linguistic predicament in not being able to ... declare what a thing is, except by saying it is something else'. All quotations in the essay are taken from *The Mill on the Floss* (Cabinet Edition, Edinburgh: William Blackwood, n.d.) Eds]

1. In Winifred Bryan Horner (ed.), *Composition & Literature: Bridging the Gap* (Chicago, 1983), pp. 38–56.

2. *Phaedrus*, 261d–2b, trans. R. Hackforth, in Edith Hamilton and Huntington Cairns (eds), *Plato: The Collected Dialogues* (Princeton, NJ, 1963), pp. 507–8. The citations from *Gorgias* are from the translation by W. D. Woodhead in the same volume, pp. 229–307.

3. See Aristotle, *The Rhetoric*, trans. Lane Cooper (New York, 1932), p. 10.

4. For example, by Joseph Litvak in a recent PhD dissertation in Comparative Literature at Yale University.

5. George Eliot, *The Mill on the Floss*, Vol. 1 (Edinburgh and London, n.d.), bk 2, ch. 1, pp. 213–17.

6. George Eliot, *Middlemarch*, Vol. 1 (Edinburgh and London, n.d.), ch. 10, p. 127.

7. The *OED* gives several examples under 'Desert' and 'Ship', the earliest dated 1615.

8. Aristotle, *Poetics*, trans. S. H. Butcher (New York, 1951), 1459a, p. 87.

9. Eliot, *Middlemarch*, Vol. 1, ch. 6, p. 86.

10. Cited by Richard A. Lanham, *A Handlist of Rhetorical Terms* (Berkeley, CA, 1969), p. 100.

11. William Wordsworth, 'Essays upon Epitaphs', in W. J. B. Owen and Jane Worthington Smyser (eds), *The Prose Works* (Oxford, 1974), Vol. 2, p. 81.

12. George Meredith, *One of Our Conquerors*, in *Works* (London, 1909–11), Vol. 17, p. 189.

13. Robert Moynihan, 'Interviews with Paul de Man', *Yale Review*, 73: 4 (July 1984), 580.

14. Paul de Man, *Allegories of Reading* (New Haven, CT, 1979), p. 10.

15. For the first see Jacques Derrida, 'Signature Event Context'; John R. Searle, 'Reiterating the Difference: A Reply to Derrida', *Glyph*, 1 (Baltimore, MD, 1977), 172–208; and Derrida, 'Limited Inc', *Glyph*, 2 (Baltimore, MD, 1977), 162–254. For the second see Paul de Man, 'Sign and Symbol in Hegel's *Aesthetics*', *Critical Inquiry*, 8: 4 (Summer 1982), 761–75; Raymond Geuss, 'A Response to Paul de Man'; and Paul de Man, 'Reply to Raymond Geuss', *Critical Inquiry*, 10: 2 (December 1983), 3375–90. For the third see M. H. Abrams, 'The Deconstructive Angel'; and J. Hillis Miller, 'The Critic as Host', *Critical Inquiry*, 3: 3 (Spring 1977), 425–47. For the fourth see Gerald Graff, *Literature against Itself: Literary Ideas in Modern Society* (Chicago, 1979); and Frank Lentricchia, *After the New Criticism* (Chicago, 1980). The literature about, for, and against deconstruction has since 1980 grown to impressive proportions.

3

The Chains of Semiosis: Semiotics, Marxism, and the Female Stereotypes in *The Mill on the Floss*

JOSÉ ANGEL GARCÍA LANDA

A semiotic-ideological aesthetics will include a typology of material forms of expression in order to understand the way ideologies arise. This typology is a historical one. In the case of literature, it includes the study of the kinds of contact available between writer and public: the existence of the printed press, of periodicals which publish instalments of novels, the extension of literacy to a wider reading public, the relationship between literacy (or kinds of literacy) and social role, etc. But it also includes a study of which is the repertory of types, conventions, genres, themes available to a writer. Once this repertory is understood to be ideological, and in no simple way 'natural', we might as well speak of 'forms of *production*'. Literary production is determined by an enormous range of factors: the existence of a privileged literary tradition, the nature of the division between the cultural elite and mass culture, the commercial, cultural, and other links between countries which allow the influence of foreign literatures, etc.

The literary work is seen by Voloshinov in a way which combines the insights of Marxism with those of the Russian Formalists: it is an instance of semiotic performance, and it does not exist outside of a communicative context.[1] The literary work is not a self-contained whole. As a signic construct, it needs the implementation of the receiver, and this changes from age to age.[2] The interplay between theme and meaning described by Voloshinov takes place at several levels. In conversation we negotiate a specific theme from the meanings that we identify at word, sentence, and textual levels. Each level is more thematic than the previous one, but none is completely thematic; all rest ultimately on the intersubjective availability of meaning. This is clearer in reading literature: the words on the page are set in a specific context, they refer to a fictional situation and we can identify an addressee-role or an implied reader who is a derivative of the communicative implementation coded in the text. This implementation does not close the text for the reader: the text remains inevitably open. The partial implementation is completed by the actual reader, or contradicted; we may feel that we do not want to become the implied reader of that text, and we implement the text in a different direction; we reject the 'evaluative accent' that we detect in the authorial attitude. It is in this sense that we might say that, even in literature, 'Any true understanding is dialogic in nature'.[3]

Moreover, the communicative context is in this case wider, and it includes the literary works of the past (at least, those which are more directly relevant to the situation of the writer and his audience). 'Each monument carries on the work of its predecessors, polemicising with them, expecting active, responsive understanding and anticipating such understanding in return.'[4] This conception amounts to a historisation of T. S. Eliot's structural limbo, where the great works of literature are arranged in an 'ideal order' which is altered each time a work of genius is created.[5] We could relate this insight of Voloshinov's to another concept introduced by him, that of 'behavioural ideology', that is, 'that atmosphere of unsystematised and unfixed inner and outer speech which endows our every instance of behaviour and action and our every "conscious" state with meaning'.[6] Behavioural ideology is linked to specific social activities, and there is a constant feedback between it and the systematised social institutions:

> The established ideological systems of social ethics, science, art, and religion are crystallisations of behavioural ideology, and these crystallisations in turn exert a powerful influence back upon behavioural ideology, normally setting its tone.[7]

Now, at least as regards literature, it is clear that it is not only an institution, a canon, etc., but also an activity: writing takes place as one more of the dialogic social activities. A writer is working in two contexts. The first is the institution of literature, consisting of works by writers of other nations or other ages, models, plots, character types, and narrative strategies. The second is his experience of social life at large. A writer – for example, George Eliot – may derive her semiotic materials from any of the 'real life' contexts she is involved in, such as the discourse on/of woman in Victorian England. These two contexts are not separate; indeed, it is one of the main tasks of the writer to bring each to bear on the other, to turn them into one. Literature, as the first of the mass media (in a historical perspective), has been an influential way of diffusing ideological representations of the self and of social relationships. Its material is not a raw one; it has been socially elaborated.[8] This material is often the ideology of everyday life. It is also a result, an important object of the writer's production.

A simple instance of this ideological production is the use of female stereotypes in *The Mill on the Floss*.[9] Eliot's use of these stereotypes is one aspect of a wholesale reflection on the gender roles favoured in her society. As a whole, *The Mill on the Floss* deals with an issue of gender representation, more specifically of female self-representation. The opening section of the book features a ghost-like authorial narrator evoking the image of a small girl looking at the mill. The closing lines of book 1, ch. 1 suggest that the girl is the narrator herself. The conclusion of the book will prove otherwise, but the empathic manoeuvre stands: Maggie Tulliver (it is a conclusion easily drawn from Mary Ann Evans's life) will be an experiment in self-representation on the part of the author. This opening movement inaugurates the tension between a system of four terms: childhood and maturity, maleness and femaleness. The tension is established by their collapsing into each other in the narrator's reverie. An old person remembers a distant childhood; the voice of male maturity (remember the *George* on the title page) suddenly becomes sexually ambiguous. The conflict of gender in *The Mill on the Floss* reaches the level of narration, but here we shall only follow the thread of some of its manifestations at story level.

The issue of gender roles is at the core of the conflicts and tensions in the Tulliver household dramatised in book 1 of the novel, a book with the revealing title 'Boy and Girl'. Mr Tulliver's patriarchal convictions are already evident in the choice of his wife '"'cause she was a bit weak, like; for I wasn't a-goin' to be told the rights o' things by my own fireside"'.[10] Male superiority is in this case accidental; the reverse, female superiority, is equally accidental in the case of the Tulliver children, Tom and Maggie. That is, generic difference is represented in the novel as *ideological* in the narrow sense of the word: it is a matter of tendentious representations on the part of the dominant group. Mr Tulliver's prejudiced views will partly bring about the catastrophe of the novel, his ruin and downfall: he wastes his money on Tom with no better reason than his being his *male heir*, in a pathetic attempt to extract from the boy the proof of his own superiority as a male, while he devotes the same unconscious obstination to curb Maggie's spontaneous growth.

The child's socialisation is portrayed in *The Mill on the Floss* as a complex of strategies of representation. Mr Tulliver, Mrs Tulliver, the epitome of alienated womanhood. Mr Stelling, Mr Riley, Tom – all foist upon Maggie the behavioural ideology of patriarchy in the field of generic self-representation: a whole catalogue of activities, hearsays, admonitions, and attitudes of the child towards her own body, which is supposed to become the emblem of her successful socialisation into female difference, a text of submission.[11] But Maggie is always portrayed as striving to escape these stereotypes: she is rebellious, intelligent, she reads difficult books (p. 11), her hair refuses to stay in place:

> Mrs Tulliver, desiring her daughter to have a curled crop, 'like other folk's children,' had had it cut too short in front to be pushed behind the ears, and as it was usually straight an hour after it had been taken out of the paper, Maggie was incessantly tossing her head to keep the dark, heavy locks out of her gleaming black eyes – an action which gave her very much the air of a small Shetland pony.
>
> (p. 7)

Everything in Maggie, her very physiognomy marks her out as the contrary of what they all wish to read into her. Her hair, most notably becomes an emblem of her irrepressible, mouldbreaking vitality, opposed to 'Mrs Tulliver's curls and capstrings' (p. 25) or her blonde cousin Lucy's 'row o' curls round her head, an' not a hair out o' place' (p. 7).

In a reflexive section of the book, Maggie and Philip Wakem are talking about literature. Maggie opposes Philip Wakem's desire to idealise her: she declines to see herself as a muse, and contests the current literary portraits of women:

> 'Take back your *Corinne* ... I'm determined to read no more books where the blonde-haired women carry away all the happiness. I

should begin to have a prejudice against them. If you could give me some story, now, where the dark woman triumphs, it would restore the balance. I want to avenge Rebecca, and Flora MacIvor, and Minna, and all the rest of the dark unhappy ones.'

'Well, perhaps you will avenge the dark women in your own person and carry away all the love from your cousin Lucy. She is sure to have some handsome young man of St. Ogg's at her feet now, and you have only to shine upon him – your fair little cousin will be quite quenched in your beams.'

(p. 299)

As Nancy K. Miller notes, Philip anticipates here the second part of the novel, but not wholly – and that is Eliot's point. This is an astonishing passage, where the character denounces a literary stereotype of which she is herself an instance, used in a deliberate and self-conscious way by Eliot.[12] The stereotypical opposition of the blonde and the dark heroine we may take to be a construct of the behavioural ideology of a monogamous (Northern European) patriarchy. The idealised, socially productive elements of the female sex are embodied in the blonde heroine, while the more disturbing elements of womanhood go to the dark one. The dark heroines are not merely powerfully sexed; they also have a strong will; they tend to be self-assertive, courageous and demanding; they are the Amazon side of womanhood. Examples abound, especially in English and American literature: the female pairs of *The Last of the Mohicans* or *The Woman in White* come to mind, apart from the heroines Maggie mentions. But George Eliot does more than recognise and denounce the stereotype; she uses it. By means of Maggie's rejection of the stereotype, Eliot deprives it of any real basis; but that does not prevent her from exploiting it in the construction of Maggie, as a literary convention which adds a powerful echo to the work. Maggie Tulliver becomes an intertextual heroine; the unconsciously accumulated images of female subjection speak through her in a new way.

These figures of dark heroines may not be wholly 'unconsciously accumulated', however. The standard example of this literary stereotype in Eliot's age was Mme de Staël's *Corinne, ou l'Italie*, and it is a self-conscious one to some extent. Ellen Moers traces the fascination of nineteenth-century writers with Corinne, a 'female Childe Harold', the superior (black-haired) woman who is crowned poetess in Rome and dies unhappily after losing her lover to her blonde cousin Lucile.[13] Corinne was a thinly disguised self-portrait of her author, also black-haired and admired as a *rara avis* in a world of men. Moers notes the symbolism of black hair in *The Mill on the Floss*: throughout the novel it represents Maggie's difficulty to settle into the conventional female role. Moers notes the use of a similar symbolism in *Corinne* and deplores Eliot's use of the allusion, and her turning Maggie, not into a Corinne (which she does not want to be anyway), 'but instead into a merely pretty and dangerous flirt who steals a rich, good-looking suitor away from her cousin Lucy' (p. 174). Accordingly, Moers accepts the usual view of Maggie's death in the flood as a *deus ex machina*: 'Maggie's convenient death in the flood is designed to smooth over, both practically and morally, her ugly revenge on blondes in the person of "dear little Lucy"' (p. 175). And Moers concludes her astonishingly inadequate reading with the comment that 'George Eliot was always concerned with the superior large-souled woman whose distinction resides not in her deeds but in her capacity to attract attention and arouse admiration' (p. 194). Moers ignores the crucial event in the plot: Maggie's *active decision* to abandon her lover and to be the object not of the admiration but of the jeers of society. The heroine she describes in the last quotation does not in the least resemble Maggie. Instead, she is the very image of Corinne. If she had accepted the last of the feminine roles foisted on her and run away with Stephen Guest, Maggie would have been a successful Corinne, and would have had her 'revenge'. But she refrains from doing it. It is clear that Eliot is rejecting the stereotype of the 'admirable woman' represented by Corinne and her literary daughters, a stereotype that declares the black-haired heroine admirable only as the exception of her sex, and on the traditional 'feminine' grounds of powerful feeling and passion. As Eliot noted elsewhere, 'Women have not to prove that they can be emotional, and rhapsodic, and spiritualistic; everyone believes that already. They have to prove that they are capable of accurate thought, severe study, and continuous self-command.'[14] This *is* a feminist programme, although it does not look like one to such feminist critics as Moers or Lynn Sukenick. According to the latter, Eliot's readers have always been surprised to find that she is not a feminist: 'she held closely for a time to the Comteian view that women are the prime receptacles of feeling in the culture'.[15] However, it is clear that to the extent that Maggie Tulliver chooses to be a 'receptacle of feeling' the author does not stand by her decision because of the fact that Maggie is a woman. 'Feeling' should not be restricted to women, in Eliot's view; consider, for instance, her masculine prototype, Adam Bede.

Anyway, 'feeling' is not the right word; '*reflexive* moral awareness' is a better description of the quality Eliot is endorsing. This is why Maggie abandons her lover and chooses moral responsibility and duty instead of romantic feeling. The choice of an image of the self which is wholly human involves the rejection of constraining ideological roles and elevation to a level of consciousness where mere sexual propriety is irrelevant.

George Eliot's attitudes towards gender can be easily deconstructed now, and shown to be, in the last analysis, a bow to the traditional generic roles. But this would be a facile manoeuvre, possible only because of our historical vantage point on the nineteenth century. Besides, some recent work on feminist theory acknowledges that the priorities defined by nineteenth-century feminists were legitimate ones for their situation.[16] Maybe we would have to live in the 1860s to fully appreciate George Eliot's project as a necessary task. It is one that she carried out consistently in her life, not least in her decision to become a 'male' novelist, a role which she could not help but subvert.

The analysis of female subjection in *The Mill on the Floss* does not stop here. With a sure instinct, Eliot portrays the material circumstances which ensure the perpetuation of ideology. Attention is drawn to the connection between the ideological immobility of the inhabitants of St Ogg and the stability of their material circumstances. The stagnant and inflexible transmission of property from one generation to another is emphasised by Eliot; beliefs are transmitted in much the same way as shops or cutlery. Mrs Glegg inherits from her grandmother a magnificent symbol of the reification of social status, 'a brocaded gown that would stand up empty, like a suit of armour' (p. 106). There is a whole constellation of associations at work here. The family pride and reactionary ideology of the nobility speak silently through the allusion to a suit of armour; also the self-defensive attitude and the instinctive fear behind Mrs Glegg's bourgeois intolerance. That the suit can stand *empty* is not a mere bow to the art of embroidery; it speaks of the inessentiality of the bourgeois self, the bourgeois (female) respectability, and of the alienation of the bourgeoisie in its possessions, in the fury of ownership. Indeed, if we are optimistic enough, George Eliot will let us read a materialist theory of conscience into her:

> If anyone strongly impressed with the power of the human mind to triumph over circumstances will contend that the parishioners of

> Basset might nevertheless have been a very superior class of people, I have nothing to argue against that abstract proposition; I only know that, in point of fact, the Basset mind was in strict keeping with its circumstances.
>
> (p. 68)

But in fact, in George Eliot's universe, ideological mobility exists only in the direction of individual growth and moral awareness; in the last analysis she regards property as inessential. The bourgeoisie is not attacked as such: it is only a convenient vehicle for the attitudes George Eliot deplores. The values she endorses and sets against the bourgeoisie (individual growth, self-examination) are also bourgeois values.

Nevertheless, this passage points to the fact that, after all, Maggie Tulliver is an exception, the result, as far as we can see, of chance and of the complex interplay of sexual roles in the Tulliver household. Elsewhere, the mind is in strict keeping with its circumstances. George Eliot shows why this is so, and why change cannot be a mere act of the will: everyone expects that we act our roles. In order to lead a normal life, Maggie would have to fight St Ogg, the bourgeoisie, and the nineteenth century. As Miller notes, 'Everywhere in *The Mill on the Floss* one can read a protest against the division of labour that grants men the world and women love.'[17] The colour and movement of Maggie's hair is a protest against this situation, a protest that only apparently is silent. Her 'implausible' death by water points to an oblique symbol of the weight of social conformity against the mobility of generic roles. Maggie is doomed from the beginning; her family's admonitions against her boyishness are interspersed with alarm that she might have drowned in the river (pp. 6, 91). Moreover, there is in this death something like a fantasy of escape through suicide; witness a scene which maybe does not lack symbolic overtones:

> The morning was too wet, Mrs Tulliver said, for a little girl to go out in her best bonnet. Maggie took the opposite view very strongly, and it was a direct consequence of this difference of opinion that when her mother was in the act of brushing out the reluctant black crop, Maggie suddenly rushed from under her hands and dipped her head in a basin of water standing near in the vindictive determination that there should be no more chance of curls that day.
>
> (p. 20)

That the parallelism with the novel's ending is most probably unconscious is all the more telling about the meaning of that ending, and of Eliot's deep compromise in this empathic self-representation. Maggie Tulliver is the result of George Eliot's work on the female stereotypes of her age as she experienced them in both life and literature. *The Mill on the Floss* is a direct attack on the subject positions available to nineteenth-century women, even those that seemed most favourable, like the Corinne myth. It is a real work effected on material-social roles, representations of gender – which is at once imaginary and real; a fiction, but a liberating one, the kind of fiction people live by.[18]

From *Papers in Language and Literature*, 27:1 (1991), 41–50.

NOTES

[This excerpt is taken from an essay which first appeared in the journal, *Papers in Language and Literature (PLL)*. In its discussion of the ideas of gender representation, female self-representation and Marxist linguistics, it can perhaps be seen as typical of the way in which feminist literary criticism borrows from other theoretical discourses. Here, Landa's specific interest is in Eliot's use of gender stereotypes, the implications of which are seen to refract back onto the characters, most notably Maggie Tulliver but also her cousin Lucy. Landa shares Fraiman's interest in the limited subject positions available to women and, like Fraiman (essay 1), discusses *The Mill* in terms of its challenge to realist conventions. Landa's particular focus is codes of representation, specifically the way in which the restrictive conventions of the light and dark heroine are played out in *The Mill*. These codes impose expected forms of behaviour on the novel's female characters from which they may or may not struggle to free themselves. All quotations in the essay are taken from *The Mill on the Floss* (New York: Bantram, 1987). Eds]

1. See V. N. Voloshinov, *Marxism and the Philosophy of Language*, trans. Ladislav Matejka and I. R. Titunik (Cambridge, 1986).

2. Cf. Roman Ingarden's distinction between a work and its concretisation, and his notion of the life of a work of art. *The Literary Work of Art*, trans. George Grabowicz (Evanston, IL, 1973), p. 333. In Voloshinov's work a more contextualised conception is advanced, if only schematically.

3. Voloshinov, *Marxism and the Philosophy of Language*, p. 102.

4. Ibid., p. 72.

5. T. S. Eliot, 'Tradition and the Individual Talent', in *Selected Essays* (London, 1951), p. 15.

6. Voloshinov, *Marxism and the Philosophy of Language*, p. 97.

7. Ibid., p. 91.

8. See Michel van Schendel, 'L'ideologème est un quasi-argument', *Texte*, 5/6 (1986–87), 93.

9. There are male stereotypes as well in George Eliot's novels, which I think are also used deliberately by the author, but in *The Mill on the Floss* they are at the service of the central figure, Maggie Tulliver.

10. George Eliot, *The Mill on the Floss* (New York, 1987), p. 13. All further references, included in the text, are to this edition.

11. With respect to the behavioural ideology of socialisation through dress, movement, and attitude, see Frigga Haug et al., *Female Sexualization* (London, 1987).

12. Northrop Frye notes several instances of this stereotype, as well as its inverted 'mate' version in *Wuthering Heights*. See *Anatomy of Criticism* (Princeton, NJ, 1957), p. 101. It may be significant that the two novels which use the stereotype in a deviant or self-conscious way are the work of women.

13. Ellen Moers, *Literary Women* (Garden City, NY, 1976), ch. 9, especially p. 176. Note the deliberate parallelism of Lucile/Lucy.

14. Eliot, *Selected Essays*, p. 334.

15. See Arlyn Diamond and Lee K. Edwards (eds), *The Authority of Experience: Essays in Feminist Criticism* (Amherst, MA, 1977).

16. See, for instance, Ellen Carol Du Bois and Linda Gordon, 'Seeking Ecstasy on the Battlefield: Danger and Pleasure in Nineteenth-century Feminist Sexual Thought', in Carole S. Vance (ed.), *Pleasure and Danger: Exploring Female Sexuality* (Boston, 1984).

17. Nancy K. Miller, 'Emphasis Added: Plots and Plausibilities in Women's Fiction', in Elaine Showalter (ed.), *The New Feminist Criticism* (New York, 1985), p. 357.

18. I would like to thank Neil Lazarus of Brown University for his comments on a first version of this paper. This and other related works were prepared during a sabbatical leave from the University of Zaragoza, and I am indebted for financial assistance to the USA-Spanish Joint Committee for Cultural and Educational Cooperation. I appreciate the support of both institutions.

4

Men of Maxims and *The Mill on the Floss*

MARY JACOBUS

> The first question to ask is therefore the following: how can women analyse their own exploitation, inscribe their own demands, within an order prescribed by the masculine? *Is a women's politics possible within that order?*
>
> (Luce Irigaray)[1]

To rephrase the question: Can there be (a politics of) women's writing? What does it mean to say that women can analyse their exploitation only 'within an order prescribed by the masculine'? And what theory of sexual difference can we turn to when we speak, as feminist critics are wont to do, of a specifically 'feminine' practice in writing? Questions like these mark a current impasse in contemporary feminist criticism. Utopian attempts to define the specificity of women's writing – desired or hypothetical, but rarely empirically observed – either founder on the rock of essentialism (the text as body), gesture toward an avant-garde practice which turns out not to be specific to women, or, like Hélène Cixous in 'The Laugh of the Medusa', do both.[2] If anatomy is not destiny, still less can it be language.

A politics of women's writing, then, if it is not to fall back on a biologically based theory of sexual difference, must address itself, as Luce Irigaray has done in 'The Power of Discourse and the Subordination of the Feminine', to the position of mastery held not only by scientific discourse (Freudian theory, for instance), not only by philosophy, 'the discourse of discourse', but by the logic of discourse itself. Rather than attempting to identify a specific practice, in other words, such a feminist politics would attempt to relocate sexual difference at the level of the text by undoing the repression of the 'feminine' in all the systems of representation for which the Other (woman) must be reduced to the economy of the Same (man). In Irigaray's terms, 'masculine' systems of representation are those whose self-reflexiveness and specularity disappropriate women of their relation to themselves and to other women; as in Freud's theory of sexual difference (woman equals man-minus), difference is swiftly converted into hierarchy. Femininity comes to signify a role, an image, a value imposed on women by the narcissistic and fundamentally misogynistic logic of such masculine systems. The question then becomes for Irigaray not 'What is woman?' (still less Freud's desperate 'What does a woman want?') but 'How is the feminine determined by discourse itself?' – determined, that is, as lack or error or as an inverted reproduction of the masculine subject.[3]

Invisible or repressed, the hidden place of the feminine in language is the hypothesis which sustains the model of the textual universe, like ether. We know it must be there because we know ourselves struggling for self-definition in other terms, elsewhere, elsehow. We need it, so we invent it. When such an article of faith doesn't manifest itself as a mere rehearsal of sexual stereotypes, it haunts contemporary feminist criticism in its quest for specificity – whether of language, or literary tradition, or women's culture. After all, why study women's writing at all unless it is 'women's writing' in the first place? The answer, I believe, must be a political one, and one whose impulse also fuels that gesture toward an elusive *écriture féminine*' or specificity. To postulate, as Irigaray does, a 'work of language' which undoes the repression of the feminine constitutes in itself an attack on the dominant ideology, the very means by which we know what we know and think what we think. So too the emphasis on women's writing politicises in a flagrant and polemical fashion the 'difference' which has traditionally been elided by criticism and by the canon formulations of literary history. To label a text as that of a woman, and to write about it for that reason, makes vividly legible what the critical institution has either ignored or acknowledged only under the sign of inferiority. We need the term 'women's writing' if only to remind us of the social conditions under which women wrote and still write – to remind us that the conditions of their (re)production are the economic and educational disadvantages, the sexual and material organisations of society, which, rather than biology, form the crucial determinants of women's writing.

Feminist criticism, it seems to me, ultimately has to invoke as its starting point this underlying political assumption. To base its theory on a specificity of language or literary tradition or culture is already to have moved one step on in the argument, if not already to have begged the question, since by then one is confronted by what Nancy Miller, in a recent essay on women's fiction, has called 'the irreducibly complicated relationship women have historically had to the language of the dominant culture'.[4] Perhaps that is why, baffled in their attempts to specify the feminine, feminist critics have so often turned to an analysis of this relationship as it is manifested and thematised in writing by and about women. The project is, and can't escape being, an ideological one; concerned, that is, with the functioning and reproduction of sexual ideology in particular – whether in the overtly theoretical terms of Luce Irigaray or in the fictional terms of, for instance, George Eliot. To quote Miller again, the aim would be to show that 'the maxims that pass for the truth of human experience, and the encoding of that experience in literature, are organisations, when they are not fantasies, of the dominant culture'.[5]

But Irigaray's 'women's politics', her feminist argument, goes beyond ideology critique in its effort to recover 'the place of the feminine' in discourse. The 'work of language' which she envisages would undo representation altogether, even to the extent of refusing the linearity of reading. 'Après-coup', the retroactive effect of a word ending, opens up the structure of language to reveal the repression on which meaning depends; and repression is the place of the feminine. By contrast, the 'style' of women – écriture féminine – would privilege not the look but the tactile, the simultaneous, the fluid. Yet at the same time, we discover, such a style can't be sustained as a thesis or made the object of a position; if not exactly 'nothing', it is nonetheless a kind of discursive practice that can't be thought, still less written. Like her style, woman herself is alleged by Irigaray to be an unimaginable concept within the existing order. Elaborating a theory of which woman is either the subject or the object merely reinstalls the feminine within a logic that represses, censors, or misrecognises it. Within that logic, woman can only signify an excess or a deranging power. Woman for Irigaray is always the 'something else' that points to the possibility of another language, asserts that the masculine is not all, does not have a monopoly on value, or, still less, 'the abusive privilege of appropriation'. She tries to strike through the theoretical machinery itself, suspending its pretension to the production of a single truth, a univocal meaning. Woman would thus find herself on the side of everything in language that is multiple, duplicitous, unreliable, and resistant to the binary oppositions on which theories of sexual difference such as Freud's depend.[6]

Irigaray's argument is seductive precisely because it puts all systems in question, leaving process and fluidity instead of fixity and form. At the same time, it necessarily concedes that women have access to language only by recourse to systems of representation that are masculine. Given the coherence of the systems at work in discourse, whether Freudian or critical, how is the work of language of which she speaks to be undertaken at all? Her answer is 'mimetism', the role historically assigned to women – that of reproduction, but deliberately assumed; an acting out or role playing within the text which allows the woman writer to know better and hence to expose what it is she mimics. Irigaray, in fact, seems to be saying that there is no 'outside' of discourse, no alternative practice available to the woman writer apart from the process of undoing itself:

> To play with mimesis is thus, for a woman, to try to recover the place of her exploitation by discourse, without allowing herself to be simply reduced to it. It means to resubmit herself – inasmuch as she is on the side of the 'perceptible', of 'matter' – to 'ideas', in particular to ideas about herself, that are elaborated in/by a masculine logic, but so as to make 'visible', by an effect of playful repetition, what was supposed to remain invisible: the cover-up of a possible operation of the feminine in language. It also means 'to unveil' the fact that, if women are such good mimics, it is because they are not simply resorbed in this function. *They also remain elsewhere.*[7]

Within the systems of discourse and representation which repress the feminine, woman can only resubmit herself to them; but by refusing to be reduced by them, she points to the place and manner of her exploitation. 'A possible operation of the feminine in language' becomes, then, the revelation of its repression, through an effect of playful rehearsal, rather than a demonstrably feminine linguistic practice.

Irigaray's main usefulness to the feminist critic lies in this half-glimpsed possibility of undoing the ideas about women elaborated in and by masculine logic, a project at once analytic and ideological. Her attack on centrism in general, and phallocentrism in particular, allows the feminist critic to ally herself 'otherwise', with the 'elsewhere' to which Irigaray gestures, in a stance of dissociation and resistance where typically characterises that of feminist criticism in its relation to the dominant culture or 'order prescribed by the masculine'. But like Irigaray herself in 'The Power of Discourse', feminist criticism remains imbricated within the forms of intelligibility – reading and writing, the logic of discourse – against which it pushes. What makes the 'difference', then? Surely, the direction from which that criticism comes – the elsewhere that it invokes, the putting in question of our social organisation of gender; its wishfulness, even, in imagining alternatives. It follows that what pleases the feminist critic most (this one, at any rate) is to light on a text that seems to do her arguing, or some of it, for her – especially a text whose story is the same as hers; hence, perhaps, the drift toward narrative in recent works of feminist criticism such as Sandra Gilbert and Susan Gubar's influential *The Madwoman in the Attic*.[8] What's usually going on in such criticism – perhaps in all feminist criticism – is a specificity of relationship that amounts to a distinctive practice. Criticism takes literature as its object, yes; but here literature in a different sense is likely to become the subject, the feminist critic, the woman writer, woman herself.

This charged and doubled relationship, an almost inescapable aspect of feminist criticism, is at once transgressive and liberating, since what it brings to light is the hidden or unspoken ideological premise of criticism itself. *Engagée* perforce, feminist criticism calls neutrality into question, like other avowedly political analyses of literature. I want now to undertake a 'symptomatic' reading of a thematically relevant chapter from Eliot's *The Mill on the Floss* (1860) in the hope that this quintessentially critical activity will bring to light if not 'a possible operation of the feminine in language' at least one mode of its recovery – language itself. I will return later to the final chapter of Irigaray's *This Sex Which Is Not One* in which an escape from masculine systems of representation is glimpsed through the metaphors of female desire itself.

Nancy Miller's 'maxims that pass for the truth of human experience' allude to Eliot's remark near the end of *The Mill on the Floss* that 'the man of maxims is the popular representative of the minds that are guided in their moral judgment solely by general rules'.[9]

Miller's concern is the accusation of implausibility levelled at the plots of women's novels: Eliot's concern is the 'special case' of Maggie Tulliver – 'to lace ourselves up in formulas' is to ignore 'the special circumstances that mark the individual lot'. An argument for the individual makes itself felt as an argument against generalities. For Eliot herself, as for Dr Kenn (the repository of her knowledge at this point in the novel), 'the mysterious complexity of our life is not to be embraced by maxims' (p. 628). Though the context is the making of moral, not critical, judgments, I think that Eliot, as so often at such moments, is concerned also with both the making and the reading of fiction; with the making of another kind of special case. Though Maggie may be an 'exceptional' woman, the ugly duckling of St Ogg's, her story contravenes the norm, and in that respect it could be said to be all women's story. We recall an earlier moment, that of Tom Tulliver's harsh judgment of his sister ('You have not resolution to resist a thing that you know to be wrong'), and Maggie's rebellious murmuring that her life is 'a planless riddle to him' only because he's incapable of feeling the mental needs which impel her, in his eyes, to wrongdoing or absurdity (pp. 504, 505). To Tom, the novel's chief upholder of general rules and patriarchal law (he makes his sister swear obedience to his prohibitions on the family Bible), the planless riddle of Maggie's life is only made sense of by a 'Final Rescue' which involves her death: 'In their death they were not divided' (p. 657). But the reunion of brother and sister in the floodwaters of the Ripple enacts both reconciliation and revenge, consummation and cataclysm; powerful authorial desires are at work.[10] To simplify this irreducible swirl of contradictory desire in the deluge that 'rescues' Maggie as well as her brother would be to salvage a maxim as 'jejune' as '*Mors omnibus est communis*' (one of the tags Maggie finds when she dips into her brother's Latin grammar) stripped of its saving Latin.[11] We might go further and say that to substitute a generality for the riddle of Maggie's life and death, or to translate Latin maxims into English commonplaces, would constitute a misreading of the novel as inept as Tom's misconstruction of his sister, or his Latin. Maggie's incomprehensible foreignness, her drift into error or impropriety on the river with Stephen Guest, is a 'lapse' understood by the latitudinarian Dr Kenn. For us, it also involves an understanding that planlessness, riddles, and impropriety – the enigmas, accidents, and incorrectness of language itself – are at odds with the closures of plot (here, the plot of incestuous reunion) and with interpretation itself, as well as with the finality of the maxims denounced by Eliot. For all its healing of division, *The Mill on the Floss* uncovers the divide between the language or maxims of the dominant culture and the language itself which undoes them. In life, at any rate, they remain divided – indeed, death may be the price of unity – and feminist criticism might be said to install itself in the gap. A frequent move on the part of feminist criticism is to challenge the norms and aesthetic criteria of the dominant culture (as Miller does in defending Eliot), claiming in effect, that 'incorrectness' makes visible what is specific to women's writing. The culturally imposed or assumed 'lapses' of women's writing are turned against the system that brings them into being – a system women writers necessarily inhabit. What surfaces in this gesture is the all-important question of women's access to knowledge and culture and to the power that goes with them. In writing by women, the question is often explicitly thematised in terms of education. Eliot's account of Tom's schooling in 'School-Time', the opening chapter of Book 2, provides just such a thematic treatment – a lesson in antifeminist pedagogy which goes beyond its immediate implications for women's education to raise more far-reaching questions about the functioning of both sexual ideology and language. Take Maggie's puzzlement at one of the many maxims found in the Eton Grammar, a required text for the unfortunate Tom. As often, rules and examples prove hard to tell apart:

> The astronomer who hated women generally caused [Maggie] so much puzzling speculation that she one day asked Mr Stelling if all astronomers hated women, or whether it was only this particular astronomer. But, forestalling his answer, she said,
> 'I suppose it's all astronomers: because you know, they live up in high towers, and if the women came there, they might talk and hinder them from looking at the stars.'
> Mr Stelling liked her prattle immensely.
>
> (p. 220)

What we see here is a textbook example of the way in which individual misogyny becomes generalised – 'maximised', as it were – in the form of a patriarchal put-down. Maggie may have trouble construing '*ad unam mulieres*', or 'all to a woman', but in essence she has got it right.[12] Just to prove her point, Mr Stelling (who himself prefers the talk of women to star gazing) likes her 'prattle', a term used only of the talk of women and children. Reduced to his idea of her, Maggie can only mimic man's talk.

Inappropriate as he is in other respects for Tom's future career, Mr Stelling thus proves an excellent schoolmaster to his latent misogyny. His classroom is also an important scene of instruction for Maggie, who learns not only that all astronomers to a man hate women in general but that girls can't learn Latin; that they are quick and shallow, mere imitators ('this small apparatus of shallow quickness', Eliot playfully repeats); and that everybody hates clever women, even if they are amused by the prattle of clever little girls (pp. 214, 221, 216). It's hard not to read with one eye on her creator. Maggie, it emerges, rather fancies herself as a linguist, and Eliot too seems wishfully to imply that she has what one might call a 'gift' for languages – a gift, perhaps, for ambiguity too. Women, we learn, don't just talk, they double-talk, like language itself; that's just the trouble for boys like Tom:

> 'I know what Latin is very well', said Maggie, confidently. 'Latin's a language. There are Latin words in the Dictionary. There's bonus, a gift.'
> 'Now, you're just wrong there, Miss Maggie!' said Tom, secretly astonished. 'You think you're very wise! But "bonus" means "good", as it happens – bonus, bona, bonum.'
> 'Well, that's no reason why it shouldn't mean "gift"', said Maggie stoutly. 'It may mean several things. Almost every word does.'
>
> (p. 214)

And if words may mean several things, general rules or maxims may prove less universal than they claim to be and lose their authority. Perhaps only 'this particular astronomer' was a woman-hater or hated only one woman in particular. Special cases or particular contexts – 'the special circumstances that mark the individual lot' (p. 628) – determine or render indeterminate not only judgment but meaning too. The rules of language itself make Tom's role learning troublesome to him. How can he hope to construe his sister when her relation to language proves so treacherous – her difference so shifting a play of possibility, like the difference within language itself, destabilising terms such as 'wrong' and 'good'?

Maggie, a little parody of her author's procedures in *The Mill on the Floss*, decides 'to skip the rule in the syntax – the examples became so absorbing':

> These mysterious sentences snatched from an unknown context – like strange horns of beasts and leaves of unknown plants, brought from

some far-off region, gave boundless scope to her imagination, and were all the more fascinating because they were in a peculiar tongue of their own, which she could learn to interpret. It was really very interesting – the Latin Grammar that Tom had said no girls could learn: and she was proud because she found it interesting. The most fragmentary examples were her favourites. *Mors omnibus est communis* would have been jejune, only she liked to know the Latin; but the fortunate gentleman whom every one congratulated because he had a son 'endowed with *such* a disposition' afforded her a great deal of pleasant conjecture, and she was quite lost in the 'thick grove penetrable by no star', when Tom called out,

'Now, then, Magsie, give us the Grammar!'

(pp. 217–18)

Whereas maxims lace her up in formulas, 'these mysterious sentences' give boundless scope to Maggie's imagination; for her, as for her author (who makes them foretell her story), they are whole fictional worlds, alternative realities, transformations of the familiar into the exotic and strange. In their foreignness she finds herself, until roused by Tom's peremptory call, as she is later to be recalled by his voice from the Red Deeps. Here, however, it is Maggie who teaches Tom his most important lesson, that the 'dead' languages had once been living: 'that there had once been people upon the earth who were so fortunate as to know Latin without learning it through the medium of the Eton Grammar' (p. 221). The idea – or, rather, fantasy – of a language that is innate rather than acquired, native rather than incomprehensibly foreign, is a consoling one for the unbookish miller's son; but it holds out hope for Maggie too, and presumably also for her creator. Though Latin stands in for cultural imperialism and for the outlines of a peculiarly masculine and elitist classical education from which women have traditionally been excluded, Maggie can learn to interpret it. The 'peculiar tongue' had once been spoken by women, after all – and they had not needed to learn it from Mr Stelling or the institutions he perpetuates. Who knows, she might even become an astronomer herself, or, like Eliot, a writer who by her pen name had refused the institutionalisation of sexual difference as cultural exclusion. Tom and Mr Stelling tell Maggie that 'Girls never learn such things'; 'They've a great deal of superficial cleverness but they couldn't go far into anything' (pp. 214, 221). But going far into things – and going far – is the author's prerogative in *The Mill on the Floss*. Though Maggie's quest for knowledge ends in death, as Virginia Woolf thought Eliot's own had ended,[13] killing off this small apparatus of shallow quickness may have been the necessary sacrifice in order for Eliot herself to become an interpreter of the exotic possibilities contained in mysterious sentences. Maggie – unassimilable, incomprehensible, 'fallen' – is her text, a 'dead' language which thereby gives all the greater scope to authorial imaginings, making it possible for the writer to come into being.

We recognise in 'School-Time' Eliot's investment – humorous, affectionate, and rather innocently self-lovingly–in Maggie's gifts and haphazard acquisition of knowledge. In particular, we recognise a defence of the 'irregular' education which until recently had been the lot of most women, if educated at all. Earlier in the same chapter, in the context of Mr Stelling's teaching methods (that is, his unquestioning reliance on Euclid and the Eton Grammar), Eliot refers whimsically to 'Mr Broderip's amiable beaver' which 'busied himself as earnestly in constructing a dam, in a room up three pairs of stairs in London, as if he had been laying his foundation in a stream or lake in Upper Canada'. It was 'Binny's function to build' (p. 206). Binny the beaver, a pet from the pages of W. J. Broderip's *Leaves from the Note Book of a Naturalist* (1852), constructed his dam with sweeping brushes and warming pans, 'hand-brushes, rush-baskets, books, boots, sticks, clothes, dried turf or anything portable'.[14] A domesticated *bricoleur*, Binny makes do with what he can find. A few lines later, we hear of Mr Stelling's 'educated' condescension toward 'the display of various or special knowledge made by irregularly educated people' (p. 207). Mr Broderip's beaver, it turns out, does double duty as an illustration of Mr Stelling's 'regular' (not to say 'rote') mode of instruction – he can do no otherwise, conditioned as he is – and as a defence of Eliot's own display of irregularly acquired 'various or special knowledge'. Like Maggie's, this is knowledge drawn directly from books, without the aid of a patriarchal pedagogue. Mr Stelling and the institutions he subscribes to (Aristotle, deaneries, prebends, Great Britain, and Protestantism – the Establishment, in fact) are lined up against the author-as-eager-beaver. Eliot's mischievous impugning of authority and authorities – specifically, cultural authority – becomes increasingly explicit until, a page or so later, culture itself comes under attack. Finding Tom's brain 'peculiarly impervious to etymology and demonstration', Mr Stelling concludes that it 'was peculiarly in need of being ploughed and harrowed by these patent implements: it was his favourite metaphor, that the classics and geometry constituted that culture of the mind which prepared it for the reception of any subsequent crop'. As Eliot rather wittily observes, the regimen proves 'as uncomfortable for Tom Tulliver as if he had been plied with cheese in order to remedy a gastric weakness which prevented him from digesting it' (p. 208). Nor is Eliot only, or simply, being funny. The bonus or gift of language is at work here, translating dead metaphor into organic tract.

Like Maggie herself, the metaphor here is improper, disrespectful of authorities, and, as Tom later complains of his sister, not to be relied on. Developing the implications of changing her metaphor from agriculture to digestion, Eliot drastically undermines the realist illusion of her fictional world, revealing it to be no more than a blank page inscribed with a succession of arbitrary metaphoric substitutions:

> It is astonishing what a different result one gets by changing the metaphor! Once call the brain an intellectual stomach, and one's ingenious conception of the classics and geometry as ploughs and harrows seems to settle nothing. But then, it is open to some one else to follow great authorities and call the mind a sheet of white paper or a mirror, in which case one's knowledge of the digestive process becomes quite irrelevant. It was doubtless an ingenious idea to call the camel the ship of the desert, but it would hardly lead one far in training that useful beast. O Aristotle! if you had had the advantage of being 'the freshest modern' instead of the greatest ancient, would you not have mingled your praise of metaphorical speech as a sign of high intelligence, with a lamentation that intelligence so rarely shows itself in speech without metaphor – that we can so seldom declare what a thing is, except by saying it is something else?
>
> (pp. 208–9)

In the *Poetics* Aristotle says: 'It is a great thing to make use of ... double words and rare words ... but by far the greatest thing is the use of metaphor. That alone cannot be learned; it is the token of genius. *For the right use of metaphor means an eye for resemblances.*'[15] Of course there's authorial self-congratulation lurking in this passage, as there is in Eliot's affectionate parade of Maggie's gifts. But an eye for resemblances (between Binny and Mr Stelling, for instance, or brain and stomach) is also here a satiric eye. Culture as (in)digestion makes Euclid and the Eton Grammar hard to swallow; Aristotle loses his authority to the author herself. On one level, this is science calling culture into question, making empiricism the order of the day. But there's something unsettling to the mind, or, rather, stomach, in this dizzy progression from culture, digestive tract, and tabula rasa to ship of the desert (which sounds like a text-book example of metaphor). The blank page may take what imprint the author chooses to give it. But the price one pays for such freedom is the recognition that language, thus viewed, is endlessly duplicitous rather than single-minded (as Tom would have it be); that metaphor is a kind of impropriety or oxymoronic otherness; and that 'we can so seldom declare what a thing is, except by saying it is something else'.

Error, then, must creep in where there's a story to tell, especially a woman's story. Maggie's 'wrong-doing and absurdity', as the fall of women often does, not only puts her on the side of error in Tom's scheme of things but gives her a history; 'the happiest women', Eliot reminds us, 'like the happiest nations, have no history' (p. 494). Impropriety and metaphor belong together on the same side as a fall from absolute truth or unitary schemes of knowledge (maxims). Knowledge in *The Mill on the Floss* is guarded by a traditional patriarchal prohibition which, by a curious slippage, makes the fruit itself as indigestible as the ban and its thick rind. The adolescent Maggie, 'with her soul's hunger and her illusions of self-flattery', begins 'to nibble at this thick-rinded fruit of the tree of knowledge, filling her vacant hours with Latin, geometry, and the forms of the syllogism' (p. 380). But the Latin, Euclid, and Logic, which Maggie imagines 'would surely be a considerable step in masculine wisdom', leave her dissatisfied, like a thirsty traveller in a trackless desert. What does Eliot substitute for this mental diet? After Maggie's chance discovery of Thomas à Kempis, we're told that 'the old books, Virgil, Euclid, and Aldrich – that wrinkled fruit of the tree of knowledge – had been all laid by' for a doctrine that announces: 'And if he should attain to all knowledge, he is yet far off' (pp. 387, 383). Though the fruits of patriarchal knowledge no longer seem worth the eating, can we view Thomas à Kempis as anything more than an opiate for the hunger pains of oppression? Surely not. The morality of submission and renunciation is only a sublimated version of Tom's plainspoken patriarchal prohibition, as the satanic mocker, Philip Wakem, doesn't fail to point out. Yet in the last resort, Eliot makes her heroine live and die by this inherited morality of female suffering – as if, in the economy of the text, it was necessary for Maggie to die renouncing in order for her author to release the flood of desire that is language itself.[16] Why?

The Mill on the Floss gestures toward a largely unacted error, the elopement with Stephen Guest which would have placed Maggie finally outside the laws of St Ogg's. Instead of this unrealised fall, we are offered a moment of attempted transcendence in the timeless death embrace which abolishes the history of division between brother and sister – 'living through again in one supreme moment, the days when they had clasped their little hands in love' (p. 655). What is striking about the novel's ending is its banishing not simply of division but of sexual difference as the origin of that division. The fantasy is of a world where brother and sister might roam together, 'indifferently', as it were, without either conflict or hierarchy. We know that their childhood was not like that at all, and we can scarcely avoid concluding that death is a high price to pay for such imaginary union. In another sense, too, the abolition of difference marks the death of desire for Maggie; 'The Last Conflict' (the title of the book's closing chapter) is resolved by her final renunciation of Guest, resolved, moreover, with the help of 'the little old book that she had long ago learned by heart' (p. 648). Through Thomas à Kempis, Eliot achieves a simultaneous management of both knowledge and desire, evoking an 'invisible' or 'supreme teacher' within the soul, whose voice promises 'entrance into that satisfaction which [Maggie] had so long been craving in vain' (p. 384). Repressing the problematic issue of book learning, this 'invisible teacher' is an aspect of the self which one might call the voice of conscience or, alternatively, sublimated maxims. In 'the little old book', Maggie finds the authorised version of her own and Eliot's story, 'written down by a hand that waited for the heart's prompting ... the chronicle of a solitary, hidden anguish ... a lasting record of human needs and human consolations, the voice of a brother who, ages ago, felt and suffered and renounced' (pp. 384–5).

Where might we look for an alternative version or, for that matter, for another model of difference, one that did not merely substitute unity for division and did not pay the price of death or transcendence? Back to the schoolroom, where we find Tom painfully committing to memory the Eton Grammar's 'Rules for the Genders of Nouns', the names of trees being feminine, while some birds, animals, and fish 'dicta epicoena ... are said to be epicene'.[17] In epicene language, as distinct from language imagined as either neutral or androgynous, gender is variable at will, a mere metaphor. The rules for the genders of nouns, like prescriptions about 'masculine' or 'feminine' species of knowledge, are seen to be entirely arbitrary. Thus the lament of David for Saul and Jonathan can be appropriated as the epitaph of brother and sister ('in their death they were not divided'), and 'the voice of a brother who, ages ago, felt and suffered and renounced' can double as the voice of a sister-author, the passionately epicene George Eliot. One answer, then, to my earlier question (why does Eliot sacrifice her heroine to the morality of renunciation?) is that Eliot saw in Thomas à Kempis a language of desire, but desire managed as knowledge is also managed – sublimated, that is, not as renunciation but as writing. In such epicene writing, the woman writer finds herself, or finds herself in metaphor.

For Irigaray, the price paid by the woman writer for attempting to inscribe the claims of women 'within an order prescribed by the masculine' may ultimately be death; the problem as she sees it is this: '[How can we] disengage ourselves, *alive*, from their concepts?'[18] The final, lyrical chapter of *This Sex Which Is Not One*, 'When Our Lips Speak Together', is, or tries to be, the alternative she proposes. It begins boldly: 'If we keep on speaking the same language together, we're going to reproduce the same history' (p. 205). This would be a history of disappropriation, the record of the woman writer's self loss as, attempting to swallow or incorporate an alien language, she is swallowed up by it in turn:

> Outside, you try to conform to an alien order. Exiled from yourself, you fuse with everything you meet. You imitate whatever comes close. You become whatever touches you. In your eagerness to find yourself again, you move indefinitely far from yourself. From me. Taking one model after another, passing from master to master, changing face, form, and language with each new power that dominates you. You/we are sundered; as you allow yourself to be abused, you become an impassive travesty.
>
> (p. 210)

This, perhaps, is what Miller means by 'a posture of imposture', 'the uncomfortable posture of all woman writers in our culture, within and without the text'.[19] Miming has become absorption into an alien order. One thinks of Maggie, a consumer who is in turn consumed by what she reads, an imitative 'apparatus' who, like the alienated women imagined by Irigaray, can only speak their desire as 'spoken machines, speaking machines'. Speaking the same language, spoken in the language of the Same ('If we keep on speaking sameness, if we speak to each other as men have been doing for centuries, as we have been taught to speak, we'll miss each other, fail ourselves'), she can only be reproduced as the history of a fall or a failure (p. 205). Eliot herself, of course, never so much as gestures toward Irigaray's jubilant utopian love language between two women – a language of desire whose object ('my indifferent one') is that internal (in)difference which, in another context, Barbara Johnson calls 'not a difference between ... but a difference within. Far from constituting the text's unique identity, it is that which subverts the very idea of identity'. What is destroyed, conceptually, is the 'unequivocal domination of one mode of signifying over another'.[20] Irigaray's experiment in 'When Our Lips Speak Together' is of this kind, an attempt to release the subtext of female desire, thereby undoing repression and depriving metalanguage of its claim to truth. 'The exhausting labour of copying, miming' is no longer enough (p. 207).

But for all Irigaray's experimentalism, the 'difference' is not to be located at the level of the sentence, as Miller reminds us.[21] Rather, what we find in 'When Our Lips Speak Together' is writing designed to indicate the cultural determinants that bound the woman writer and, for Irigaray, deprive her of her most fundamental relationship: her relationship to herself. In fact, what seems most specifically 'feminine' about Irigaray's practice is not its experimentalism as such but its dialogue of one/two, its fantasy of the two-in-one: 'In *life* they are not divided', to rephrase David's lament. The lips that speak together (the lips of female lovers) are here imagined as initiating a dialogue not of conflict or reunion, like Maggie and Tom's, but of mutuality, lack of boundaries, continuity. If both Irigaray and Eliot kill off the woman engulfed by masculine logic and language, both end also – and need to end – by releasing a swirl of (im)possibility:

> These rivers flow into no single, definitive sea. These streams are without fixed banks, this body without fixed boundaries. This unceasing mobility. This life – which will perhaps be called our restlessness, whims, pretences, or lies. All this remains very strange to anyone claiming to stand on solid ground.
>
> (p. 215)

Is that, finally, why Maggie must be drowned, sacrificed as a mimetic 'apparatus' (much as the solidity of St Ogg's is swept away) to the flood whose murmuring waters swell the 'low murmur' of Maggie's lips as they repeat the words of Thomas à Kempis? When the praying Maggie feels the flow of water at her knees, the literal seems to have merged with a figural flow; as Eliot writes, 'the whole thing had been so rapid – so dreamlike – that the threads of ordinary association were broken' (p. 651). It is surely at this moment in the novel that we move most clearly into the unbounded realm of desire, if not of wish fulfilment. It is at this moment of inundation, in fact, that the thematics of female desire surface most clearly.[22]

We will look in vain for a specifically feminine linguistic practice in *The Mill on the Floss;* 'a possible operation of the feminine in language' is always elsewhere, not yet, not here, unless it simply reinscribes the exclusions, confines, and irregularities of Maggie's education. But what we may find in both Eliot and Irigaray is a critique which gestures beyond cultural boundaries, indicating the perimeters within which their writing is produced. For the astronomer who hates women in general, the feminist critic may wish to substitute an author who vindicates one woman in particular or, like Irigaray, inscribes the claims of all women. In part a critic of ideology, she will also want to uncover the ways in which maxims or *idées reçues* function in the service of institutionalising and 'maximising' misogyny, or simply deny difference. But in the last resort, her practice and her theory come together in Eliot's lament about metaphor – 'that we can so seldom declare what a thing is, except by saying it is something else'. The necessary utopianism of feminist criticism may be the attempt to declare what is by saying something else – that 'something else' which presses both Irigaray and Eliot to conclude their very different works with an imaginative reaching beyond analytic and realistic modes to the metaphors of unbounded female desire in which each finds herself as a woman writing.

From Mary Jacobus, *Reading Women: Essays in Feminist Criticism* (London, 1986), pp. 62–79.

NOTES

[This essay can be read as part of an ongoing debate about the creation of a female language as an appropriate expression of female experience. In the essay reproduced here, Mary Jacobus continues the discussion of a politics of women's writing, showing that rather than attempting to produce an *écriture féminine*, Eliot positions herself critically in relation to the dominant male discourse. Bringing together literary criticism and cultural critique, Jacobus argues that the character of Maggie, and the text more generally, offer examples of women's troubled relationship with language. This is resolved in the novel's ending, 'an imaginative reaching beyond analytic and realistic modes to the metaphors of unbounded female desire'. Jacobus thus reads *The Mill on the Floss* in order to deal with important questions posed by Luce Irigary concerning the complex politics of women's language: how, it is asked, can women liberate themselves from its concepts? All quotations in the essay are taken from *The Mill on the Floss* (Harmondsworth: Penguin, 1979). Eds]

1. Luce Irigarary, 'The Power of Discourse and the Subordination of the Feminine' in her *This Sex Which Is Not One* (Ithaca, NY, 1985), p. 81.

2. See Hélène Cixous, 'The Laugh of the Medusa', Elaine Marks and Isabelle de Courtivron (eds), *New French Feminisms*, pp. 245–64 (Amherst, MA, 1980). The implications of such definitions of '*écriture féminine*' are discussed briefly in 'The Difference of View' section 11.1, and by Nancy K. Miller, 'Emphasis Added: Plots and Plausibilities in Women's Fiction', *PMLA*, 96:1 (January 1981), 37; my own essay is indebted to Miller's account of *The Mill on the Floss* in the context of 'women's fiction'.

3. See Irigarary, *This Sex Which Is Not One*, pp. 68–85, and her *Speculum of the Other Woman* (Ithaca, NY, 1985), pp. 133–46. See also Carolyn Burke, 'Introduction to Luce Irigarary's 'When Our Lips Speak Together', *Signs*, 6:1 (Autumn 1980), 71.

4. Miller 'Emphasis Added', p. 38.

5. Ibid., p. 46.

6. Irigarary, *This Sex Which Is Not One*, pp. 74–80.

7. Ibid., p. 76.

8. See, for instance, Sandra Gilbert and Susan Gubar, 'Toward Feminist Poetics', Part 1 of *The Madwoman in the Attic: The Woman Writer and the Nineteenth-Century Literary Imagination* (New Haven, CT, 1979), pp. 3–104; Gilbert and Gubar's is above all a work of literary (her)story.

9. George Eliot, *The Mill on the Floss*, ed. A. S. Byatt (Harmondsworth, 1979), p. 628; subsequent page references in the text are to this edition. I am especially indebted to Byatt's helpful annotations.

10. See Gilbert and Gubar, *The Madwoman in the Attic*, who succinctly state that Maggie seems 'at her most monstrous when she tries to turn herself into an angel of renunciation' (p. 491), and Gillian Beer, 'Beyond Determinism: George Eliot and Virginia Woolf', in Mary Jacobus (ed.), *Women Writing and Writing About Women* (London, 1979), p. 88, on an ending that 'lacks bleakness, is even lubricious' in its realisation of 'confused and passionate needs'.

11. '*Mars omnibus est communis* would have been jejune, only [Maggie] liked to know the Latin': Eliot, *Mill*, pp. 217–18.

12. '*Astronomer: ut* – "as", *astronomus* – "an astronomer", *exosus* – "hating", *muleres* – "women", *ad unum* – mulierem – "to one" [that is general].' (*Eton Grammar*, 1831 edn, p. 279); Eliot, *Mill*, p. 676, n. 55.

13. See Virginia Woolf, 'George Eliot', *Collected Essays of Virginia Woolf*, 4 vols, ed. Leonard Woolf (London, 1966–7), I:204: 'With every obstacle against her – sex and health and convention – she sought more knowledge and more freedom till the body, weighted with its double burden, sank worn out.'

14. See Eliot, *The Mill on the Floss*, pp. 675–6, n. 44.

15. *Poetics*, 22:16 (my italics); see Eliot, *The Mill on the Floss*, p. 676, n. 46. J. Hillis Miller notes apropos of this passage that it 'is followed almost immediately by an ostentatious and forceful metaphor [that of a shrewmouse imprisoned in a split tree (p. 209)], as if Eliot were compelled ... to demonstrate that we cannot say what a thing is except by saying it is something else': 'The Worlds of Victorian Fiction', *Harvard English Studies*, 6 (1975), 145n.

16. See Carol Christ, 'Aggression and Providential Death in George Eliot's Fiction', *Novel*, 9:2 (Winter 1976), 130–40, for a somewhat different interpretation.

17. See Eliot, *The Mill on the Floss*, p. 676, n. 53.

18. Irigarary, 'When Our Lips Speak Together', *This Sex Which Is Not One*, p. 212.

19. Miller 'Emphasis Added', p. 46.

20. Barbara Johnson, *The Critical Difference* (Baltimore, MD, 1981), pp. 4, 5.

21. Miller 'Emphasis Added', p. 38

22. Cf. Gillian Beer, 'Beyond Determinism', in Jacobus (ed.), *Women Writing*, p. 88: 'Eliot is fascinated by the unassuageable longings of her heroine. She allows them fulfilment in a form of plot which simply glides out of the chanelled sequence of social growth and makes literal the expansion of desire. The river loses its form in the flood.'

5

Nationhood, Adulthood, and the Ruptures of *Bildung*: Arresting Development in *The Mill on the Floss*

JOSHUA D. ESTY

The Mill on the Floss has always stood out among Eliot's works as an unusual case – prickly, undigested, 'immature', but the terms of its difference have not always been satisfactorily articulated. My argument holds that the novel's intractability – what Susan Fraiman calls its 'portion of radical discontent'[1] – is fuelled by its resistance to historical, generic and psychological conventions of development. Specifically, *The Mill on the Floss* throws into question the most typical modern narrative of social identity – nationalism – and, in a tightly coordinated allegorical logic, undermines the most typical modern narrative of individual progress – the *Bildungsroman*. Eliot does not simply cast doubt on the idea that societies or individuals *improve* over time, but asks the more radical question of whether societies or individuals can be said to possess any kind of continuous identity over time. A careful look at the novel reveals a doubly anti-teleological stance whereby both national and individual histories unfold as sequences of rupture and loss, of separate and disjunctive states.

Let us first consider the wider social narrative of *The Mill on the Floss* (1860). The novel's 'historical' setting in the 1820s allows Eliot to locate Maggie Tulliver in the breach between two societies with competing value systems. The narrator quickly establishes and rigorously maintains a fault line between the 'premodern' village life of St Ogg's and the 'modern' conditions of mid-Victorian England. The basic motor force that generates this historical divide is modernisation. However, rather than narrate the continuous 'development' of Victorian capitalism out of a traditional agricultural and trading economy, Eliot implies the dramatic difference between the two.[2] By describing drastic changes (not smooth transitions), the text implicitly casts doubt on recuperative, organic versions of English history wherein the land and the folk remain mystically constant despite the complete reorganisation of their economy.

Of course, Eliot is ambiguous on this point: Victorian readers are asked to recognise that they are on the near side of a historical divide from the rural English past, but they are also invited to feel a symbolic connection to the villagers of St Ogg's. Taking the latter half of this formulation to heart, critics have often recruited Eliot's writing into the service of an abiding national myth – the yeoman farmer as quintessential Englishman.[3] The nativist reading of Eliot, especially of *The Mill on the Floss*, conceals a host of clues indicating that the rural past is in fact disconnected from modern readers (including Eliot's contemporaries). Far from invoking yeomanry as a form of life with enduring relevance for England, the novel marks its passage from economic viability to historical obscurity.

The novel's setting, Dorlcote Mill, constitutes a *locus classicus* of English yeomanry. Owned by the economically autonomous Tulliver family, the mill is both a domestic and a productive site. Uncle Glegg, a wool stapler, and Uncle Pullet, a prosperous farmer, also belong to the yeoman class. But the early agrarian capitalism that gave rise to such yeoman changed dramatically between 1830 and 1850 as a result of entailments and other concentrations of land and capital.[4] This economic transformation, a *fait accompli* for Eliot's readers, can barely be glimpsed by the characters in the novel. Indeed, faced with inevitable modernisation, the St Ogg's families are 'constituted ... a race' by dint of their archaic economic habits (p. 188). Eliot attributes a quaint (which is to say dim) mercantilist understanding of commerce to the village merchants, who share the precapitalist assumption that trade is a zero-sum game in which the participants dicker face to face. In short, the inhabitants of St Ogg's do not fully understand the abstract, anonymous, legal-financial capitalism that is overtaking them. Mr Tulliver's loss of Dorlcote Mill to lawyer Wakem – the crisis that triggers the novel's plot – is a paradigmatic instance of the yeoman fallen prey to modernisation.[5]

Modernisation in this novel kills off central characters and social practices, making them victims ripe for historical obscurity rather than candidates for commemoration. While Eliot's general position on historical commemoration certainly allows for recovery of the past, this particular novel demands the recognition that some losses are absolute. In later novels, Eliot takes pains to imbue her own mundane era with some of the emotional and literary force of tragedy. For example, *Middlemarch* grants its provincial bourgeoisie an unsuspected dignity and moral significance. But in *Mill*, rather than use redemptive language to rescue her characters from history's ashcan, the narrator admits to a 'cruel conviction' that the Dodsons and Tullivers 'will be swept into ... oblivion with the generations of ants and beavers' (p. 362). The point receives an entirely different emphasis in the final passage of *Middlemarch*, where we are told that 'the growing good of the world is partly dependent on unhistoric acts'.[6] In *Middlemarch*, Eliot betrays a more confident investment in the memorialising mission of her own narrative. Serious and sympathetic treatment of obscure provincial subjects has made them relevant to 'the world'. In *Mill*, by contrast, Eliot struggles with the possibility that the Dodsons and Tullivers may finally be irrelevant, which is to say drastically discontinuous from the modern world of her readers. By proposing that elements of the past become radically unavailable to the present, *The Mill on the Floss* pays tribute more to an unblinking historicism than to the familiar operations of recuperative Victorian history.

For Eliot, one of the chief differences between Victorian England and premodern St Ogg's is historical consciousness itself. In the village, we are told, there is no need to invent communal identity through the devices of formal history: 'The mind of St Ogg's did not look extensively before or after. It inherited a long past without thinking of it' (p. 184). *Mill* is a novel about people who have no need for historical novels. Eliot makes an implicit comparison between the village and her own society which, rather than enjoying a tacit assumption of shared origins, must construct its collective national past. In representing the village as a version of what

Raymond Williams calls the 'knowable community', the text seems to be installing St Ogg's as the symbolic core of modern England and providing fodder for nativist myth-making. But the narrator also takes pains to suggest that St Ogg's cannot in any simple way be imagined as the 'inner child' of modern England.

For example, although *Mill* contains nostalgic envy of St Ogg's (as a place where nostalgia is unnecessary), Eliot also indicates that this version of the traditional community is itself a literary invention. In an early description of the village, Eliot writes: 'It is one of those old, old towns which impress one as a continuation and outgrowth of nature' (p. 181). The language of autochthony invoked here is one of the key tropes for land-based myths of tribal identity. Yet the narrator's phrasing makes it clear that there is only the *impression* of organicism. Almost immediately, the ahistorical notion that St Ogg's was always, simply, St Ogg's gives way to a more complex local history. Rather than tell of an eternal connection between land and *ethnos*, the rest of the passage tells a story of colonisation and cultural intermingling among Romans and Saxons, Normans and Danes. Furthermore, when Eliot does evoke the myth of the yeoman, she draws attention to its fictive and conventional quality – warning off literal-minded readers who might take St Ogg's as the essence of modern England. At one point, the narrator drives the wedge between her readers and the Dodson–Tulliver clan by mentioning that the former already know the life of St Ogg's 'through the medium of the best classic pastorals' (p. 181). As the particular setting of 1820s St Ogg's dissolves into a blandly 'classic' agrarianism, the novel checks the notion that its Victorian readership has any specific genealogical interest in these rural folk. It is no longer 'us' thirty years ago, but *them* – the peasantry doing its timeless peasant dance. Such rueful admissions that the English village is more an idealised national myth than a concrete historical antecedent qualify the novel's apparently nativist romance.

Throughout the novel, the narrator's self-consciously modern voice brims with authority about a rural existence that is nonetheless distant from it and its presumably metropolitan audience. In regard to its provincial subjects, the novel adopts an ethnographic tone that reflects the difference between modernised observer and premodern object. But the narrator is no naïve tourist; in fact, Eliot – often recognised for her excellence as a domestic historian – might also be considered a prescient anthropological theorist. She notes, for example, that a modern writer needs irony in order to describe 'unfashionable families'. Moreover, she identifies irony as the product of a 'national life' imagined in explicitly metropolitan-rural terms.[7] In a fascinating passage, Eliot recognises that the nation, predicated on economic injustice and the inclusion of unfashionable rustics, supports both the material and representational needs of 'good society' (p. 385). As a political container for regional and class heterogeneity, the nation allows for the 'gossamer wings of light irony' that leaven the Victorian novelist's treatment of her archaic country cousins. This meditation on irony contains a ready awareness of the ethnographic conceit of *The Mill on the Floss*.

At such moments, Eliot acknowledges that metropolitan representations of the rural often depend on a rhetoric of nationhood that yokes together diverse populations otherwise separated by class and religion as well as by space and time. By revealing the self-consciousness involved in national myths of identity and continuity, she draws attention to such myths as inventions that tend to obscure England's essential 'lack of self-presence'.[8] The novel further undermines its own romantic nativism by insisting on the historical incommensurability between 1820s St Ogg's and the modern industrial nation of 1860. Eliot's strong commitment to historicism – the idea that different epochs are irreducibly different – requires the novel to execute a complicated double manoeuvre. First, the text shows that modernisation generates absolute losses both materially and epistemologically: there are objects, documents, people, values, experiences, and knowledge that can neither be preserved nor recollected from the past. Second, the novel exposes and challenges the recuperative rhetoric of nationalism that seeks to deny those losses and to emphasise the survival of a rural English core. This double movement – which is integral to the novel's representation of social history – also informs its representation of Maggie Tulliver's individual history. The process of maturation generates absolute losses for Maggie: there are moods, sensations, relationships, and experiences that cannot survive into adulthood. And the novel bravely challenges the recuperative rhetoric of 'development' that seeks to deny those losses and to posit instead a continuous self that remembers, preserves, and endures it all.

Eliot represents the passage from childhood to adulthood as more disjunctive than additive. For example, although the narrator describes memories of youth as the 'mother tongue of the imagination', this Wordsworthian sentiment quickly gives way to the recognition that childhood experiences are in fact frustratingly

inaccessible (p. 94). Memories of youth carry such drastically different emotional value from the original experiences that they seem
almost to belong to another person. Just as the novel implies a 'lack
of self-presence' in the modern nation, it also voices doubt about the
mature self's relationship to its childhood incarnation. Where the
conventional idea of development posits a core identity that accu-
mulates new 'layers', Eliot's text recognises the gains and the losses
associated with the protagonist's 'progress' towards adulthood.

Historical and individual nostalgia recur throughout the novel,
each cast by Eliot in terms of the other. In the Wordsworthian
passage cited above, for instance, the narrator describes personal
memory in ethno-linguistic terms ('mother tongue of the imagination') and indicates the unsatisfactory quality of recollected youth by
declaring that no 'tropic palms' could thrill the same fibres as a May
day in England (p. 94). Conjuring images of the colonies, this
passage establishes an analogy whereby the far-flung empire represents a lapsed national adulthood, no longer fully connected to the
authentic native setting of its English childhood.[9] Later, Eliot
addresses the metropolitan reader whose experience of home cannot
match that of the legendary yeoman: 'Our instructed vagrancy
which has hardly time to linger by the hedgerows but runs away
early to the tropics and is at home with palms and banyans – which
... stretches the theatre of its imagination to the Zambesi can hardly
get a dim notion of what an old fashioned man like Tulliver felt for
this spot where all his memories centred' (p. 352). Again the rural
English past stands in contrast to the extended colonial sphere. The
modern economy of industry and empire has forced England to
develop into something quite different from what romantic nationalism would identify as its essential core. The political entity
'Britain' is no longer coextensive with its founding *ethnos* – a difference measured metaphorically by the psychological rupture between
child and adult.

The maturation of the protagonist and the modernisation of the
nation unfold as parallel narratives. Indeed, the novel's deviation
from *Bildungsroman* formulae depends on the thematic power of
these mutually allegorical stories of disjunction and of loss. But
modernisation is not only a figurative parallel to maturation: the
two stories also intersect causally, so that England's economic
changes play a direct role in arresting the development of Maggie
(and Tom) Tulliver. The economic transformations that Eliot documents (including, for example, the loss of Dorlcote Mill) leave

Maggie stranded in the historical gap between old St Ogg's and modern industrial England. It is, in fact, entirely unclear what kind of society is meant to provide the setting for Maggie's evolving adult identity. Thus although *The Mill on the Floss* is often read as a conventional *Bildungsroman*, it departs from the generic model on several counts. Unlike the standard novel of education, wherein the protagonist undergoes continuous moral development towards the goal of an integrated personality, Eliot's novel moves disjunctively among various moments in the conflict-ridden life of Maggie Tulliver.[10] There is a stepped chronology, but no continuity and little promise of durable social adjustment.

In the standard novel of education, as described by Jerome Buckley, the young protagonist develops autonomously within a knowable social world.[11] Indeed, as Franco Moretti suggests, the classical *Bildungsroman* of Goethe or Austen establishes a set of stable public values and then presides over the successful 'adjustment' of the protagonist.[12] *Mill* turns this generic formula on its head so that a narrative of historical change impedes, and ultimately prevents, the adjustment of Maggie Tulliver. Rapid changes in England's social conditions are thrown into relief by a heroine who cannot adapt to them. Where most *Bildungsromane* make the historical backdrop a function of the protagonist's all-important 'formation', this novel makes the protagonist's fate a function of its uncompromising historical scheme. In this way, the novel invites us to read beyond the generic model towards a more complex recognition of the intertwining of 'self' and 'society'. Along these lines, Susan Fraiman has recently argued that *Mill* replaces notions of the self-determining bourgeois subject with a more relational and socially-embedded model of character formation.[13] In my reading, the novel's challenge extends not just to the bounded bourgeois ego, but also to the notion of a persistently self-identical subject. *The Mill on the Floss*'s critique of development cuts into bedrock liberal assumptions about continuous identity in both maturing women and modernising nations. As an anti-*Bildungsroman*, it disrupts the usual metaphorical affirmation between narratives of national progress and stories of individual growth.

Modernisation in *The Mill on the Floss* has different effects on women than on men and creates different narrative problems for Maggie Tulliver than for her brother, Tom. As I hinted above, it is the novel's *female* hero who, for the most part, reveals *Bildung* to be a disjunctive and tragic process. At one point, the narrator acknowledges that there would be neither reason nor means for telling Maggie Tulliver's story were Maggie not trapped in the class and provincial margins of pre-Victorian England: 'for the happiest women, like the happiest nations, have no history' (p. 494). Once again, Maggie and her society operate in figurative parallel; both illustrate the idea that narrative itself is an index of unhappiness. In this postlapsarian epigram, ideal or innocent states always give way to historical awareness. And, after the fall, grown women, like modernised societies, can only tell and retell their histories in an impossible attempt to reinhabit imaginary, innocent sites like premodern St Ogg's or the girlhood of Maggie Tulliver.

If unhappy women are (in Elliot's broad figurative sense) similar to modern nations, they are also (in Eliot's keen historical view) subject to certain new limitations in power within modern nations. Modernisation reorganises the culture of St Ogg's, converting yeoman into wage-earners and dividing domestic from productive space. These conversions, combined with the rise of professions and bureaucracies, move normative power from the local community to national institutions. They also transfer such power from women to men. In old St Ogg's, women like the Dodson sisters enforce the customary rules of conduct which, though rooted in the domestic space, are not limited to household matters. Although the village is no feminist utopia, Eliot's account of the Dodson Aunts as *policières des moeurs* shows that distinct powers accrued to women in the kinship systems of rural England. Jane Glegg's expertise in matters of tradition gives her sway over an extended family that includes the Tullivers; with power relocated in the male-run nuclear family, Aunt Glegg will have considerably less influence.[14] By registering the potential losses for women when male institutions replace female-regulated customs, Eliot gives special relevance to the historical obscurity of a 'generation of ants [aunts]' (p. 362).

As for Maggie Tulliver, she lives in the liminal zone between traditional and modern arrangements of gender and power. Local customs, regulated by Glegg of St Ogg's, are the binding force at the centre of young Maggie's life – signalled by the Anglo-Saxon velar stop (gg) at the centre of her name. But she does try to break away from that social network at various points in the novel. One early escape attempt – Maggie's flight to the gypsies – serves as a good example of how Eliot coordinates gender and national identity. In the scene, Maggie rebels against the prospect of sexual and economic development – processes that threaten to alienate her from Tom and to replace her Edenic childhood at Dorlcote Mill with a 'fallen' modern/adult world. When Tom and his cousin, Lucy Deane, form a bond which excludes her, Maggie flees the constraints of her tribe and joins the gypsies. At this point, Tom conforms to the kinship rules and customary expectations of St Ogg's in a way that Maggie cannot. Discovering that life as a reformist queen of the gypsies is not possible, however, Maggie returns home and signals acceptance of her identity by evincing a new attachment to the bonnet she had earlier spurned. She pays the price in a gender adjustment for the reassurance of belonging to a familiar, if constraining, community.

The gypsy episode prefigures Maggie's attempt to escape down the river Floss with Stephen Guest – a journey which is equally abortive. After Maggie returns, the women of St Ogg's ostracise her for what is apparently a sexual transgression. But the older women are not simply punishing a libidinal crime; they are also reclaiming their power to regulate the behaviour of village youths. By floating out of the sphere of St Ogg's on their way to establish a 'modern' nuclear family, Maggie and Stephen threaten to erode the power of the kinship system. The consequences of this escape are more than just sexual, but so is Maggie's interest in Stephen Guest. In fact, Maggie's desire for Stephen runs through channels that are created by her predicament as an unhappy provincial woman. Maggie cannot adjust to the values of old St Ogg's (especially insofar as those values are losing historical viability). But neither can she find an escape route out of St Ogg's. Stephen seems to offer Maggie a potential pathway to a more modern existence not only through his family's capitalist success, but also through his pedagogical wooing. As Mary Jacobus and Nancy Miller have suggested, education represents all that Maggie cannot have; she is recurrently and painfully excluded from male-dominated chambers of culture. Thus when Stephen courts her 'as if he had been the snuffiest of old professors and she a downy-lipped alumnus', he seems to answer Maggie's fervent desire for intellectual exchange (p. 489). She acquiesces to the illicit journey with Stephen, making a grab for modernity and for the metropolitan privileges of literate culture. But the attempt fails; Maggie does not and cannot escape from St Ogg's.

Even if Maggie could surmount the constraints of her backward and provincial circumstances, however, she would find herself in a metropolitan culture dominated by men. This is another ambiguity in the novel: Eliot seems to indicate that Victorian Englishwomen have gained a certain amount of intellectual freedom even if they have lost the customary powers enjoyed by Aunt Glegg. For example, the narrator describes the 1820s as 'a time when ignorance was much more comfortable than at present ... a time when cheap periodicals were not, and when country surgeons never thought of asking their female patients if they were fond of reading but simply took it for granted that they preferred gossip: a time when ladies in rich silk gowns wore large pockets in which they carried a mutton bone to secure them against cramp' (p. 185). Victorian women have gained freedom from quackery and medical condescension. But the passage also suggests, with gentle irony, that the advances in women's cultural freedom have only really afforded them access to cheap periodicals. Does this compensate for the quarantining of middle-class Victorian women in the domestic space? Clearly, Victorian society does not represent a paradise for emancipated women any more than old St Ogg's. Maggie Tulliver thus inhabits the intermediate zone between two almost equally – but not mono-lithically – unattractive historical options for women of her region and class.

Maggie's location in this historical breach is further confirmed by the outcome of libidinal subplots involving Philip Wakem and Tom Tulliver. As we have seen, the non-recuperative logic of Eliot's his-toricism keeps Maggie from entering into the value system of either traditional St Ogg's or modern England. This logic also conditions Maggie's investment in Philip Wakem, who, like Stephen, initially promises to satisfy Maggie's wish for cultural fulfilment. Philip's tutelage helps disengage Maggie from her place within the retrenched values of old St Ogg's; the currency of their relationship is entirely intellectual and aesthetic. But Philip has roots in the village: he is neither a 'Guest' nor a viable escape route from St Ogg's to metropolitan England. When they are together in the Red Deeps, Philip and Maggie inhabit an enclosed and aestheticised environment which, like the novel itself, is finite and temporary.

Marrying neither Philip nor Stephen, Maggie is barred from per-manently entering into either traditional or modern gender arrange-ments. The absence of a marriage plot for Maggie is the most important index of the novel's break from *Bildungsroman* conven-tions: without a husband, she cannot be recognised as a fully 'formed' woman. In at least one important way, Eliot's uncompro-mising historical logic determines that neither Maggie nor Tom will be able to marry and reproduce. After all, if modernisation consigns the yeoman to history's ashcan, it makes sense that the yeoman class – as represented by the Dodson sisters and their families – cannot reproduce itself. Consider the statistics: the Pullets and Gleggs are childless; the Tullivers and Deanes have only three children between them. The only families in the novel whose procreative pace exceeds zero population growth (the peasant Mosses and the capitalist Guests) fall on either side of the class zone staked out by the dwindling Dodson clan.

In keeping with Eliot's ethnographic narrative stance, we might think of St Ogg's as an endogamous village whose viability is suddenly threatened by modernisation. The narrator implies that, under ordinary circumstances, the tribe would produce a marriage between Tom Tulliver and Lucy Deane. Economic changes, however, force the yeoman class into retrenchment – a condition expressed by Eliot in her extreme application of the rules of endogamy to the Tulliver offspring, who end up bound to each other. The loss of Dorlcote Mill causes an artificial and premature circumscription of the Tulliver family, cutting them off from the larger Dodson clan. In a disastrous 'premature birth' of the nuclear family, the Tullivers lose their status as members of an extended kinship system and become an economically fragile, socially independent unit. This crisis in turn precipitates the imploding family romance whose outcome is the final union and death-embrace of Tom and Maggie.[15] This manoeuvre does more than simply thwart a literary convention, it delivers an appropriately antidevelopmental conclusion to the historical crisis facing old St Ogg's.

Tom's development, like Maggie's, is arrested by uneven modernisation; he never passes the conjugal and vocational rites that we expect in a typical *Bildungsroman*. At first, Mr Tulliver ships Tom out of the family circle and into the wide world of letters and commerce. But the crisis of the Wakem lawsuit intervenes, drawing a net of obligation and class insecurity tightly around the family. This turn of events initiates an odd trajectory for Tom, who begins moving towards a modernised education, then succeeds in a capitalist-style trading venture, but finally doubles back in a relentless drive to reinstate the economic life of the yeoman and reinhabit Dorlcote Mill. In the process, Tom not only foils his father's Oedipally-driven economic scheme to remove him from the scene of the mill, but also effectively bars himself from sexual or reproductive possibilities outside the family. Facing a similar familial and historical trap as his sister faces, Tom has no access to the relatively unfettered character formation of the conventional *bildungsheld*. The novel's refusal of *bildung*, though initially driven by gendered factors particular to Maggie, crosses over into Tom's narrative line.

When brother and sister are united in a final moment of hyperendogamy, the novel accepts the implications of its unblinking historicism. Given the figurative links between personal and social development, Eliot needs an outcome in which the losses suffered by a given class are also suffered by its particular representatives. Along the same lines, Lukács praises Walter Scott for remaining faithful to the logic of historical necessity by killing off sympathetic characters whose death represents the demise of an obsolescent way of life.[16] The exogamous plot (Maggie marries Stephen Guest) – or even the appropriately endogamous one (Tom marries Lucy Deane) – cannot occur because such marriages would provide an allegorical basis for the yeoman community to 'mature' smoothly into the social fabric of modern England (while, of course, preserving its tribal essence). Such an outcome would, as we have seen, run counter to the novel's emphasis on the ruptures rather than the continuities of national history.

Still, Eliot makes a belated concession to an integrative history by hinting, in a kind of epilogue, at the marriage between Stephen Guest and Lucy Deane (p. 656). The narrator cannot resist establishing – though to be sure only at the outer margins of the narrative arc – a family unit that gives the properly Victorian bourgeois resolution. The linkage of Lucy (the blond Dodson force of custom) with Stephen (the dark Guest force of capitalism) does create a pathway leading from old St Ogg's to modern England.[17] Such a marriage is precisely the resolution Eliot refuses for Maggie and Tom Tulliver. And, on the allegorical level, it is precisely the resolution whose synthetic and recuperative version of national history the novel otherwise eschews.

In discussing the historical factors that determine Maggie Tulliver's suspension on the threshold of womanhood and modernity, I have no doubt implied that her arrested development is an unfortunate narrative outcome. In a certain sense, however, it would be still more unfortunate if Maggie's energies, desires, and talents were subordinated to the strictures of womanhood in either St Ogg's or Victorian England. Female protagonists like Maggie challenge the conventions of *Bildung* because they so often imply a kind of social adjustment that restricts women's freedom. In *The Mill on the Floss*,

Eliot manages to short-circuit the generically ordained process of social adjustment.

It is especially surprising for readers of the mature Eliot to consider *Mill* in this light. Where the exquisitely wrought narrative machinery of a novel like *Middlemarch* grinds out an accommodation between major characters and their social environment, this novel does not, finally, subject Maggie to her Victorian norms of class, gender, region and religion.[18] The standard Eliot heroine grows up and makes her peace with social exigencies (an outcome which, despite Eliot's belief in the Christian value of submission, often seems tantamount to defeat for her talented female protagonists). But *Mill* represents Maggie's childhood in and for itself, not as mere prelude to the demands of full Victorian womanhood.[19] *Mill* refuses the socialisation plot precisely in order to forestall the conversion of Maggie into a mature 'angel of the house'. From this perspective, we can endorse F. R. Leavis's famous identification of the novel as an 'immature' work while reversing its valuation. The novel's immaturity is neither accident nor flaw, but the necessary formal premise and thematic goal of its entire operation.

Of course, given that Maggie dies in the novel's climactic flood, readers may legitimately wonder whether she – socially adjusted or not – is an apt vehicle for feminist resistance. Taken in the context of the novel's general critique of development, however, her watery death has formal justification. In the first place, it seems a fitting device, given that Eliot so regularly deploys the language of hydraulic currents and pressures. In fact, the flood confirms Eliot's investment in a rich figurative system built around images of land and water, of Mill and Floss. The language of flows and currents dominates the novel's representation of desire and becomes quite literal when Maggie and Stephen drift downstream. The river Floss plays an equally important role in the novel's wider historical scheme, where it acts as the conduit for economic modernity into St Ogg's. Merchant ships from beyond the village borders open the gates to the capitalist economy and disrupt the traditional yeoman world.

Bearing the seeds of economic change, the river runs like an epistemological fault line through St Ogg's. As Raymond Williams suggests, nineteenth-century capitalist dynamism tends to produce fractures in the 'knowability' of the community and to place strains on literary realism.[20] Ordinarily, realism functions in the *Bildungsroman* to make visible the worldly codes that the protagonist must learn. Here, however, modernisation places Maggie and

Tom on the historical margins where those codes are no longer intelligible or viable. Thus the river represents not only unauthorised desire, but also the disintegration of traditional community. In this figurative scheme, the flood serves as the ultimate figure for modernisation itself – for the drastic transformations wrought by capitalism. Eliot's modernisation is an implacable Hegelian force that renders an entire cast of characters quite literally antediluvian. In a different novel, one whose historical logic conformed more to our stereotypes of Victorian liberalism, modernisation might figure as a controlled form of progress that gradually improved conditions for these provincial Britons. However, instead of the humanist and recuperative bourgeois tragedy of, say, *Middlemarch*, *Mill* expresses the stern fatalism of classical tragedy, with the flood as its naturalised, secularised *deus ex machina*.

The Mill on the Floss concludes with a final indication that, although nature and society can rebuild themselves after the flood, some losses are absolute: 'if there is a new growth, the trees are not the same as the old, and the hills underneath their green vesture bear the marks of the past rending. To the eyes that have dwelt on the past, there is no thorough repair' (p. 656). Like most flood stories, this one describes a quasi-apocalypse through which selected elements of the past survive. Lévi-Strauss has taught us that myths use natural analogies to explain (and thereby muffle the threat of) social contradictions. Eliot's flood story seems at first to perform this mythic trick: it explains the chief contradiction of recuperative history by showing that, even when drastic changes occur, the essential landscape remains the same. But this story ends on a different note: it registers the losses associated with modernisation and maturation by recognising that, for modern nations and Victorian women, there is *no thorough repair*.

Maggie's non-adjustment to society exposes and resists the conventions of *bildung*, but it also works as a formal sentence to death. Critics like Elaine Showalter have read Maggie's drowning as an almost punitive foreclosure on Eliot's part. Maggie's exit from *Bildungsroman* conventions is thus only a Pyrrhic victory over the constraints of gender, genre, and history. Indeed, the end of *Mill* provokes the same kind of difficult questions for feminist readers as the end of Kate Chopin's *The Awakening* (or, in more contemporary narrative, Ridley Scott's *Thelma and Louise*). Does the heroine's death disqualify a novel from positive feminist interpretation? In my view, the answer is no. Maggie's death testifies to the costs paid by women as both maturation and modernisation unfold. A more integrative and recuperative closure that spared Maggie's life might have muted the novel's demonstration of the sacrifices attendant on Victorian womanhood.[21]

Critics of Eliot's tendency to thwart female characters have pointed out that Maggie Tulliver, to all appearances a fictional self-portrait, is nonetheless denied the options enjoyed by George Eliot herself. Despite the parallels between the fictional Maggie Tulliver and the real Marian Evans, the latter gained access to metropolitan privileges denied the former: intellectual achievement, escape from sexual and social conventions (the non-marriage to G. H. Lewes), escape from national rootedness (the extended continental travels), and escape of a kind even from assigned gender roles (the assumption of the male pseudonym). And yet, as the pseudonym cannot help but remind us, these advances for Eliot also entailed a certain drastically self-alienating process – a process from which Maggie Tulliver is 'spared by death'. The novel is less an autobiography than a counter-autobiography: it imagines the fate of Marian Evans without the social compromises made by George Eliot. Its apparently paradoxical conceit – the recovery of irrecoverable material from a childhood past – seems less paradoxical when we recognise the theory of memory operative in the text. For Eliot, the recovery of the past (whether personal or national) is perforce an act of invention – the half-blind gropings of a remembering subject that is only nominally identical to its previous incarnations.

Eliot's investment in Maggie's girlhood runs athwart the generic ethos of maturity and eschews the standard method for ending a *Bildungsroman*. In the ordinary (male-centred) 'novel of socialisa-tion', as Franco Moretti describes it, the protagonist's achievement of maturity provides the necessary symbolic closure, preventing the novel from becoming an endless story of change. Moretti holds that the narrative of youthful development (which represents the dynamic growth of nineteenth-century capitalism) must be con-tained by the imposition of an artificial and static endpoint – adult-hood. But of course the modernisation process itself never reaches such an endpoint – a fact that is swept under the carpet by the *Bildungsroman*'s symbolic closure. By refusing the genre's normal *telos* of adulthood, Eliot fully and honestly assimilates the logic of capitalism and accords genuine power to modernisation as a con-stant, ruthless process.[22] Eliot's unwillingness to posit an 'adult Maggie' undermines psychological and historical fantasies of com-pletion. The novel does not ratify adulthood as a final and static form, nor does it provide an allegorical basis for believing that

English society had or has arrived at its final, stable form. Just as moral and psychological change proceed without regard to received ideas about the mature self, social and economic change proceed without regard to romantic illusions about national permanence.

In this sense, the novel sides with narrativity itself as the literary expression of historicism (change always occurs). But the book must come to a stop, even if it does not reach the expected kind of closure. Enter the flood, which provides a kind of artificial or arbitrary endpoint. This literary device draws attention to the losses attendant on the conventional process of *Bildung*. The image of Maggie permanently suspended at the threshold of committed and constrained womanhood cannot last. That image is, nevertheless, the lyric possibility at the heart of this anti-developmental narrative.

A female anti-*Bildungsroman*, *The Mill on the Floss* unsettles national and personal myths of development. At a number of levels, it expresses the heterodox notion that individuals and societies do not always maintain their essences while undergoing radical transformation. Here Eliot combines feminist complaint with conservative lament in complex and paradoxical ways. Nostalgia for girlhood fuses with nostalgia for traditional community in a joint rejection of the progressivist assumptions of the male-oriented *Bildungsroman* and modern nationalism. As a woman surveying the transition to capitalism in nineteenth-century England, Eliot occupies the same kind of tragic, non-aligned position that Lukács ascribed to Walter Scott. According to Lukács, Scott's perspective on the bourgeois revolution was unbiased precisely because he knew that his class (the provincial low aristocracy) was doomed no matter what the outcome. If *The Mill on the Floss* evinces an especially clear-eyed vision about the losses that result from ceaseless modernisation, perhaps it is because Eliot knew that women were unlikely to share equally in the spoils of Victorian capitalism. To explore this connection, we might consider other women writers who, like Virginia Woolf, register suspicion of male-oriented narratives of social progress and male-oriented narratives of individual growth. Does their awareness of the costs of mature womanhood in most societies make available special insights about the costs of economic modernisation? Such an inquiry would doubtless advance our understanding of the organic metaphors that connect novels of development and narratives of romantic nationalism – metaphors embedded not only in the fabric of Victorian literature, but in the wide discursive networks of contemporary culture.

In 1857, George Eliot wrote: 'I feel every day a greater disinclination for theories and arguments about the origins of things in the presence of all this mystery and beauty and pain and ugliness that floods one with conflicting emotion'.[23] Three years later, she published *The Mill on the Floss*, in which the incidental choice of the verb 'floods' becomes a full-blown narrative and thematic device. The letter points up the novel's central tension between 'arguments about the origins of things' and the 'conflicting emotions' embodied by the flood. Eliot pits the ark of origins – both national and individual – against a flood of ruptures and discontinuities.[24] She thus posits a *terra firma* that supports the recuperative promises of nationalist history and the assumed continuities of personal development while, in the same text, she unleashes the disruptive floodwaters that force our recognition of the groundless breach between past and present, between the unregenerate girl-ghost of Maggie Tulliver and the mature Victorian angel of the house. If there is any doubt, finally, whether this is a myth of the Ark or a narrative of the Flood, then we must remember the narrator's impulsion towards the stream, enunciated from the very first: 'I am in love with moistness' (p. 54).[25]

From *Narrative*, 4:2 (1996), 144–59.

NOTES

[Joshua Esty's essay first appeared in the journal *Narrative* in 1996. It forms part of a growing body of work (see Jim Reilly, essay 9 in this collection) which has sought to integrate Eliot's engagement with historical events and the meaning of history. It also builds on readings which focus on the ambiguous and divided nature of Eliot's work and the novelist's problematic relations to concepts of national identity and community. In its integration of these issues Esty's essay reinforces the argument that to regard Eliot as a nostalgic writer or an uncritical traditionalist is to underestimate the extent to which *The Mill on the Floss*, rather than simply mourning the past, reinforces and examines the process by which social and cultural change within a community or a nation comes about in a complex and highly analytical way. Esty's essay examines questions central to Eliot's work: How is change generated? How is it incorporated into people's lives? All the quotations in the essay are taken from *The Mill on the Floss* (New York: Penguin, 1985). Eds]

1. Susan Fraiman, '*The Mill on the Floss*, the Critics, and the *Bildungsroman*', *PMLA*, 108 (1993), 137. [Reprinted in this volume pp. 31–56 – Eds]

2. In a recent article on class and gender relations in Eliot's early fiction, Margaret Homans suggests that *Mill* projects high Victorian elements onto a pre-Victorian setting. See her 'Dinah's Blush, Maggie's Arm: Class, Gender and Sexuality in George Eliot's Early Novels', *Victorian Studies* (1993), 169. Homan's argument looks at many of the same modernisation processes as mine, but sees them in the service of a historical conflation that universalises middle-class experience. In my view, Eliot is more committed to making historical distinctions than anachronistic fusions, though the novel's complexity depends on the use of both devices. Eliot's challenge to a nationalist rhetoric of continuity, in other words, demands that she also make that rhetoric available and plausible in the text. Similarly, as we will see, Eliot's revision of the conventional *Bildungsroman* requires her to reproduce (in order to question) some of the genre's basic structural elements.

3. Consider, for example, F. R. Leavis's anointment of Eliot in *The Great Tradition* (New York, 1949). Leavis recognises historical change and in fact seems to lament the loss of organic rural communities, but his criticism emphasises certain essential continuities in what becomes a normative discourse of Englishness. Leavis's reading of Eliot in some way secures the imprimatur of the English yeoman ideal for what Francis Mulhern identifies as Leavis's own up-by-the-bootstraps, white, heterosexual middle class. See Francis Mulhern, 'English Reading', in Homi Bhabha (ed.), *Nation and Narration* (New York, 1990), p. 259. It should be noted that Leavis's general admiration for Eliot did not extend to *Mill*, which he dismissed as 'immature'. Although the terms of his dismissal were rather more formal, perhaps Leavis intuitively grasped this novel's challenge to recuperative national history.

4. Raymond Williams, *The Country and the City* (Oxford, 1973), p. 98.

5. Franco Moretti in *The Way of the World* (London, 1987) suggests that Jane Austen's economic plots depend on the amalgamation of industrial and agrarian capitalism (pp. 63–4). By representing these two economic modes in conflict rather than in cooperation, *Mill* already reverses the conventional operations of the classical *Bildungsroman*.

6. George Eliot, *Middlemarch* (Boston, 1956), p. 613.

7. Eliot's awareness of these issues no doubt draws on the cultural context so well described by Nancy Armstrong in her recent article on *Wuthering Heights* – 'Emily's Ghost: The Cultural Politics of Victorian Fiction, Folklore, and Photography', *Novel*, 25 (1992). Armstrong locates that novel within an early Victorian cultural system in which 'modern literate urban' Britons expressed a folkloric interest in their 'primitive' rural compatriots (p. 245). Armstrong's discussion also points out the way that Victorian literary and photographic representations of a putatively authentic English past often 'destroyed the very thing [they] sought for' (p. 247). In similar terms, Eliot's ethnographic

'observer's voice' derives from the sad recognition that her literary attempts to recover the life of St Ogg's only widen the gap between nostalgic modern intellectuals and the vanishing past.

8. I borrow this phrase from Andrew Parker, Mary Russo, Doris Sommer and Patricia Yaeger, *Nationalisms and Sexualities* (New York, 1991), who suggest that, as a rule, the modern nation has an 'insatiable need' for representations that will 'supplement its founding ambivalence, the lack of self-presence at its origin or in its essence' (p. 5).

9. As Armstrong demonstrates, the idea that rural or provincial life somehow constitutes 'the idyllic childhood of the modern nation' saturated the rhetoric of English folklorists during the 1830–50 period. See Armstrong, 'Emily's Ghost: The Cultural Politics of Victorian Fiction, Folklore, and Photography', p. 253. Here Eliot exploits but also casts doubt on that kind of organic rhetoric.

10. In this sense, the novel runs athwart the ideal of the *Bildung* in its classical German sense. Perhaps the novel might better be described by the term *Entwicklungsroman* which, G. B. Tennyson points out, admits a broader and less teleological description of the protagonist's trajectory than does the term *Bildungsroman*, with its inevitable goal of 'harmonious cultivation of the whole personality'. See G. B. Tennyson, 'The *Bildungsroman* in Nineteenth-Century English Literature', in *Medieval Epic to the 'Epic' Theater of Brecht*, ed. Rosario P. Armato and John M. Spalek (Los Angeles, 1968), p. 142.

11. See Jerome Buckley, *Season of Youth: The Bildungsroman from Dickens to Golding* (Cambridge, 1974).

12. See Moretti, *The Way of the World*.

13. Fraiman, '*The Mill on the Floss*, the Critics, and the *Bildungsroman*', p. 138.

14. These observations are indebted to Eve Kosofsky Sedgwick's discussion of 'sphere ideology' in Eliot's *Adam Bede* (pp. 138–46). Following Mary Poovey – *Uneven Developments: The Ideological work of Gender in Mid-Victorian England* (Chicago, 1988) – in placing the domestic sequestration of women within the context of economic histories, Sedgwick argues that *Adam Bebe* creates a foundation for restrictive class and gender relations in the Victorian period.

15. I think it makes sense to analyse the Tulliver family romance in historical terms, but for a fairly strict Lacanian account of these issues, see Ranjini Philip, 'Maggie, Tom and Oedipus: A Lacanian Reading of *The Mill on the Floss*', *Victorian Newsletter*, 82 (1992), 35–40.

16. Georg Lukás, *The Historical Novel* (Boston, 1962), p. 55.

17. The Stephen–Lucy pairing recalls the synthesising, reproducing pair at the end of *Wuthering Heights* (dark Hareton Earnshaw and blonde Catherine Linton). In fact, the various sexual, ethnic, and economic attributions Eliot gathers around blonde and dark features throughout *Mill* suggest an extended comparison with *Wuthering Heights*. In that novel, dark Heathcliff represents (like Maggie) a principle of will, passion, and sexual energy. Heathcliff also represents (like Stephen) a principle of economic advance, an infusion of modern capital into the sluggish provincial economy. In both novels, a faded blonde English rural population (Lintons, Dodsons) cannot reproduce itself and requires revitalisation from dark, alien characters (Heathcliff as Black Irish, Stephen the Guest). For more on ethnic attributions in *Wuthering Heights*, see Elsie Michie, 'From Simianized Irish to Oriental Despots: Heathcliff, Rochester and Racial Difference', *Novel*, 25 (1992), 125-40.

18. Christina Crosby in her *The Ends of History: Victorians and 'the woman question'* (New York, 1991) finds in Eliot a general pattern of subordinating the specific claims of female characters to the unfolding of a Hegelian historical totality, but goes on to note that *The Mill on the Floss* presents an anomalous – and much debated – case (pp. 161-3). Even more suggestively, Crosby claims Eliot's *Daniel Deronda* as a participant in the Victorian historical industry that provided a 'secular guarantee' of 'origins and ends' (p. 5). I am arguing that *Mill* departs from Eliot's normal historical commitments precisely by challenging 'origins and ends' with a thoroughly historicist vision of *continual* change.

19. Here I concur with Charlotte Goodman, who sees the final reunion of Tom and Maggie as an affirmation of childhood values (against the gender separations precipitated by adolescence). See Charlotte Goodman, 'The Lost Brother, the Twin: Women Novelists and the Male–Female Double *Bildungsroman*', *Novel*, 17 (1983), 28–43.

20. Williams, *The Country and the City*, p. 165.

21. Chopin's heroine also drowns – a resemblance that raises the possibility of reading Maggie's death as an immersion in some specifically feminine (and potentially redemptive) symbolic zone such as the one described by the liquid language of French feminist Luce Irigaray. I am inclined to concur with Mary Jacobus's reading of the novel in terms informed by Irigaray. In Jacobus's view, the flood is a sign of the near-impossibility of fully resisting male-oriented conventions, even if it also entails a moment of symbolic access to unmediated female desire. See Luce Irigaray, *This Sex Which Is Not One* (Ithaca, NY, 1985), p. 215; Mary Jacobus 'The Question of Language: Men of Maxims and *The Mill on the Floss*, *Critical Inquiry*, 8 (1981), p. 222. My argument depends less on declaring the drowning either a defeat or a victory

than on pointing out its inevitability within the historical narrative that Eliot weaves around Maggie Tulliver.

22. Thus *The Mill on the Floss* performs the 'assimilation of real historicist time' that Bakhtin sees as crucial to the *Bildungsroman* – but which few orthodox *Bildungsromane* are able to maintain. M. M. Bakhtin, 'The *Bildungsroman* and its Significance in the History of Realism: Toward a Historical Typology of the Novel' in *Speech Genres and Other Late Essays* (Austin, TX, 1986), p. 21.

23. Gordon S. Haight, *The George Eliot Letters*, Vol. 2 (New Haven, CT, 1954), p. 341. In her Introduction to the Penguin *The Mill on the Floss*, A. S. Byatt aptly cites this letter as evidence for her claim that the novel resists totalising historical schemes. See A. S. Byatt (ed.), *The Mill on the Floss* (London, 1979).

24. In his discussion of nationalism's mythic repertoire, Regis Debray cites the Ark as an especially potent symbol. More to the point, Debray suggests that the Ark is to embody national origins, preventing the society from dissolving into 'an infinite regression of cause and effect' and allowing a symbolic 'defeat of the irreversibility of time'. Regis Debray, 'Marxism and the national question', *New Left Review*, 105 (1977), 27. It is only fitting, then, that Eliot's Flood should represent both the symbolic victory of irreversible time and the infinite regress of modernisation.

25. I would like to thank Eve Kosofsky Sedgwick, Marianna Torgovnick, Clyde Ryals, Heather Hicks, and Carolyn Gerber for their comments on earlier versions of this essay.

6

Narcissistic Rage in *The Mill on the Floss*

PEGGY R. F. JOHNSTONE

In *The Mill on the Floss*, Maggie Tulliver's unresolved childhood rage, which results from her sense that she is devalued by her family and society, is transformed into her adult misuse of sexual power in her relationships with Philip, Stephen, and Dr Kenn. Her creator, George Eliot, rationalises Maggie's behaviour with men and even turns her into an idealised heroine in the last section of the book. Eliot's apparent inability to see the aggression in her heroine's actions seems to derive in part from the autobiographical nature of the novel and possibly reflects the patterns of her own relationships with men in her young adult life.

Psychoanalytic literary critics have discussed the closeness between Maggie and her brother Tom, who serves as a substitute in Maggie's life for her rejecting mother and her weak father.[1] Emery's Freudian analysis stresses Maggie's need to identify with Tom, a male, in a family which devalues females. Paris' Horneyan analysis emphasises Maggie's morbid dependence on Tom: Maggie, the 'self-effacing person', is drawn to Tom, the 'arrogant-vindictive person ... because [she] needs to be protected by and to live vicariously through someone who can master life aggressively'.[2] Both Paris and Emery emphasise Maggie's childhood fear of being openly aggressive toward Tom because she needs him so much. Paris observes that '[Maggie] suppresses awareness of her vindictive drives and acts them out only in direct or disguised ways'.[3] Emery notes further that Eliot portrays as accidental some of Maggie's aggressive actions toward Tom: letting his rabbits die when she has promised to take care of them while he is away at school (p. 82)[4] and upsetting his pagoda (p. 147) and knocking against his wine (p. 155) during a visit with their relatives.

Maggie's excessively close attachment to Tom reflects her underlying need to be accepted by her parents; yet at the same time, her recurring aggression toward him enacts her anger at her parents' rejection. Emery explains that because Maggie feels rejected by her mother, she 'remains "hungry" for love, and ... her loving retains the quality of narcissistic need'.[5] The intensity of her attachment to Tom along with her repeated expressions of aggression toward him, reflect this hunger for love. Maggie's later relationships with other men also combine the need for attachment with the need to express aggression, as she attempts to revive her childhood sense of closeness to Tom. But her involvements with Philip, Stephen, and Dr Kenn only cause Tom's rejection of her and cannot satisfy her voracious need for his love.

Maggie's expression of aggression follows the pattern of the Prodigal Son story, which is told in a series of pictures on the wall at Luke's house, where she goes for comfort after she learns that Tom's rabbits are dead. Maggie's behaviour follows a cyclical pattern of impulsive and/or aggressive action and flight, followed by guilt and reparation. For example, after she lets the rabbits die, she tries to persuade Tom to forgive her, but he rebuffs her, and she runs upstairs to the attic. When the family notices that Maggie is missing, Mr Tulliver sends Tom to look for her. Maggie, seeking reparation, 'rushe[s] to him and [clings] round his neck', and Tom finally kisses her and offers her a piece of cake (p. 91). On another occasion, when Mrs Tulliver's visiting relatives make negative comments about Maggie's skin and hair, she seeks revenge by running upstairs and cutting her hair (p. 120). She soon feels sorry for what she has done, and when she returns to face her relatives' inevitable reactions, she seeks reparation by running to her father: she 'hid her face on his shoulder and burst out into loud sobbing' (p. 126). And when Maggie pushes the family's model female, Lucy, in the 'cowtrodden mud' (p. 164) as a way of getting back at Tom, Lucy, her mother, and her aunts, she runs off to the gypsies. One of the gypsies finally takes her home, and Mr Tulliver once again rescues and comforts her (p. 180). Thus Maggie's aggression in all three incidents follows the pattern of aggressive action and flight, followed by guilt and finally, reparation with the father (figure).

The cyclical pattern of Maggie's expression of aggression reflects the underlying low self-esteem that results from her family's ongoing devaluation of her. Maggie's is a 'narcissistic rage': a chronic and disproportionate anger in response to any incident perceived as a narcissistic injury – any incident that attacks her already weak sense of self, or that repeats the pattern of rejection by her parents and society. When Tom goes away to school, Maggie, the female, stays at home, receives inferior educational opportunities despite her superior intelligence, and is even expected to care for Tom's rabbits. When Maggie is with her relatives, they criticise her and look upon Lucy as an example of femininity; even her beloved Tom ignores her in favour of Lucy. These situations provoke her underlying sense of outrage and result in her aggressive actions.

According to Heinz Kohut, mature aggression is direct, proportionate, and under the control of the ego; it dissipates as soon as the cause of the provocation is removed. Narcissistic rage, however, is not dissipated by aggressive action; the rage continues to return until the underlying problem of low self-esteem is resolved – hence Maggie's continuing cycles of rage and reparation. Kohut refers to an early work on aggression, which, by way of explaining human aggressive responses, presents the 'schema of a self-perpetuating cycle of psychological phenomena'. The Paper describes 'the dynamic cycle of hostility – guilt – submission – reactive aggression – guilt, etc.'.[6] This cycle can be applied to Maggie: she behaves aggressively, she feels guilty, she submits to her father or Tom; then she gets angry at her inferior status and reacts aggressively again. Kohut also describes the fight/flight pattern of narcissistic rage: 'the narcissistically vulnerable individual responds to actual (or anticipated) narcissistic injury either with shamefaced withdrawal (flight) or with narcissistic rage (fight).[7] In all three of the above examples, Maggie, ambivalent about expressing hostility, responds with both 'fight' and 'flight': after she lets the rabbits die, she runs to Luke's house, and then upstairs to the attic when Tom refuses to forgive her; when her relatives criticise her, she runs upstairs to cut her hair; after she pushes Lucy in the mud, she runs to the gypsies; later in life she repeats the pattern when she goes away from her family and refuses to let Tom support her[8] after her father dies, and when she runs away with Stephen. Her pattern of running away is bound up with her pattern of expressing aggression.

Although Ermarth, Steig, Woodward[9] and other critics have discussed some of the effects of the rigid, provincial society on Maggie, none has fully considered the effect of the family's status in the community on Maggie's self-esteem. The sense of personal disgrace that marks Mr and Mrs Tulliver's lives at the outset becomes self-fulfilling in them as they move toward their financial fall and later in Maggie as she finds ways to disgrace herself.

Mrs Tulliver begins with a low position in her own family: she is compared unfavourably to her sisters, and 'is always on the defensive towards [them]' (p. 227). There are many references to Mrs Tulliver's inferiority: Mr Tulliver has picked his wife because she is 'a bit weak' (p. 68); he is proud to have 'a buxom wife conspicuously his inferior in intellect' (p. 73); she is the 'feeblest' member of the Dodson family (p. 97). Mrs Tulliver's own sibling rivalry comes out in her worries that Maggie can't compare to her sister's daughter Lucy: 'It seems hard as my sister Deane should have that pretty child' (p. 61). She is always concerned about the impression Maggie will make on her sisters. When Maggie dips her head in a basin of water 'in the vindictive determination that there should be no more chance of curls that day', Mrs Tulliver warns Maggie that the aunts won't love her, and then adds her fears for herself: 'Folks'ull think it's a judgment on me as I've got such a child – they'll think I've done summat wicked' (p. 78).

Maggie is said to resemble Mr Tulliver's sister, who suffers the disgrace of marriage to a poor man and has the burden of raising eight children in poverty. Both she and Maggie are said to take after Mr Tulliver's mother. Mr Tulliver wants to take care of his sister, just as he wants Tom to take care of Maggie (p. 116). The implication is perhaps that her aunt's existence is what awaits Maggie: marriage to a poor man. As the unappealing daughter of the lowest in status in the family, she could not expect more. One important source of Maggie's rage, then, in addition to that which she feels toward the rejecting members of her nuclear family, is her low position in a rigid society which allows very little room for upward mobility, especially for women.

Maggie's low position in society is made worse by her father's financial fall. Eliot emphasises the Tulliver's sense of disgrace following the loss of the lawsuit to Wakem. Mr Tulliver suffers a physical collapse, and Maggie and Tom are devastated: 'Tom had never dreamed that his father would "fail": *that* was a form of misfortune which he had always heard spoken of as a deep disgrace, and disgrace was an idea that he could not associate with any of his relations, least of all with his father. A proud sense of family respectability was part of the very air Tom had been born and

brought up in' (p. 267). The Dodson family proves to be unsupport-
ive and judgmental. They, like Tom, feel disgraced because 'one of
the family [has] married a man [who] has brought her to beggary'
(p. 294). Both Tom and Maggie are angry with their relatives' reactions, but since Tom shares some of their feeling of blame toward
his father, 'he felt nothing like Maggie's violent resentment against
them for showing no eager tenderness and generosity' (p. 308).
Maggie is openly angry with her mother and Tom whenever they
seem to be joining the relatives in blaming her father. She 'hated
blame' and only wants to remember how her father 'had always
defended and excused her' (p. 284).

Maggie's 'Valley of Humiliation' (Book IV), however, her own
reaction to the family's fall, sets the stage for the beginning of a new
cycle. During the monotonous period of time when Tom is working
to pay off the family debt and Maggie is at home taking care of her
sick father, she falls into the despair which is described in the three
chapters of Book IV. Chapter 1 provides the context for her despair
by emphasising the oppressiveness of life in a society which holds up
respectability as its chief virtue. In chapter 2, Maggie, unable to
count on her ailing father's customary warmth to distract her from
her predicament, is becoming weighed down by her family's disgrace. Her father is unresponsive to 'her little caresses' (p. 371) and
seems preoccupied with Maggie's 'poor chance of marrying, down
in the world as they were' (p. 372). In chapter 3, Maggie turns to
books for comfort, although she is easily distracted by her sorrow.
She has fits of anger and hatred 'towards her father and mother who
were so unlike what she would have them to be – toward Tom, who
checked her and met her thought or feeling always by some thwarting difference' (p. 380). Then she reacts to her own anger with 'wild
romances of a flight from home in search of something less sordid
and dreary: – she would go to some great man – Walter Scott,
perhaps, and tell him how wretched and how clever she was, and he
would surely do something for her' (p. 381). Her real father would
inevitably interrupt her fantasy and complain, for example, that she
had failed to bring his slippers. In desperation, Maggie finally discovers Thomas à Kempis and begins to try to apply his ideas to her
situation: 'renunciation seemed to her the entrance into that satisfaction which she had so long been craving in vain' (p. 384). As time
goes on, her mother notices and approves her new submissiveness;
her father, also approving the change, but still worrying about her
prospects for marriage, shifts his plaint to: 'there'll be nobody to

marry her as is fit for her' (p. 388). Thus in chapter 3 Maggie repeats her pattern: she feels angry toward her family for her inferior position in society, she flees (in fantasy), she feels guilty (when her father interrupts her fantasy) and then regains her parents' approval with her new found submissiveness, brought on by her misguided attempts to apply Thomas à Kempis to her life.

After the Thomas à Kempis incident, there is little mention of Maggie's anger, and there are no accounts of overtly aggressive action on her part.[10] At this point in the story Maggie begins to act out her rage in her relationships with men. Her childhood aggression is transformed into her young adult misuse of sexual power. Neither Philip, nor Stephen is a suitable or appealing choice for Maggie, but she becomes involved in them as a means of hurting them and others around her. Yet just as Eliot portrays Maggie's aggressive actions toward Tom as accidental, so she portrays her heroine's actions toward other men as innocent. Furthermore, by the end of the novel, Eliot idealises Maggie on the grounds of her struggle of conscience over her involvements with the two men.

Maggie's long period of renunciation has prepared her for a new cycle: her sense of inferiority, exacerbated by her father's financial fall, his illness, and her own self-deprivation and recent growth into 'early womanhood' (p. 393), are motivating factors in the action that follows. Maggie's expression of aggression takes the form of pursuing a relationship with Wakem's son, Philip. By becoming involved with him, Maggie expresses her anger toward her family for their inadequacies, and toward Tom,[11] who has forbidden her to speak to Philip (p. 279). And although she has never acknowledged any feelings of anger toward Philip for his father's role in Mr Tulliver's failure, she typically acts out her resentment indirectly.

The foundation for friendship is laid when Maggie meets Philip as a child on a visit to Tom's school. Maggie feels 'growing interest' in Philip, despite his and Tom's antagonism toward each other, because he is so 'clever', and because she has 'rather a tenderness for deformed things' (p. 252). During the visit, Philip becomes Maggie's replacement for Tom, whose troubles with his studies had 'made him more like a girl than he had ever been in his life before': his 'boyish self-satisfaction' had been replaced by 'something of the girl's susceptibility' (p. 210). When Philip becomes a student at the school, his academic successes add to Tom's ongoing need to prove himself as a fighter. Finally Tom bribes the school drill master into lending him his sword, which he plans to 'tie around his waist' and show off to Maggie as his own. But when the time comes, 'his wrist trembles' as he lowers the sword, drops it on his foot and wounds himself (p. 255) – a symbolic castration which reveals his sense of inadequacy. Soon after, Maggie, needing a male to complete her sense of identity, 'turns toward Philip, and identifies not with what she would like to be, but with something that resembles her own need'.[12] His humpback represents her own low self image. In chapter 6, 'A Love Scene', which immediately follows the scene in which Tom is injured, Maggie expresses her feelings toward Philip in relation to her need to be loved by Tom: first she tells him that she doesn't think she could love him better than Tom, 'But I should be so sorry ... for you' (p. 259); then she corrects her allusion to his deformity by saying that she wishes he were her brother; finally she concludes, 'I think you're fonder of me than Tom is' (p. 260). The relationship that develops later in their young adult years follows from Maggie's ongoing need to be loved by Tom at the same time she needs to express aggression toward him.

Maggie meets Philip again a few years later on one of her solitary walks in the 'Red Deeps'. Although Philip initiates their conversation, Maggie, glad to see him despite the rift between their families, responds warmly. But although Eliot assures her readers of Maggie's innocence, her behaviour toward Philip is actually flirtatious. When Maggie, who has grown into 'early womanhood' (p. 393), asks Philip if she is like what he expected, Eliot comments, 'The words might have been those of a coquette, but the full bright glance Maggie turned on Philip was not that of a coquette. She really did hope he liked her face as it was now, but it was simply the rising again of her innate delight in admiration and love' (p. 395). Philip tells her she is much more beautiful than he expected, which Eliot intimates is a surprise to Maggie, who, during her renunciation, has 'abstain[ed] from the looking glass' (p. 396). Maggie then tells Philip that she must not see him again (p. 396), but Philip plays on her sympathies and finally says, 'I should be contented to live, if you would let me see you sometimes' (p. 398). Maggie, beginning to wonder whether she might do him some good in seeing him, wavers, and then postpones the decision by submitting to his suggestion that he come to the woods as often as he can until he meets her again on one of her walks. By failing to prevent his meeting her again, she chooses to pursue the relationship. She lets Philip appear to make the decision in which she actually participates. Meanwhile, she inwardly plans to tell him the next time they meet of her determination not to keep seeing him.

Maggie's aggression is not only evident in the choice of Philip against her family's wishes, but also in the portrayals of her interactions with him. Her cycles of giving Philip hope and then rejecting him reveal the latent cruelty in her behaviour. For example, in the passage in Book V, chapter 3, 'The Wavering Balance', Maggie tells Philip that they cannot meet again (p. 425), and Philip responds by asking her to talk for half an hour before they part. When he takes her hand, 'Maggie felt no reason to withdraw it' (p. 425). Thus she declares she will not see him again, but then immediately gives in to his advances. Then Philip flatters her by asking to study her face one last time so that he can finish her portrait; he elicits her sympathy and her own discontent about her lot by expressing bitterness about his deformity (p. 426); finally, he argues vehemently against her practice of self-deprivation (p. 427). Maggie, still seeing the relationship in terms of her need for Tom, says, 'What a dear, good brother you would have been' (p. 427). By the end of the conversation, in which Philip continues to argue against her determination to renounce him, Maggie finally gives in to his suggestion that he continue to walk in the woods and meet her 'by chance' (p. 429). It is clear in this passage that Maggie wants to continue seeing Philip ('her heart leap(t) at this subterfuge of Philip's' [p. 429]), yet 'even to Maggie he was an exception: it was clear that the thought of his being her lover had never entered her mind' (p. 430) – i.e., his deformity stands in the way of his attractiveness to Maggie. Although Philip's interest in Maggie is clear to the reader, Eliot claims Maggie's innocence of his intentions; so Maggie continues to lead him on, although her rejection of him is inevitable.

A year later they are still meeting. Philip finally declares his love and asks Maggie whether she loves him. She replies, 'I think I could hardly love any one better: there is nothing but what I love you for' (p. 435). Later in the conversation when Philip asks if she is forcing herself to say she loves him, she repeats the thought: 'I don't think I could love any one better than I love you. I should like always to live with you – to make you happy' (p. 437). But she also says she will never do anything to wound her father, and adds that it is impossible for them ever to be more than friends. Philip continues to try to get her to clarify her feelings, but by this time, Maggie is feeling that she must return home: 'the sense that their parting was near, made her more anxious lest she should have unintentionally left some painful impression on Philip's mind. It was one of those dangerous moments when speech is at once sincere and deceptive – when feeling, rising high above its average depth, leaves flood-marks which are never reached again' (p. 437). Philip says, 'We do belong to each other – for always – whether we are apart or together?' And Maggie responds, 'Yes, Philip: I should like never to part: I should like to make your life very happy' (p. 437). Philip, however, aware of the ambiguity of her answer, is 'waiting for something else – I wonder whether it will come' (p. 438). Maggie stops to kiss him and has 'a moment of belief that if there were sacrifice in this love [because of Philip's deformity] – it was all the richer and more satisfying' (p. 438). Her feeling for Philip is more a need to be 'worshipped' (p. 426) than the kind of love that Philip wants.

Tom inevitably discovers their meetings, and Maggie promises not to see Philip again without Tom's knowledge (p. 446). He confronts and insults Philip (pp. 447–8). After they leave Philip, Tom asks her, 'Pray, how have you shown your love that you talk of either to me or my father? By disobeying and deceiving us. I have a different way of showing my affection.' Maggie's response, 'Because you are a man, Tom, and have power, and can do something in the world' (p. 450), reveals a motive for pursuing the friendship: her sense of powerlessness as a female. Shortly after the discussion with Tom, Maggie inwardly acknowledges her relief that the relationship is over (p. 451). The implication in this passage and those cited above is that she does not want to be seriously involved with Philip. After she becomes involved with Stephen, she quickly loses interest in Philip: she 'shivers' at Lucy's offer to contrive a way for her to marry Philip (p. 498); she is 'touched not thrilled' when Philip sings to her in the presence of Lucy and Stephen (p. 533). Although Maggie and Philip share many interests, her feeling for him never gets beyond her need to be admired; he plays on her sympathies when he persuades her to see him, and she continues to submit to his suggestions to meet. But despite Philip's declarations of love, she never actually declares hers. Relieved when Tom breaks up the relationship, she lets him verbalise what she represses. Through her brother, she vicariously lives out her own unacknowledged feelings of aggression toward Philip, whose father has ruined hers.

The relationship is not all Maggie's fault; Philip has sought her out and pressured her into declaring her love. His motives interact with hers. He feels bitter about his deformity (pp. 398, 430), discouraged about his painting, and 'had never been soothed by [a] mother's love' (p. 431). Perhaps a relationship with Maggie could also be seen as an expression of his (and his father's) power over the Tullivers. In any case, the story of the relationship between Maggie and Philip is suspended when Mr Tulliver dies and Maggie and Tom are reconciled. When Maggie asks Tom's forgiveness, 'they clung and wept together' (p. 465). Maggie completes her cycle: by becoming involved with Philip she takes revenge on Tom, her family, and the Wakems; 'weary of her home' (p. 436), she flees her family by habitually meeting him at the Red Deeps; she feels guilty afterwards, especially after her father's death; finally, she is reconciled to Tom.

Maggie's next period of submissiveness follows during her lonely, monotonous two years as a teacher after her father's death. By the time she visits Lucy in Book VI, she is ready for a new cycle. She meets Stephen, Lucy's intended fiancé, and soon finds herself tempted to run away with him. Although he seems to be an unlikely object of her affections, the reasons for her involvement with him become clear if the relationship is seen in the context of Maggie's recurring cycles of submission and rage.

Book VI, which traces the relationship with Stephen, emphasises Maggie's low position in the society at St Ogg's, especially in contrast to Stephen, who represents the established society.[13] Unlike Maggie, the daughter of a failure, Stephen is in the privileged position of being the son of the owner of 'the largest oil-mill and the most extensive wharf in St Ogg's' (p. 469). Lucy's father and Tom both work for him. Stephen feels superior to all the people around him: he speaks with 'supercilious indifference' of Mr Tulliver (p. 471); he makes fun of Mrs Tulliver's 'conversational qualities' (p. 472); he refers to Tom as 'not a brilliant companion' (p. 473); he has even chosen Lucy 'because she did not strike him as a remarkable rarity' (p. 477). He is conscious of her inferior position as 'the daughter of his father's subordinate partner; ... he had had to defy and overcome a slight unwillingness and disappointment in his father and sisters – a circumstance which gives a young man an agreeable consciousness of his own dignity' (p. 478). Stephen's sisters, too, 'associated chiefly on terms of condescension with the families of St Ogg's, and were the glass of fashion there' (p. 512). For Maggie, it is supposed to be 'a great opportunity' (p. 512) to be included in the parties of such a group.

One of the earlier conversations between Maggie and Philip reveals the motivation for her later involvement with Stephen. When

Maggie tells Philip she would like to read a book in which the dark-haired lady triumphs, Philip jokes, 'perhaps you will avenge the dark women in your own person, and carry away all the love from your cousin Lucy'. Maggie, insulted, denies that she is 'odious and base enough to wish to be her rival' (p. 433) and insists that 'It's because I always care the most about the unhappy people. ... I always take the side of the rejected lover in the stories.' Then when Philip asks her if she would ever have the heart to reject a lover, she responds: 'I think perhaps I could if he were very conceited; and yet, if he got extremely humiliated afterwards, I should relent' (p. 434). Stephen is the kind of conceited person that Maggie tells Philip she would be able to reject. The infatuation for Stephen is bound up with her hostility toward him and others around her. By running away with him, she repeats the pattern of the gypsy incident: angry with her father and jealous of Lucy, she pushes her in the mud, runs away to the gypsies, where she fantasises that she is queen – 'in Lucy's form',[14] and then returns to be rescued by her father.

The nature of infatuation has been explored by psychoanalysts, although there is relatively little literature on the subject. One study stresses that such an attraction is 'based on resemblance to a fantasy which, for both sexes, derives from the "original love object" – the mother'. Another asserts that 'falling in love represents an attempt to undo the original separation from mother, as well as subsequent separations'. A third says that 'people who become infatuated have an incapacity for establishing [constant relationships with others]: infatuation is a repetition compulsion whose origins are in developmental failures'. Werman and Jacobs build on these and other studies in stating their belief that infatuation has its roots in the earliest years of life. Its 'shifting and inconstant nature reflects the experience of the child prior to the formation of [love] object constancy' and suggests 'the existence of difficulties in the mother-infant relationship that contribute to the development of critically important aggressive conflicts in the child'; this accounts for the latent hostility in infatuations. They can occur normatively during adolescence, a time when oedipal conflicts are revived at the same time the individual is struggling for a sense of identity. They can also occur repeatedly during a person's life, or in some people, only during a particularly stressful time: '[an infatuation] may come about when an individual is in a crisis of defensive regression, subsequent to severe stress, intense anxiety, or during time of depression'.

An infatuation 'typically condenses both narcissistic and oedipal wishes'.[15]

Maggie's infatuation for Stephen comes about as a cyclical reaction to her underlying narcissistic rage against her family and society; it also comes about during a time of special stress and depression: Maggie has suffered the death of her father, has grown bored with her teaching position, and is suddenly in a social setting in which she is continually reminded of her low status.

In a conversation with Lucy in chapter 2 of Book VI, Maggie expresses her discontent by comparing herself to a bear confined in a cage. She says she often hates herself 'because I get angry sometimes at the sight of happy people' (p. 481). She feels that she has slipped back 'into desire and longing' (p. 482). When she goes for a ride in the boat with Stephen and Lucy, 'She felt lonely, cut off from Philip – the only person who had ever seemed to love her devotedly, as she had always longed to be loved' (p. 491). Renewed anger at her relatives adds to her feelings of discontent. When her mother and aunt make remarks about her brown skin, Maggie laughs, but feels 'impatient' (p. 492). When Tom expresses his distrust of her, 'she rebelled and was humiliated at the same time' (p. 504). She tries to be reconciled to him at the end of the conversation, and he does kiss her, but has to rush off to a consultation with Deane. Her anger appears in flashes in her relationship with Stephen· after he takes her for a walk in the garden (p. 521) and after he kisses her arm at the dance (p. 561).

Maggie's first meeting with Stephen recalls the first meeting with Philip in the Red Deeps. Maggie is aware that Stephen thinks her attractive; in this case she pretends to rebuff his compliment. Once again, Eliot denies her heroine's flirtatious behaviour: when Maggie mentions that she has had to earn money by plain sewing, Eliot comments, 'but if Maggie had been the queen of coquettes she could hardly have invented a means of giving greater piquancy to her beauty in Stephen's eyes' (p. 487).

True to the pattern established in her relationship with Philip, Maggie makes her choices about Stephen indirectly – by allowing Stephen to appear to be making the decisions. For example, when it becomes clear that neither Lucy nor Philip will be able to go along on the planned boat ride, Maggie says to Stephen, 'We must not go' (p. 588). But when she asks Stephen to tell the man who is waiting for them with the boat cushions, Stephen says, 'What shall I tell him?' And 'Maggie made no answer.' Stephen then says, 'Let us go' at the same time he rises and takes her hand, thus relieving her of the burden of openly making the decision for herself.

Maggie's feeling for Stephen, however, is different from what she had experienced for Philip. The relationship with Stephen satisfies her underlying need to feel attached to a stronger person. When she and Stephen return from the first boat ride, Maggie's foot 'slips', 'but happily Mr Stephen Guest held her hand and kept her up with a firm grasp ... It was very charming to be taken care of in that kind graceful manner by someone taller and stronger than oneself. Maggie had never felt just in the same way before' (p. 492). And just before the last boat ride, Maggie feels 'that she was being led down the garden ... by this stronger presence that seemed to bear her along without any act of her own will' (p. 588). Maggie experiences the sense of union with a powerful love object that is part of the fantasy of infatuation.

Werman and Jacobs emphasise the 'intense, irrational, and dream like' state of infatuation.[16] After the first evening with Stephen, Maggie feels 'the half-remote presence of a world of love and beauty and delight, made up of vague, mingled images from all the poetry and romance she had ever read, or had ever woven in her dreamy reveries' (p. 495). When they walk in the garden, they are 'in the same dreamy state as they had been in a quarter of an hour before' (p. 521). At the dance, Maggie says that the flowers seem to be part of 'an enchanted land' (p. 560). When they go away in the boat, they are enveloped in an 'enchanted haze' (p. 589). And on the Dutch vessel, 'Stephen's passionate words made the vision of such a life more fully present to her than it had ever been before; and the vision for the time excluded all realities' (p. 594).

Infatuation is a condensation of the narcissistic wish for the infant's blissful sense of union with the mother and the oedipal wish to marry the parent of the opposite sex; it thus provides for a female a means of being united in fantasy with both parents at the same time. Maggie's fantasies when she is with Stephen recall her blissful childhood moments with Tom, her substitute for both parents, at the 'Round Pool' when they would imagine that 'they would always live together and be fond of each other'. As a child Maggie thought of sitting by the pool as 'a very nice heaven'. She would 'look dreamily at the glassy water' and feel as though nothing could 'mar her delight in the whispers and the dreamy silences' (p. 93). The scene at the Round Pool, 'deep ... almost a perfect round, framed in with willows and tall reeds', a symbolic womb,[17] suggests Tom's and Maggie's ongoing need to be together with their lost love object, their mother – a need temporarily met for Maggie later in the dream-like infatuation for Stephen. And because the 'triangle between Stephen, Lucy, and Maggie is a recasting of the Oedipal triangle',[18] Maggie is also able to be temporarily united in fantasy with her father when she and Stephen elope.

Maggie's interactions with Stephen repeat the pattern of her cruelty to Philip. She encourages and rejects him in cycles. For example, at the dance in Book VI, chapter 10, Maggie and Stephen walk together feeling 'that long grave mutual gaze which has the solemnity belonging to all deep human passion'. When they pause to look at some flowers, Stephen, overwhelmed by the strength of their feeling, suddenly takes Maggie's arm and 'shower[s] kisses on it'. Maggie, reacting with rage and humiliation, refuses to have anything to do with him for the rest of the evening because she feels 'Stephen thought more lightly of her than he did of Lucy' (pp. 561–2). In their next scene (chapter 11), Stephen comes to see her while she is staying at her aunt's house and tries to persuade her to marry him. Maggie seems on the verge of giving in to her impulses, but just as 'his lips are very near hers', Maggie 'opened her eyes full on his for an instant, like a lovely wild animal timid and struggling under caresses, and then turned sharp round towards home again' (pp. 569–70). When they are alone in the boat together, Maggie fails to notice that they have drifted past the village where they had planned to stop. When Stephen tries to persuade her to marry him before they return home, Maggie feels 'angry resistance'. She accuses him of wanting 'to deprive me of any choice. You knew we were come too far – you have dared to take advantage of my thoughtlessness. It is unmanly to bring me into such a position' (p. 591). The pattern repeats itself again after they board the 'Dutch vessel', where Maggie paces 'up and down the deck leaning on Stephen', yet soon realises 'that the condition was a transient one, and that the morrow must bring back the old life struggle' (pp. 594–5). The next day she tells Stephen she cannot marry him, and finally Stephen, worn out and exasperated, say, 'Go, then – leave me – don't torture me any longer – I can't bear it.' Even then, Maggie 'involuntarily … leaned towards him and put out her hand to touch his', but this time Stephen, not wanting to be hurt again, '[shrinks] from it as if it had been burning iron' (p. 606).

Maggie's low self-esteem prevents her from disentangling herself from her old patterns of behaviour. She is at the mercy of a repetition-compulsion which causes her to re-enact her sense of injury by repeatedly injuring others. By getting involved with Stephen, Maggie hurts everyone around her – Stephen, by repeatedly encouraging and rejecting him; Lucy, her long-term rival[19] by taking away her intended fiancé just when Lucy is being kind to her; Philip, by failing to be clear about 'the position they must hold towards each other', thus continuing to lead him on (p. 527); Wakem, who finally consents to let Philip marry her, and then suffers embarrassment when she goes away with Stephen (p. 632); Tom, whose happiness over regaining the mill is destroyed by her flight with Stephen, and who, it is implied, is already hurting from his own loss of Lucy to Stephen (p. 501). Finally, she hurts all her other relatives, who will suffer from the disgrace she brings on the family.

Yet Eliot's portrayal of the flight with Stephen emphasises the nobility of Maggie's decision not to marry him. Maggie is implicitly praised as she parts from Stephen for not thinking about 'what others would say and think of her conduct' on the grounds that 'Love and deep pity and remorseful anguish left no room for that' (p. 606). Maggie's superiority to the rest of the community is implied through the words of Dr Kenn, who lets her know after her return how harshly the community is judging her: 'The persons who are the most incapable of a conscientious struggle such as yours, are precisely those who will be likely to shrink from you; because they will not believe in your struggle' (p. 626). At the end of the conversation with Dr Kenn, his thoughts shift to the narrator's commentary in the last two paragraphs of chapter 2, Book VII, in a defence of Maggie's struggle: 'moral judgments must remain false and hollow, unless they are checked and enlightened by a perpetual reference to the special circumstances that mark the individual lot' (p. 487).

The relationship with Stephen, like the one with Philip, is not all Maggie's fault. Stephen repeatedly seeks her out and finally pressures her into leaving with him. His 'inward vision of her which perpetually made part of his consciousness' (p. 559) is evidence that he is suffering from infatuation himself. Like Philip, Stephen's motives interact with Maggie's. His involvement with her can be seen as an outgrowth of his feelings of superiority over those around him – an expression of power over the Tullivers, Lucy, Philip, and even his own father.

Book VII opens with Tom as master at Dorlcote Mill: he has fulfilled the family's wish to own it again; but his success is spoiled by Maggie's disgrace upon her return from the failed elopement with Stephen. From Tom's point of view, it is a disgrace worse than death (p. 611). 'You have disgraced us all – you have disgraced my father's name. You have been a curse to your best friends' (p. 612). Maggie attempts to repent and be reconciled to him, but Tom's refusal is final: he does not even want her under his roof. Mrs Tulliver comes to her rescue, however, and they go to Bob Jakin's house together. Maggie goes through a period of extreme guilt in the form of (belated) anxiety for Stephen, Lucy, and Philip (p. 621). While she claims a desire for financial independence (p. 622), she thinks of Dr Kenn, the Anglican clergyman she met at Lucy's bazaar, and 'the momentary feeling of reliance that had sprung in her when he was talking with her'. She determines to see him, despite her knowledge that he is grieving over the recent death of his wife (p. 623). She attempts reparation through her confession to him, a new father figure.

Maggie's Aunt Glegg offers her shelter at her house, but Maggie, insisting on her 'independence', takes a position with Dr Kenn instead, thus again establishing a connection with a strong male. But in chapter 5, 'The Last Conflict', Dr Kenn, who has grown sensitive to the local gossip and feels he should avoid even the 'appearance of evil', has asked her to leave and offered to find her a position in another town. Maggie suffers an overwhelming sense of abandonment: 'There was no home, no help for the erring' (p. 646).

On the third day of her despair she receives another letter from Stephen, who is still pleading for her love. She wavers, and then burns the letter, but puts off writing him 'the last word of parting' until the next day (p. 649). Maggie is caught in a cycle which only death can bring to an end. Conveniently, just as she wishes for death, she feels the flood water at her feet.

Psychoanalytic interpretations of the flood ending, which has been the focus of literary criticism of *The Mill on the Floss* because of the novel's sudden shift from a realistic to a symbolic mode, emphasise Maggie's need to be reunited with Tom, whom no other man can replace. Smith, describing the relationship between Maggie and Tom as incestuous, sees the flood scene as the symbolic consummation of their passion. Emery sees many levels of meaning: the flood represents the outpouring of Maggie's repressed rage toward Tom at the same time it fulfils oedipal and oral wishes (to be reunited with both father and mother, for whom Tom is a substitute), and finally, the wish to return to the womb (to be at one with her mother and Tom), which is simultaneously a wish for death (p. 23). Tom is the focus of Maggie's infantile attachments, from whom she is unable to separate. Her unmet need to be accepted by her parents creates her hunger to be attached to symbols of them (first Tom, and then other men) in later life.

Kohut explains that narcissistic rage is 'aggression mobilised in the service of an archaic grandiose self and that it is deployed within the framework of an archaic perception of reality'.[20] In other words, images of self and other in the person who suffers narcissistic rage are confused and distorted. The most violent forms of narcissistic rage arise in individuals in whom 'the maintenance of self-esteem – and indeed of the self – depends on the unconditional availability of the approving-mirroring functions of an admiring self-object, or on the ever-present opportunity for a merger with an idealised one'.[21] Maggie's sense of self depends on her perception of herself as attached to Tom, the symbolic substitute for her parents – hence her ongoing need to seek reparation with him. The flood ending brings Maggie and Tom permanently back together through death.

Eliot's friend Sara Hennell thought *The Mill on the Floss* 'unfinished' because of '[Eliot]'s intense sympathy with Maggie. ... In every word of the book ... she could hear [Eliot]'s voice of ten years before'.[22] Many twentieth-century critics have also seen Eliot's over-identification with Maggie as a flaw in the novel. Leavis refers to 'a tendency toward the direct presence of the author' and to Maggie's 'lack of self-knowledge shared by George Eliot'.[23] Paris, essentially agreeing with Leavis, writes that Eliot 'succeeds brilliantly' in the characterisation of Maggie, but 'fails to interpret her correctly'.[24] Hardy refers to the problem of 'under-distance' of the narration toward the ending and to the relation between personal need and artistic shaping at each stage of the novel.[25] Emery refers to a particular point at the beginning of chapter 13 in Book VI, when Maggie and Stephen drift off together, where 'the narrator's point of view [merges] with Maggie's'.[26]

The autobiographical nature of the novel is well known. McDonnell is among the critics who have noted parallels between the Maggie–Tom relationship and the relationship between Eliot[27] and her brother Isaac, who although close in early childhood, had rejected her as an adult because of her liaison with George Lewes.[28] But there are also parallels in the patterns of Maggie's and Eliot's young adult relationships with other men – relationships which involved dependence on men unavailable for marriage. In 1843, at age twenty-four, Eliot became involved in a friendship with a much older married man, Dr Brabant, whose wife became jealous and insisted that she be put out of the house.[29] After her father's death in 1849, she formed a friendship with François D'Albert Durade, a forty-five year old married painter whose deformity calls to mind Philip Wakem, and whom Eliot loved 'as a father and brother'.[30] Her involvement in 1851 with John Chapman, who already had a wife and mistress, precipitated her departure from his household;[31] McDonnell suggests that her infatuation for Chapman 'may have influenced her depiction of Stephen Guest'.[32] In 1854, when Eliot left England with Lewes, who was married but permanently separated from his wife, they left for Germany by boat: 'Like Maggie and Stephen Guest aboard the Dutch vessel, [Eliot] paced up and down the deck, leaning on George's arm'.[33] The series of relationship with unavailable men perhaps suggests that Eliot's 'dependence on the arm of man'[34] was combined with aggression in the form of defiance toward society's values.

Eliot's choice of Lewes, as Emery suggests, might have been a self-perpetuation of her childhood sense of alienation from family and society. The separation from family and past that the liaison provoked served as an impetus for her fiction writing: it became 'possible and even urgent for her to create'.[35] The close attachment to Lewes, which apparently fulfilled both oedipal and pre-oedipal needs[36] and which seems to have successfully replaced her childhood love for her brother Isaac, also provided her with the nurturing she needed in order to write. Eliot herself referred to their 'Siamese-twin condition'.[37] Throughout her fiction writing career, she relied on Lewes's unfailing encouragement and protection from criticism.

Eliot's failure to see Maggie as readers see her probably derives from her own faulty self-perception. It can be argued that Eliot projects the idealised self-image of her youth on to Maggie. By rationalising Maggie's behaviour with Philip, Stephen, and Dr Kenn, Eliot justifies her own pattern of behaviour which culminated in her choice of Lewes, and defends herself against her family's and society's judgement. Her failure to separate her own life from her heroine's results in a work of art flawed by decreasing control over the narrative as the novel approaches its deus ex machina ending.

From *Literature and Psychology*, 36: 1–2 (1990), 90–109.

NOTES

[This essay first appeared in the journal *Literature and Psychology* in 1990. It falls within the confines of biographical criticism but also within the mode of criticism based on the insights of Sigmund Freud, Heinz, Kohut, Jacques Lacan, Julia Kristeva and many others which take the text, as well as the author, as a subject and in which events of the narrative are read as symptoms, both real and metaphoric, of a psychic structure. As a psychoanalytic critic Johnstone thus reads *The Mill* in a similar way to that in which a psychoanalyst reads the words of a patient. She argues that Eliot's novels illuminate her life, suggesting, for example, that in this novel, Eliot's presentation of Maggie's relationships with men can be read as her author's therapeutic confrontation with men in her own life: her brother Isaac Evans, the painter, François D'Albert Durade, and the publisher John Chapman. In her essay Johnstone also traces the paths that Maggie's/Eliot's desire follows through a complex series of significant symbols and metaphors. Eds]

1. See Laura Comer Emery, *George Eliot's Creative Conflict: The Other Side of Silence* (Berkeley, CA, 1976), p. 17 and p. 23.

2. Bernard Paris, 'The Inner Conflicts of Maggie Tulliver', in *A Psychological Approach to Fiction: Studies in Thackeray, Stendhal, George Eliot, Dostoevsky, and Conrad* (Bloomington, IN, 1974), p. 170.

3. Ibid., p. 171.

4. The page numbers in the text, unless otherwise indicated, refer to the Viking Penguin edition of *The Mill on the Floss* (New York, 1979), p. 82.

5. Emery, *George Eliot's Creative Conflict*, p. 16.

6. See Heinz Kohut, 'Thoughts on Narcissism and Narcissistic Rage', *The Psychoanalytic Study of Child*, Vol. 27 (New York, 1973), p. 380. The study that Kohut refers to is F. Alexander's 'Remarks about the Relation of Inferiority Feelings to Guilt Feelings', *Psycho-Analysis*, 19 (1938), 41–9.

7. Kohut, 'Thoughts on Narcissism and Narcissistic Rage', p. 379.

8. Emery also sees Maggie's insistence on supporting herself as evidence of her 'unconscious anger' toward Tom. 'Maggie offends Tom by seeking work too ostentatiously.' Emery, *George Eliot's Creative Conflict*, p. 25.

9. Ermarth discusses the sexist social norms that Maggie has internalised and which have caused her to be 'self-effacing and dependent, buying her identity at the price of her autonomy' (p. 592). Steig shows how the anal traits of the society, represented by the older generation of

Dodsons, have affected Maggie's 'shame', 'self-doubt', and 'fantasy of dominance' (p. 40). Woodward shows how Maggie is ostracised from the rigid community of women at St Ogg's because she is 'bold and "unwomanly"' (p. 47). See Elizabeth Ermarth, 'Maggie Tulliver's Long Suicide', *Studies in English Literature*, 14 (1974), 587–601; Michael Steig, 'Anality in *The Mill on the Floss*', *Novel*, 5 (1971), 42–53; Wendy Woodward, 'The Solitariness of Selfhood: Maggie Tulliver and the Female Community at St Ogg's', *English Studies in Africa*, 28 (1985), 46–55.

10. Emery writes that after Thomas à Kempis, 'Maggie takes a distinctively different attitude toward her impulses, especially rage ... [W]hile Maggie seeks peace the action of the novel becomes suddenly more violent' (p. 29). Emery is referring to Maggie's 'intense participation' (in fantasy) in Tom's verbal assault on Philip and in her father's violence toward Wakem (pp. 30–1). See Emery, *George Eliot's Creative Conflict*.

11. Emery also sees the involvement with Philip as an aggressive action against Tom, whose sense of triumph over repaying his father's debts is spoiled when he learns of the secret meetings. Ibid., p. 25.

12. Ermarth, 'Maggie Tulliver's Long Suicide', p. 19.

13. Graver also writes about Stephen as representing the 'good society' in the context of a discussion about 'the shift in the portrait of Stephen from privileged gentleman to romantic lover' (p. 194), which she believes is a flaw in the last section of the novel: 'George Eliot evades in the end what she earlier so forcefully confronts: the outer world that frustrates and defeats Maggie's desire for work, attainment, and even marriage. Instead, the concerns of the novel move inward, in part by forgetting how Stephen Guest and the narrow attitudes of good society drove Maggie out of the world altogether into her ultimate emphasis of want' (p. 199). See Suzanne Graver, *George Eliot and Community: A Study in Social Theory and Fictional Form* (Berkeley, CA, 1984).

14. Emery, *George Eliot's Creative Conflict*, p. 38.

15. David S. Werman and Theodore J. Jacobs, 'Thomas Hardy's The Well-Beloved and the Nature of Infatuation', *International Review of Psychoanalysis*, 10 (1983), 447–56.

16. Ibid., p. 450.

17. Emery, also referring to the Round Pool as a symbolic womb, adds that the wish to return to the womb is one of the structural elements which unifies the novel. See Emery, *George Eliot's Creative Conflict*, p. 10.

18. Ibid., p. 37.

19. Jane McDonnell in '"Perfect Goodness" or "The Wider Life": *The Mill on the Floss* as *Bildungsroman*', *Genre*, 15 (1982), notes the 'long-smouldering revenge' that is enacted in the Stephen–Maggie relationship (p. 392).

20. Kohut, 'Thoughts on Narcissism and Narcissistic Rage', p. 385.

21. Ibid., p. 386.

22. Gordon S. Haight, *George Eliot: A Biography* (New York, 1968), p. 335.

23. F. R. Leavis, *The Great Tradition* (New York, 1950), p. 33 and p. 43.

24. Paris, 'The Inner Conflicts of Maggie Tulliver', p. 186.

25. Barbara Hardy, 'Life and Art in *The Mill on the Floss*, in R. P. Draper (ed.), *The Mill on the Floss and Silas Marner* (New York, 1977), p. 173 and p. 179.

26. Emery, *George Eliot's Creative Conflict*, p. 49.

27. The name George Eliot is used throughout the essay, even when, in reference to her early life, her name was still Mary Ann Evans (until 1851), or Marian Evans (until 1856).

28. McDonnell in '"Perfect Goodness" or "The Wider Life"', p. 381.

29. Haight, *George Eliot: A Biography*, p. 50.

30. Gordon S. Haight, *The George Eliot Letters*, 7 Vols (New Haven, CT, 1954–5), Vol. 1, pp. 316–17.

31. Gordon S. Haight, *George Eliot: A Biography*, p. 85.

32. McDonnell in '"Perfect Goodness" or "The Wider Life"', p. 381.

33. Gordon S. Haight, *George Eliot: A Biography*, p. 148.

34. Ibid., p. 52.

35. Emery, *George Eliot's Creative Conflict*, p. 224.

36. Ibid., p. 223.

37. Haight, *The George Eliot Letters*, Vol. 3, p. 23.

7

'Light enough to trusten by': Structure and Experience in *Silas Marner*

TERENCE DAWSON

Silas Marner (1861), always a favourite with readers, was until recently considered too obvious and too lightweight to merit serious critical discussion. In 1949, F. R. Leavis echoed the views of many when he described it as 'that charming minor masterpiece', an evident 'moral fable'.[1] In only one respect was the work seen as unusual: it appeared to have no direct bearing on its author's life.[2] Ever since the mid-1950s, however, it has gradually gathered advocates who have shown that it is not only as rich in ideas but also as firmly rooted in George Eliot's personal concerns as any of her other works and, somewhat surprisingly, these two issues have been increasingly seen as one.[3] In 1975, Ruby Redinger explored the theme of hoarding and concluded that 'the transformation of gold into Eppie justified George Eliot seeking and accepting money for her writing'.[4] Lawrence Jay Dessner looked at a wide range of parallels between the events of the novel and the author's circumstances at the time of writing, and noted that 'fear of being abandoned, fear of having one's secret revealed, antagonism towards a brother, love for a lost sister, concern for moral reputation [are all] common to the fact and the fiction'.[5] It was not until 1985, however, when Sandra Gilbert argued that Eppie is the central character and that the novel's principal theme is the riddle of daughterhood, that anyone specifically explored the implications for a woman of the relationship between Eppie and Silas. Through Silas, she affirms, George Eliot was able to examine 'the dispossession that she herself had experienced as part of the empty pack of daughterhood'.[6] The common element in these otherwise different readings is that they are all, and almost exclusively, concerned with themes. They have established that many of the motifs at the heart of the text are pertinent to the situation in which Eliot found herself in 1860, but they have not explained the novel's structure as a whole. In the following pages, I re-examine the narrative structures in order to illustrate that this novel occupies a much more significant place in its author's literary development than has been recognised.

On the surface, the main plot would seem to be about the regeneration of a middle-aged weaver through love and his reintegration into the community in which he lives. Interlinked with this 'story' is another, generally described as the story of Godfrey Cass, the local squire's eldest son, who turns over something of a new leaf in the course of the events described. Faced by a novel in which there are two distinct plots, the critic's first task is to discover the connexion between them. The most frequent definition of the relation between the two stories in *Silas Marner* is that they are parallel, but move in opposite directions.[7] Not only is this view too vague to be helpful, it is also misleading, for there is no similarity whatsoever between Silas's situation at the beginning and Godfrey's at the end, or vice versa. Nevertheless, the two plots are unquestionably related: indeed, I shall argue that they show many more similarities than have been identified to date.

In purely narrative terms, the main events of the novel would seem to trace the parallel stories of the weaver and Godfrey Cass: I do not wish to argue otherwise. But in psychological terms, because the novel was written by a woman, one would expect it to reflect and describe a woman's experience. Such a view assumes that the events of a novel are shaped by the nature of a dilemma uppermost in its author's mind at the time of writing. In 1860 Eliot, having completed her preliminary studies for *Romola*, a novel about the Florence of Savonarola, had fallen into one of her periodic fits of depression. Just how much of this novel's action she had sketched when the idea of *Silas Marner* 'thrust' itself upon her so insistently that she shelved her historical novel in order to write her tale about the weaver of Raveloe we shall never know.[8] All that is certain is that Savonarola occupied a major place in her thoughts immediately prior to the vision (the word is not too strong) of 'a linen weaver with a bag on his back' (p. 382) which provided the initial seed from which *Silas Marner* quickly grew. If we can assume that a connexion exists between George Eliot's preoccupation with Savonarola, who may be described as a 'dark' father-figure who influences Romola for as long as she is attracted to the worthless Tito, and her own depression, then one can read this vision of a benevolent father-figure as a 'compensatory' urge which emerged, spontaneously, from her unconscious in order to shake her out of her increasingly gloomy thoughts. A primary aim of these pages is to argue that embedded in the surface narrative of *Silas Marner* are numerous thematic concerns which suggest that the events it describes are shaped by a psychological dilemma pertinent to Eliot at the time of writing. My intention is to show that the very structures of the text invite the reader to read this novel as an expression of a woman's psychological concerns.

My first objective is to demonstrate that the events of *Silas Marner*, not only those of the main plot but all the major events, including such scenes as the wonderfully comic conversation in the Rainbow Inn, can be shown to be directly related to a female character who functions as the 'carrier' of the author's unconscious personality. This character, I shall show, is Nancy Lammeter, an apparently minor figure hitherto almost completely ignored by critics.[9]

The basis for this claim is derived from the analysis of the major episodes of the novel, all of which reveal thematic parallels with the dilemma of confronting Nancy. Even when she does not actually feature in the episodes in question, or plays only a minor role in them, the insistence with which their theme is related to her amounts to evidence that the entire narrative constitutes a symbolic representation of the dilemma facing her. My aim, then, is to demonstrate that not only is the so-called sub-plot principally about a process affecting Nancy, but so too is the entire novel: in other words, to reveal that the interconnected plots of the novel tell *one* story on two distinct 'levels' of fictional representation and to argue that, in psychological terms, both pertain to Nancy. In the first section, I look at the parallels between the two 'plots' to show that the events in which Godfrey features can indeed be said to be told from Nancy's perspective. In the next, I identify the nature of the dilemma confronting her by reference to some of Jung's key concepts.[10] I then examine the relation between the Silas plot and the way in which Nancy achieves a tentative resolution to this problem and, lastly, as my reading tacitly implies that the experience at issue was highly relevant to the author, I briefly relate the conclusions to George Eliot's situation in 1860–61.

First, let us remind ourselves of the main stages of Silas's story. At the outset of the novel, he is living in complete isolation, nursing the hurt of a wrong done to him some fifteen years previously by William Dane and the arbitrary result of the drawing of lots by the Lantern Yard brethren. On the day of Mrs Osgood's birthday party, his gold is stolen. A month later, he sees lying on his hearth a baby girl, the sight of which awakens 'old quiverings of tenderness' in him (p. 168). Sixteen years later, contrary to his fear that she might abandon him, Eppie chooses to stay with him, and the novel ends with her marrying Aaron. This pattern is remarkably similar to that of Nancy's story. At the time the novel opens, Nancy is privately nursing the hurt of a wrong done her by Godfrey. On the night of Mrs Osgood's birthday party, Dunstan falls to his death in the stone-pits, and some four weeks later, Molly dies while on her way to claim recognition, thus making it possible for Nancy to marry the man whom she loves. Fifteen years later, Godfrey, afraid that she might want to leave him, reveals his past to her. To his surprise, she forgives him and they consolidate their relationship.

These similarities are striking. Each plot begins with a contrast between two men, one of whom is well-intentioned but weak (Silas, Godfrey); the other, more dynamic but morally reprehensible (William Dane, Dunstan). The men are either brothers or the very best of friends (Silas and Dane are called 'David and Jonathan' by the Lantern Yard brethren [p. 57]). In the 'present', Godfrey's only remaining possession is his horse, appropriately called 'Wildfire'. Even this he is prepared to sacrifice rather than admit to his marriage with a barmaid, Molly Farren, because he knows that his father would disinherit him for such a folly. In the 'past', when William Dane falsely accuses Silas, the latter is literally cast out by the community to which he belongs. Both stories are thus instigated by a similar combination of factors. In each case, a more vital, 'daring and cunning' brother is endeavouring to steal the birthright of a better but weaker brother (p. 87).

There is, however, a very considerable difference between the two situations. Godfrey does not want his 'degrading marriage' with Molly Farren brought to light; he is guilty of deceiving not only his wife but also Nancy, whom he has continued to court. Silas, on the other hand, does *not* commit the crime he is accused of. If there is a parallel between the events in the 'present' and those in the 'past', it is between Silas and Nancy, who are equally blameless.

One notes that Godfrey's conduct is constantly being excused. We are asked to believe that he really is 'a fine open-faced good-natured young man' (p. 73). The facts do not bear this out: he is secretive and has behaved abominably towards both Molly and Nancy. He deserved to be disgraced. Why, then, should he not be exposed? Who stands to gain by his behaviour's not being revealed? Most obviously, of course, himself. One remembers that Nancy is proud and could not stand knowing that Godfrey has been deceiving her. At the end, he reminds her why he did not tell her about his marriage with Molly Farren: 'With your pride and your father's, you'd have hated having anything to do with me after the talk there'd have been' (p. 224). He is, of course, making excuses, but he is also probably right. Everything we learn about Nancy in Part 1 would corroborate his assertion. If she reacts differently in Chapter 18, it is because she has 'changed' by the time he reveals his past to her. In other words, it is essential that Nancy does not learn of his affair with Molly until she is ready to assimilate such information. Nancy would like Godfrey to be exonerated from as much censure as possible, for he can be the man that *she* wants him to be only if *his* shoddy behaviour is not a reflection of his own personality but has been provoked by another character. Thus Dunstan's function is ambiguous. At one level of reading, he seeks to inculpate Godfrey, whom he 'traps' into marrying a barmaid of whom he is ashamed because he wants his older brother 'turned out of house and home' by their father (pp. 74, 80). But at another, Dunstan, by his very existence, serves to extenuate Godfrey's guilt, and in this latter capacity, no matter how paradoxical this may seem, Dunstan serves Nancy's interests.

I shall look more closely at the similarities between Dunstan and William Dane in a moment. Meanwhile, it is worth noting those between Molly and Sarah, each of whom is associated with the stronger but morally reprehensible man: Molly becomes involved with Godfrey through Dunstan, and Sarah marries William Dane. The most striking feature that they have in common is their weakness. Sarah slips into marriage with William Dane and is never mentioned again, and Molly is kept away from Raveloe, in a neighbouring village called Batherley, where she slides into laudanum addiction until she finally succumbs to a longing for oblivion (pp. 164–5). There is a clear parallel with Nancy's situation. When

Godfrey fails to propose to her, Nancy determines not to marry him and withdraws to her own home. Molly's isolation corresponds to Nancy's isolation, and Sarah's preference for William Dane corresponds to Nancy's continuing interest in Godfrey after his behaviour has become as hypocritical as that of William Dane. In thematic terms, then, the fifteen years of Silas's self-imposed isolation correspond to the period of about three years of Nancy's bitter doubts.

In corroboration of this, one notes the parallels between the ways in which Silas and Nancy react to the various wrongs done to them. They both ward off despair by devoting themselves to work. When the lots pronounce against him, Silas ceases to trust in a 'God of lies' (p. 61). To forget his pain, he abandons his home town, settles in as isolated a community as possible, and devotes himself to his work. Weaving, one of the dominant images of the novel, symbolises the slow growth of a pattern through the patient interconnexion of opposites. Similarly, when Godfrey fails to propose to her, Nancy abandons all hope of marrying him. To forget her pain, she buries herself in domestic duties: her hands 'bore the traces of butter-making, cheese-crushing, and even still coarser work' (p. 147). Like linen, butter and cheese are the products of patient toil. Thus, at the outset of the events, both Silas and Nancy have been wronged, and have reacted in a similar fashion. They are both leading isolated and restricted lives, immersing themselves in transformative work in order to forget their hurt.

Nancy is equally central to the crucial events which take place on the evening of Mrs Osgood's birthday party and Squire Cass's New Year party. Mrs Osgood is Nancy's aunt: Godfrey's relations play virtually no part in the story. The night of her birthday party, we learn that Godfrey is very pleased to see Nancy. The same evening, Silas's gold, which stands in lieu of a 'purpose' in his life and is the visible symbol of his 'hard isolation' (p. 65), is stolen, causing him for the first time since his self-imposed exile to become aware of a 'lack' in his life. A few moments later, the thief, Dunstan, disappears from view (we subsequently learn that he has fallen to his death). This not only frees Godfrey from the negative influence upon him which Dunstan represents, but thereby opens the way for him to make things up with Nancy. We know that Nancy is still deeply attached to Godfrey: it is surely legitimate to infer that his pleasure in seeing her causes Nancy to become conscious of the distance that has grown between them – that is, of a 'lack' in *her* life. The theft of Silas's gold thus coincides with Nancy's becoming dimly aware of how she too has 'undergone a bewildering separation from a supremely loved object' (p. 166).

The parallelism between the two plots is even more apparent on the night of Squire Cass's New Year party. In the course of the festivities at the Red House, Ben Winthrop comments to Mr Macey: 'Well, I think Miss Nancy's a-coming round again' (p. 160). This remark not only tells the reader that Nancy's determination not to marry Godfrey is not as firm as she would like people to believe (p. 143), but also, at least in the eyes of one villager, lays the blame for the delayed engagement not with Godfrey, but with Nancy. This is so contrary to one's assumptions about the situation that it requires attention. Only Dunstan knows about Godfrey's secret marriage. No one else suspects Godfrey of anything other than coming under Dunstan's influence (p. 73). Ben's comment tells us that Nancy appears to have resolved to end her self-imposed isolation by responding to Godfrey's devotion. The dance in the Red House coincides with two crucial events, one occurring just outside the weaver's cottage and the other inside. Molly dies of laudanum intoxication and Silas discovers Eppie on the hearth and begins to feel 'old quiverings of tenderness' for the first time in several years (p. 168), thereby discovering a 'purpose' in life. Nancy's change of heart thus coincides not only with the death of a woman who is an obstacle to her ambition to marry Godfrey but also with the beginning of Silas's redemption through love. Moreover, the phrases used to describe Silas's emotions are equally applicable to Nancy: she also feels 'old quiverings of tenderness' towards Godfrey and thereby discovers a new 'purpose' in *her* life. Thus, just as Nancy's intimation of Godfrey's continuing affection for her, on the night of Mrs Osgood's birthday party, coincides with Silas becoming conscious of a lack, so her 'a-coming round again' in her attitude towards Godfrey, noticed by Ben on New Year's Eve, coincides with the awakening of Silas's love for another human being. [...]

I have looked at some parallels between Silas's story and Nancy's story. There is however one all-important difference. Silas is acted upon. Things happen to him. He is expelled from the Lantern Yard brethren. His money is stolen and he later discovers Eppie on his hearth. He is not abandoned at the end. When he acts (for example, when he decides to leave the Lantern Yard community, or to look after Eppie) it is compulsively. Silas is never an agent. In contrast, each of the main stages in Nancy's story is characterised by a decision which *she* makes. Her isolation corresponds to *her* determination not to marry Godfrey. Her resolve then wavers, she warms to him once again; at exactly the same time (although she knows nothing of this), she is liberated to marry him. At the end, when provided with a reason which, earlier, would have been sufficient for her to abandon him, she chooses to stay with him. The main events in Nancy's story correspond to her various attitudes and decisions. She *is* an agent. In this section, I want to show, by means of an analysis of the relation between Nancy and the other characters, that all the events are directly related to her: the opening situation offers a symbolic representation of a challenge facing her, and the course of events described in the novel reflects how she reacts to it.

The surprising number of attributes that Nancy and Godfrey have in common provides the most striking indication of the nature of their relation one to the other. Priscilla chides Nancy for 'sitting on an addled egg for ever, as if there was never a fresh un in the world' (p. 150). Godfrey is defined by his similar vacillation and moral cowardice (p. 77). His father describes him as a 'shilly-shally fellow' and adds: 'You take after your mother. She never had a will of her own' (p. 125). Nancy's mother died when she was a small child, and so too did Godfrey's. Although Nancy is reluctant to admit she loves him, she does not want to marry anyone else (pp. 224, 151), and Godfrey constantly puts off declaring that he loves her, while conceding that there is no other woman whom he wants to marry (p. 125). One way of looking at the characteristics they have in common is to maintain that they are drawn to one another because of their similar backgrounds. Such an explanation is insufficient. The parallels suggest rather that they 'mirror' one another: in other words, that their relationship is conditioned by psychological factors. Because the Nancy–Godfrey plot tells *her* story, one must conclude that Nancy is drawn to Godfrey largely because he 'personifies' or 'mirrors' aspects of her own weakness. This, in turn, implies that Godfrey is not so much an autonomous male character as a type or, more specifically, an 'image of a man' to which she is instinctively drawn.

According to Jung, just as every man has an inherent, albeit unconscious, mental image of the feminine that reflects his relationship with women, so every woman has a similar image of the masculine that mirrors her relationship with men. The image of a man encountered by a woman in her dreams and waking fantasies, personifying her inner or unconscious attitudes towards men, he called the *animus*.[11] That Godfrey's attributes so clearly mirror Nancy's suggests that he may be defined as an animus-figure.[12] In short, not only do the events in which Godfrey features tell Nancy's story, but this story may be defined as essentially psychological. It is not so much about two individuals as about the relation between a young woman and her own inherent image of masculinity: her animus. Clearly, regarding the relation between Nancy and Godfrey in this light invites one to read the novel not as a succession of episodes that represent a real situation, but as a reflection of a psychological process in which Nancy serves as the carrier of the author's unconscious personality.

Read in this way, the elements that compose the initial situation symbolise the impasse in which Nancy finds herself. At the time the novel opens, both Nancy and Godfrey live in houses dominated by a father-figure (The Warrens by Mr Lammeter, The Red House by Squire Cass). Nancy's sister, Priscilla, is entirely contained in her relationship with her father, she is proud that she 'features' his family and spurns all other men:

> 'The pretty-uns do for fly-catchers – they keep the men off us. I've no opinion of men, Miss Gunn – I don't know what you have. And as for fretting and stewing about what *they'll* think of you from morning till night, and making your life uneasy about what they're doing when they're out o' your sight – as I tell Nancy, it's a folly no woman need be guilty of, if she's got a good father and a good home. [...] As I say, Mr Have-your-own-way is the best husband, and the only one I'd ever promise to obey.'
>
> (pp. 148–9)

This is not the speech of a liberated woman; it is an expression of Priscilla's over-attachment to her father and a corresponding confusion of 'father' and 'home' that prevent her from even contemplating a relation with a male 'other'. Priscilla does not change: at the end of the novel, she is as attached to her father as she was sixteen years before. She thinks of him as unique and is correspondingly scornful of other men: 'But joyful be it spoken, our father was never that sort o' man' (p. 213). She never distances herself from him.[13]

At the outset, in spite of her continuing love for him, Nancy has turned her back on Godfrey and is living at home with her sister and father: in other words, she has adopted her sister's maxim. This implies that Priscilla personifies an attitude which Nancy has adopted in spite of its being detrimental to her happiness. Jung used the term *shadow* to describe alter-ego figures of the same sex as the dreamer which he or she encounters in dreams and waking fantasies. The shadow personifies 'the "negative" side of the personality, the sum of all those unpleasant qualities we like to hide' (*CW*, vii, 103 n. 5). More specifically, it illustrates the way in which an individual *actually is behaving*, even when he or she is utterly unconscious of acting in such a manner. Nancy would like to marry Godfrey; instead, she is sitting at home pretending she has forgotten him. If Priscilla personifies an aspect of Nancy's character of which she is unaware, then her opinion about men in general tells the reader what Nancy is unconsciously afraid of: Nancy is worried at what Godfrey might be doing when he is out of her sight. Given that Nancy has no inkling of Molly's existence, her fears must represent tendencies in her own character.

The corresponding events in the Silas plot not only corroborate this claim, but also constitute a direct comment on what she is doing. One remembers that it is on becoming engaged to Silas that Sarah's manner towards him 'began to exhibit a strange fluctuation between an effort at an increased manifestation of regard and involuntary signs of shrinking and dislike' (p. 58). That is, as soon as Sarah becomes engaged to him, she begins to have negative feelings towards him. She is afraid of his epilepsy, and epilepsy may be defined as an 'absence' from oneself. Silas's 'absences' are equivalent to Nancy's feelings of emptiness when Godfrey goes away for 'days and days together' (p. 73). We are told that everyone in Raveloe thinks they would make 'a handsome couple' (pp. 73, 159–60), but Nancy turns her back on him in much the same way as Sarah abandons Silas. Imagining that Godfrey is unreliable, she retires to her own home. Yet, although she pretends she does not want to marry him, she continues to treasure some dried flowers for his sake (p. 151). She cannot bring herself to forget him; later, she asserts that there is no other man that she would ever have contemplated marrying (p. 224). In other words, she has surrendered herself to Godfrey, but only in her imagination. In reality, she is shunning him. *Silas Marner* offers a vivid representation of how and why such opposite tendencies arise.

The key to an individual's conflicting tendencies is the nature of his or her shadow-personality. I have defined Priscilla as Nancy's shadow, but an individual's shadow is often multiple. Priscilla represents Nancy's 'personal' shadow; Molly Farren can be defined as an archetypal aspect of her shadow. The events surrounding Molly are implausible in realistic terms, for it is equally improbable that a young village barmaid should have had access to laudanum and that Godfrey's relation with her could have been kept secret for so long in such small and tightly-knit communities as Raveloe and

Batherley. The reason Godfrey's interest in her must remain secret is that Nancy could not bear its being disclosed. As Dunstan says to Godfrey, 'Miss Nancy wouldn't mind being a second, if she didn't know it' (p. 76). Even at the end, when Godfrey tells her about his first marriage, she asks him not to tell either her father or Priscilla about his affair with Molly (p. 236). None of the villagers learns of it. In other words, she does not want to face the fact of Molly's existence and, in psychological terms, whatever aspect of our personality we seek to repress belongs to our 'shadow'. Molly can therefore be defined as another, deeper or more archetypal aspect of Nancy's shadow. If Molly's concealed existence corresponds to Nancy's self-imposed isolation, then her addiction to laudanum symbolises the narcotic quality of Nancy's fantasy surrender to Godfrey. She personifies a deeply unconscious aspect of Nancy, whose unnatural isolation and exaggerated fantasies about the man whom she loves are psychologically destroying her.

Not surprisingly, it is Priscilla who provides an explanation of why Nancy is doing this. Priscilla clings to the image she has of her father; Nancy does the same. For, although we are told little about Nancy's relationship with her father, there is much we can deduce about it. The narrator, describing Nancy's attitude, tells us that her father 'was the soberest and best man in the countryside, only a little hot and hasty now and then, if things were not done to the minute' (p. 144). One remembers that Squire Cass also thinks of his family as being the best in the neighbourhood, and he, too, easily loses his temper (pp. 121, 123). Godfrey lives in constant fear of being censured and perhaps disinherited by his father. If he is an animus-figure, it follows that *his* weakness (lack of confidence in himself) can be ascribed to *Nancy*'s lack of confidence in herself owing to her equal fear of being reproved by her father or of separating herself from him. The doubts she entertains about Godfrey are therefore directly related to her over-attachment to her father. Thus, for Nancy to 'imagine' Godfrey married to a woman who would degrade him signals not so much a petty jealousy as a lack of confidence in her own worth: compare her 'perpetually recurring thought': '"I can do so little – have I done it well?"' (pp. 214–15). Nancy, while isolating herself from Godfrey, *unconsciously* thinks of herself as an unsuitable partner for such an eligible young man as Godfrey.

On the surface, everything pertaining to Nancy is 'of delicate purity and nattiness' (p. 147); but the other elements which compose the initial situation leave room to doubt whether this is the whole picture. They suggest that she is unconsciously projecting her doubts and suspicions onto those around her, and even weaving plots in order to disguise her fear of committing herself to Godfrey. Indeed, so unconscious is she of this tendency that she ascribes it not to any female character (any aspect of her female identity) but to male characters: not only to Godfrey but also to Dunstan and William Dane (aspects of her *animus*).

The connexion between Dunstan and William Dane needs little insistence. Dunstan 'traps' Godfrey into a degrading marriage and William Dane has 'woven a plot' in order to have Silas expelled from the Lantern Yard brethren (pp. 80, 61). Just as Godfrey falls easy prey to Dunstan's blackmail because he does not have the courage to stand up to his father, so Silas falls easy prey to William Dane because he does not have the courage to stand up to the arbitrary decision of the Lantern Yard brethren. Indirectly, however, this trait reflects something happening to Nancy, for Dunstan can be defined as a destructive aspect of her animus that has undermined Godfrey's worth (that is, the worth of the true animus). He is, so to speak, the 'shadow' of the animus. In the same way as Nancy has adopted Pricilla's views, so Godfrey has come under Dunstan's negative influence. Thus, the quarrel between the two brothers can be seen as a conflict between two components of a woman's animus. The question, then, becomes: 'What reason does the text offer to explain why Nancy should imagine men as behaving in this way?'

Surprisingly, the answer is provided by the two scenes which feature groups of men, for they, too, can be shown to be related to Nancy. The Lantern Yard brethren are defined by their manner of arbitrarily judging a man by drawing lots. Although they are called 'brethren', they act towards Silas more like father-figures. According to Jung, the animus may well be experienced as 'rather like an assembly of fathers or dignitaries of some kind who lay down incontestable, "rational", *ex cathedra* judgments' (CW, vii, 332). He observed that a woman whose animus behaves in this way is prone to act upon just such arbitrary opinions as she unconsciously ascribes to all father-figures. One notes that Mr Lammeter is described as a 'grave and orderly senior' (p. 153), a phrase which could equally apply to the Lantern Yard brethren who fill Silas with awe, and that Nancy is described as having an opinion about everything: her opinions 'were always principles to be unwaveringly acted on. They were firm not because of their basis, but because she held them with a tenacity inseparable from her mental action' (p. 216; see p. 148).

Astonishingly, although the conversation at the Rainbow has occasioned a great deal of critical interest, no one has ever offered a reason why it should be entirely about Nancy's father. It consists almost exclusively of groundless and tenaciously defended opinions. The butcher, the farrier, Mr Macey, Mr Tookey, and Mr Winthrop all argue fiercely, each convinced that he alone knows what is right (p. 97), and its most significant feature is that it is *entirely* about Mr Lammeter: first, about his cows, then about his father's arrival in Raveloe, then about his unusual 'Janiwary' marriage, and finally about the previous owner of his home. One need scarcely add that this is not because he is a close friend of any of them: Mr Lammeter lives a retired existence. A literal reading of the events leads to observations about either social life in an isolated community or typically masculine attitudes. But given the tendency I have noted in Nancy, who is 'as constant in her affection towards a baseless opinion as towards an erring lover' (p. 148), we can infer that the villagers constitute yet another aspect of her animus. Thus, both groups of men described in the novel are associated with arbitrary opinionatedness. The Lantern Yard brethren offer an archetypal representation of the consequences of such a tendency. The villagers tell us that it stems from Nancy's father.

The culminating tale in the extraordinary conversation at the Rainbow is about the previous owner of The Warrens, and it provides the only lengthy description we are given of Nancy's home. Nancy is described as 'slightly proud and exacting' (p. 148). She is interested only in 'the young man of quite the highest consequence in the parish' and dreams of one day becoming '"Madam Cass", the Squire's wife' (p. 151). Her pride seems to come from her father. Mr Lammeter, like Godfrey, 'always *would* have a good horse' (p. 213). Appearances matter to them. It is fitting, therefore, that the previous owner of Nancy's home was a jumped-up tailor with an exaggerated concern with appearances. Determined to impress his neighbours at no matter what cost, Mr Cliff (or Cliff, as he is usually called) built and ran an enormous stables. He so bullied his son into acting like a gentleman that the boy died and, mentally unbalanced, he himself died soon after. The Warrens, where Nancy lives, is still haunted by the sound of stamping horses and cracking whips, which the terrified locals call 'Cliff's holiday' (pp. 102–3). Nancy has a similar determination to have her own way; Priscilla remarks how Nancy behaved as a child: 'If you wanted to go to the field's length, the field's length you'd go; and there was no whipping you, for you looked as prim and innicent as a daisy all the while' (p. 150). The reference to 'whipping' is perhaps not entirely fortuitous. The tale of Cliff's holiday, with the stamping of horses and the cracking of a whip, symbolises Nancy's periodic fits of irrational, headstrong determination, a tendency that has emotionally isolated her.

That the Lantern Yard brethren function as father-figures for Silas, and the conversation in the Rainbow is entirely about Mr Lammeter, suggest that Nancy's problem with Godfrey stems from her relation with her father. This corresponds exactly to Jung's views on the animus. He held that a woman who has little understanding about the nature of her own animus will very often develop a tendency to express forceful and arbitrary opinions that 'have the character of solid convictions that are not lightly shaken, or of principles whose validity is seemingly unassailable' (CW, 55vii, 331). Not surprisingly, such a tendency usually stems from an exaggerated attachment to her father in her childhood (CW, 55xiv, 232). Thus, Mr Cliff's relationship with his son may be read as a symbolic representation of the psychological effect that Mr Lammeter has had, unwittingly, upon Nancy. The son who dies is 'equivalent' to the Godfrey on whom Nancy has turned her back. Cliff's holiday is a symbolic description of the irrational aggression which can take possession of a woman and its origins in the foibles of a doting father. The Lantern Yard's arbitrary judgement of Silas symbolises the manner in which a woman whose animus demonstrates wildly conflicting tendencies might arrive at a decision of significance to her. His expulsion is therefore an archetypal representation of Nancy's need to distance herself from the 'assembly of fathers' that make up such a large part of her animus.

The surface narrative and the deeper structures implied by the text thus produce radically different readings of the events. On the surface, it appears that the reason for Nancy's self-imposed isolation is that her fiancé has jilted her, that the Lantern Yard brethren are just a narrow-minded sect, and that the villagers represent the conversation of rustics. A literal reading of the events can lead only to the conclusion that we should not look too closely at the novel's coherence. A psychological analysis of both structures and themes allows one to admire its coherence. It suggests that Godfrey's irregular attentions correspond to Nancy's fears that the two groups of men described in the novel symbolise the reason for these fears: she is still so attached to her father that she is reluctant to trust any other man.

Jung defined the condition in which a woman falls prey to her own fantasies about her animus as animus-possession. By this term, he meant to indicate that opinionatedness that can be shown to be conditioned by her animus does not reflect a woman's essential personality: it merely signals a maladjustment in her notions about men (*CW*, 55 vii 331; ix, ii, 29). The situation at the outset of the novel, in which Nancy is living in self-imposed isolation, in a home which is haunted by the sound of stamping horses and cracking whips, thus symbolises a 'loss' of her true female identity. She has withdrawn into herself to the point of being almost invisible, and Eppie (the other important female character) is suffering from inadequate attention. In a novel written by a woman, their situation is not only significant but also disturbing.

[...]

Silas's discovery of Eppie on his hearth, and the unexpected birth of his love for an abandoned creature, represent the renewal of Nancy's love for Godfrey. In other words, Eppie personifies an aspect of her nature that Nancy had been denying (or, in psychoanalytic terminology, repressing). Thus, if the rehumanisation of Silas corresponds to Nancy's warming again to Godfrey, then Eppie personifies Nancy's burgeoning love. This is why Eppie has and requires no depth of character: she is an archetypal image of a daughter-figure in an older woman's imagination. It is because Nancy's difficulties stem directly from her over-attachment to her father that Eppie's education is entirely entrusted to a symbolic foster-father. Silas's growing devotion to Eppie signals a process deep in Nancy's unconscious, working towards the correction of her self-doubts.

Had Godfrey acknowledged Eppie at his father's New Year party, Nancy would have withdrawn still further from society and become another Priscilla: competent, no doubt, but never having had the experience of a relationship. In other words, he would have taken Eppie into the Red House, and she would have been left with only the dried leaves that she treasures for his sake, longing to marry him and have his child. The novel traces the 'process' she has to go through before she is ready to overcome her tendency to long for 'what was not given' (p. 215). Her dilemma determines not only the course of its two separate stories but also the nature of the interconnexions between them. Silas's redemption through love is a symbolic representation of the way in which Nancy gradually overcomes instinctive tendencies in her personality which might have become detrimental to both her aims and her happiness.

[...]

In psychological terms, the novel is not composed of two 'plots' of equal value. It tells one story on two different levels of fictional representation. It is about Nancy's relation with Godfrey, which has been made difficult as a result of an over-attachment to her father and a corresponding tendency to suspect the worth of any other man. It tells how Nancy gradually overcomes a self-destructive tendency to indulge in unconscious fears, fantasies, and arbitrary decisions detrimental to the happiness she desires. By working at her relationship with Godfrey, she gradually overcomes those deeply-ingrained tendencies in her character which could so easily have led her into increasing emotional isolation and prevented her from making her peace with Godfrey, as she so evidently wants to do. The novel traces the process Nancy unconsciously goes through before she finally, albeit only tentatively, comes to terms with her situation: she is (and in all likelihood will remain) childless, but she now knows that the 'partner' in her own imagination fully accepts their situation.

Although I have endeavoured to show that one can deduce Nancy's central function in the novel only from textual evidence, the basis of my argument supposes that the dilemma facing Nancy must also be relevant to George Eliot. There are, however, few obvious parallels between Nancy and Marian Evans. The fictional character is clearly not the carrier of the author's conscious personality, but the carrier of an aspect of her unconscious personality. A good description of the distinction between these two concepts is supplied by Edward Whitmont's definition of the difference between the ego and the dream-ego:

> In any normal person's dream the 'I' as identity-carrier may appear altered and dissociated. It may seem to have lost the conscious ego's value and action capacities and to have taken on strange new ones; the dream-ego frequently feels and acts in a way which is uncharacteristic of the waking ego, or it cannot act at all, as in the dream of wanting to run away but instead standing paralysed on the spot.[14]

There is no reason why the pivotal character in a novel should resemble the author. But, just as the dream-ego's *behaviour* will always reveal an important aspect of the ego's unconscious personality, so too, in a novel, will the pivotal character's reactions to the dilemma facing him/her reveal an important aspect of its author. Nancy's reactions have much in common with those of George Eliot.

Silas is about forty years old at the beginning of the novel, and Nancy is about forty years old at the end – Eliot's age at the time of writing. We know that the novelist's early life was considerably affected by her relation with her father.[15] When Nancy separates herself sufficiently from her father to set her hopes on Godfrey she is about the same age as Marian Evans was in 1842, when her refusal to go to church led to a violent quarrel with her father. In spite of this, however, he continued to influence her greatly, even after his death. Marian met G. H. Lewes in October 1851: he was still married, even though he was no longer attached to his wife. She knew the indignity of having to keep her affair with him secret – the parallel with Molly is obvious; Nancy, one notes, suffered no less for her 'secret' love for Godfrey. Her instinct to withdraw into herself and to cross-question herself mercilessly was shared by her creator, who was unusually depressed throughout 1860, occasioned at least in part by society's continued refusal to accept her relation with Lewes. In spite of all the love by which she was surrounded, and for all her literary success, she continued to be prey to an astonishing lack of confidence in herself. Dessner and others have drawn attention to a great many parallels between the life and the fiction.[16] There is ample evidence to suggest that the dilemma I have identified as confronting Nancy is comparable to that which faced Eliot in 1860. Its ending represents a tentative resolution to an enormously painful personal experience that 'thrust' itself upon Eliot in 1860.

Perhaps the most significant feature of this reading, however, is that it provides a substantial link between her previous and her subsequent novels. Maggie Tulliver loses her chance of true happiness when she rejects Stephen Guest and Romola is attracted to an opportunist who conceals both his character and Tessa from her: the parallel with Nancy's situation is self-evident. The vulnerability of both Maggie and Romola stems from their relationships with their respective fathers, relationships which prevent them from discovering their own independent worth until they have forfeited any possibility of the happiness they sought. All three works are centrally concerned with a father's unwittingly negative influence on a female character: the same, one might add, could also be held for *Middlemarch*. Thus, whilst in many ways surprising, this reading of *Silas Marner* in effect re-places the novel in its context. As to why it assumed the form it has, which seems to centre on two male characters, one can only speculate: for my part, as I maintained at the outset, I believe that the figure of Savonarola so weighed upon Eliot's spirits that her creative imagination spontaneously produced a 'compensatory' image whose purpose was to give her 'light enough to trusten by'.[17] If this was indeed so, *Silas Marner* is no less therapeutic than her other novels.

This conclusion raises one further question, and one must touch on it even though it cannot be satisfactorily resolved. To what extent was Eliot conscious of the nature of the dilemma I have outlined? We can never know, but that Nancy never fully realises the debt that she, no less than Godfrey, owes to Silas signals that the ending represents but a tentative solution to the problem with which the novel is concerned. Nancy may never again give way to such fears as occasioned her initial withdrawal from life, but her author might. Indeed, one notes that a considerable part of *Felix Holt* is a development of the theme explored in *Silas Marner*, which would suggest that Eliot only very partially integrated the lesson learned by Nancy at the end of her tale about the weaver of Raveloe. One remembers Mrs Transome's bitter remark: 'A woman's love is always freezing into fear. She wants everything, she is secure in nothing [...] God was cruel when he made woman.'[18] *Silas Marner* illustrates how a woman who is uncertain of her feminine worth risks falling victim to negative fantasies of her own devising and illustrates the psychological origin of Eliot's own deep-rooted insecurity, succinctly expressed by Nancy's 'longing for what was not given'. It tells how a woman whose love had frozen into fear unconsciously discovered a 'light enough to trusten by' that allowed her to achieve at least a partial escape from her own self-doubts and a partial fulfilment of her desires.

From *Modern Language Review*, 88:1 (1993), 26–45.

NOTES

[This essay is taken from Terence Dawson's article '"Light enough to trusten by": Structure and Experience in *Silas Marner*', which provides a useful introduction to the novel and its critical history. As with Johnstone's essay (6), Dawson proceeds in the assumption that there is a direct relationship between life and literature. Thus Dawson contends that Eliot's novels as a whole illuminate her life. In *Silas Marner*, the character of Nancy Lammeter can be read as the 'carrier' of the author's unconscious self. Dawson draws heavily on the work of Carl Jung, notably his concept of the 'animus', the mental image of the opposite sex held by an individual which affects his/her relationships. Dawson is also interested in the structure of the novel, particularly in Eliot's use of parallels, binary opposites and 'shadow' personalities, the latter offering insights into why a particular character acts as s/he does.

All quotations in the essay are taken from *Silas Marner* (Harmondsworth: Penguin, 1967). Eds]

1. F. R. Leavis, *The Great Tradition* (Harmondsworth, 1970), p. 60.

2. W. J. Harvey, *Victorian Fictions: A Guide to Research*, ed. Lionel Stevenson (Cambridge, MA, 1964), p. 296. See also R. T. Jones, *George Eliot* (Cambridge, 1970), p. 31 and William E. Buckler 'Memory, Morality, and the Tragic Vision in the Early Novels of George Eliot', in *The English Novel in the Nineteenth Century: Essays on the Literary Meditations of Human Values*, ed. George Goodin (Urbana, IL, 1972), p. 159.

3. The most important of these early re-evaluations of *Silas Marner* are: Jerome Thale, 'George Eliot's Fable: *Silas Marner*', in *The Novels of George Eliot* (New York, 1959); Fred C. Thomson, 'The Theme of Alienation in *Silas Marner*', *Nineteenth-Century Fiction*, 20 (1965), 69–84; Ian Milner, 'Structure and Quality in *Silas Marner*', *Studies in English Literature*, 6 (1966), 717–29; David R. Carroll, '*Silas Marner*: Reversing the Oracles of Religion' in *Literary Monographs 1*, ed. Eric Rothstein and T. K. Dunseath (Madison, WI, 1967), pp. 167–200, 312–14.

4. Ruby Redinger, *George Eliot: The Emergent Self* (London, 1976), p. 438.

5. Lawrence Jay Dessner, 'The Autobiographical Matrix of *Silas Marner*', *Studies in the Novel*, 11 (1979), 251–82. Redinger's and Dessner's findings have been questioned by Alexander Welsh in *George Eliot and Blackmail* (Cambridge, MA, 1985), p. 167.

6. Sandra M. Gilbert, 'Life's Empty Pack: Notes Towards a Literary Daughteronomy', *Critical Inquiry*, 11 (1985), 355–84 (p. 360).

7. John Preston, 'The Community of the Novel: *Silas Marner*', *Comparative Criticism*, 2 (1980), 121; also Susan R. Cohen, '"A History and a Metamorphosis": Continuity and Discontinuity in *Silas Marner*', *Texas Studies in Literature and Language*, 25 (1983), 414.

8. See George Eliot's Journal entry for 28 November 1860: 'I am engaged now in writing a story, the idea of which came to me after our arrival in this house, and which has thrust itself between me and the other book [*Romola*] I was meditating', *The George Eliot Letters*, ed. Gordon S. Haight, 7 vols (London, 1954–56), III, 360.

9. A striking exception is Lilian Haddakin, who writes that Nancy is 'vitally important in the rendering of "feeling and form" on the realistic level'. She thereupon drops the point: see '*Silas Marner*', in *Critical Essays on George Eliot*, ed. Barbara Hardy (London, 1970), p. 74.

10. Interest in Jung has concentrated too much on his ideas about archetypal images (the 'object' of experience), and not enough on the need to identify the 'subject' – the perceiving consciousness – of the experience in question. Clearly, how one interprets a dream depends on the identity of the subject whose dream it is. The same, I believe, is true of a novel.

11. C. G. Jung, *The Collected Works*, 20 vols (London, 1953–76), ix, ii, paras 29–33; hereafter cited as *CW* followed by volume and paragraph number.

12. The need to define him as such as self-evident. If one is reading the novel in psychological terms, then one should be wary of assuming a one-to-one relation between any character and a possible real-life original. Godfrey certainly shares at least one major attribute of G. H. Lewes: devotion. But it would be mistaken to infer from this that Godfrey = Lewes. The alternative is to view Godfrey as an image of masculinity spontaneously produced by the author's imagination, towards which Nancy Lammeter is instinctively, almost irrationally, drawn.

13. One notes that at the end of the novel she is treating her father almost as if he were a substitute child: see pp. 211–12.

14. Edward C. Whitmont, *The Symbolic Quest* (Princeton, NJ, 1978), p. 234.

15. Gordon S. Haight, *George Eliot: A Biography* (Oxford, 1968), esp. chs 2 and 100; or Jennifer Uglow, *George Eliot* (London, 1987).

16. Dessner, 'The Autobiographical Matrix of *Silas Marner*'; see also Redinger, *George Eliot: The Emergent Self*.

17. One of Jung's major theories was, of course, that the unconscious 'compensates' the one-sidedness of the individual's conscious attitude(s): for example, 'The unconscious processes that compensate the conscious ego contain all those elements that are necessary for the self-regulation of the psyche as a whole' (*CW*, vii, 279; also 282–3; vi, 574–5).

18. George Eliot, *Felix Holt*, ed. Peter Coveney (Harmondsworth, 1972), p. 488. For a discussion of parallels between *Romola, Silas Marner,* and *Felix Holt*, see Elizabeth Deeds Ermarth, 'George Eliot's Conception of Sympathy', *Nineteenth-Century Fiction*, 40 (1985), 23–42.

8

The Miser's Two Bodies: *Silas Marner* and the Sexual Possibilities of the Commodity

JEFF NUNOKAWA

I

What could be simpler than *Silas Marner*'s support for family values? Forsaking her customary tact, Eliot fills the story with simple maxims and paeans promoting a life with wives and children, and emphatic caveats about a life without them. A faith in the family she is elsewhere content confiding to the implications of her narrative is here urged, and urged again, as conspicuous doctrine. Pulling out the stops, Eliot pours her formidable but usually discreet didactic energy into a straightforward channel of simple exhortation: 'the Squire's wife had died long ago, and the Red House was without that presence of the wife and mother which is the fountain of wholesome love and fear in parlour and kitchen';[1] men without women inhabit houses 'destitute of any hallowing charm' (p. 73) and filled instead with the 'scent of flat ale' (p. 73); men without women live in a region barren of the 'sweet flowers of courtesy' (p. 121); men without women dwell in a twilight zone of tedium vitae whose only source of light is the memory of what is lost to them:

pass[ing] their days in the half-listless gratification of senses dulled by monotony ... perhaps the love of some sweet maiden, the image of purity, order, and calm, had opened their eyes to the vision of a life in which the days would not seem too long, even without rioting; but the maiden was lost, and the vision passed away, and then what was left to them, especially when they had become too heavy for the hunt ... ?

(p. 79)

The pains that patient Dolly Winthrop takes to teach the errant weaver the work of raising a child are surely no greater than the pains that *Silas Marner* takes to promote it. It is hard to imagine how the difference between the wholesome delights of the semi-traditional family life Silas Marner manages to sustain with his step-daughter and the debilitating bleakness of his money love could be remarked more blatantly or more often. The fine calibrations of a moral scale able to weigh with utmost precision the specific densities of characters as various as Mr Farebrother, Nicholas Bulstrode and the Princess Halm-Eberstein are abandoned for the blunt dichotomy of the primer when Eliot comes to assess the evil of the gold and the goodness of the child:

> The gold had kept his thoughts in an ever-repeated circle, leading to nothing beyond itself; but Eppie was an object compacted of changes and hopes that forced his thoughts onward ... to the new things that would come with the coming years, when [she] would have learned to understand how her father Silas cared for her ... The gold had asked that he should sit weaving longer and longer, deafened and blinded more and more to all things except the monotony of his loom and the repetition of his web; but Eppie called him away from his weaving, and made him think all its pauses a holiday, re-awakening his senses with her fresh life.
>
> (p. 184)

Silas Marner's commerce with his gold looks less dull in an earlier description, where its deviation from the purity and order of tradi-tional familial arrangements verges on forms of sexuality that both Victorian and contemporary champions of those arrangements apprehend as enemy number one:

> It was pleasant to him to feel them in his palm, and look at their bright faces ... He handled them ... till their form and colour were like the sat-isfaction of a thirst to him; but it was only in the night ... that he drew them out to enjoy their companionship ... at night came his revelry: at night he closed his shutters, and made fast his doors, and drew forth his

gold. He ... felt their rounded outline between his thumb and fingers, and thought fondly of the guineas that were only half-earned by the work of the loom as if they had been unborn children.

(pp. 65, 68, 70)

The pleasure that Eliot's miser takes in this illicit atmosphere ('only in the night'; 'at night came his revelry', 'at night he closed his shutters, and made fast his doors') resembles a condensed catalogue of sexual deviance – incest, of course – the 'rounded outlines' which are the object of his nocturnal fondlings are the bodies of his own children 'begotten by his labour' – but also the range of perversions that surround the 'secret sin' of masturbation. Eliot's account of the revelry of this 'pallid, undersized' man, isolated amongst full-bodied strangers, reads like a case study of the solitary practice and enervating consequences of self-abuse imagined by nineteenth-century sexology, consequences which range from bodily debilitation to homosexuality. Intimations of solitary and more than solitary vices are enfolded in the hard cash whose 'rounded' and 'resistant outlines' the miser fondles, outlines and 'faces' not only 'his own', but also *like* his own.[2] The miser's self-love suggests one that dares not speak its name, a love whose definition is glimpsed in the shadow of Sodom (whose eponymic reputation was as active in the nineteenth century as it is now) that hovers over 'the city of Destruction' from which the miser is saved when the gold is replaced by the girl:

> In the old days there were angels who came and took men by the hand and led them away from the city of destruction. We see no white-winged angels now. But yet men are led away from threatening destruction: a hand is put into theirs, which leads them forth gently towards a calm and bright land, so that they look no more backward; and the hand may be a little child's.
>
> (pp. 190–1)[3]

What is remarkable about Eliot's propaganda campaign on behalf of familial propriety is less the lengths that she goes to in its prosecution, or even the alarming shapes that threaten it, than the deficiency indicated by the very need for such a campaign in the first place. Her frank efforts to propagate a preference for family ties, or, more to our point here, her efforts to propagate an aversion for other kinds of congress, marks a loosening in *Silas Marner* of the quieter methods by which these things are usually inculcated in her fiction; a loosening whose promiscuous consequences verge on the regions of perversity; a loosening that we will eventually return to as a crisis of capital.

II

The appearance of impropriety that clings to the miser's fondlings is an affront to rules of proper bodily conduct, or more precisely, of proper bodily *contact*; a flouting of restrictions imposed by a not just Victorian standard of propriety on the body's intercourse with others, a challenge to the frequently informal bylaws charged with the work of regulating sexual relations. Often dwelling outside the annals of official or even explicit dictates, inhabiting instead 'the seemingly most insignificant details of *dress, bearing*, physical and verbal *manners*', the rules of bodily propriety are easier to observe in their breach:[4] like the sudden realisation of speed limits prompted by the sound of a siren, proper distances between bodies in and beyond the Eliot novel are typically measured by what happens when those which should not, get too close; when intercourse between a man and woman who are not married, or between a man and another man, exceed correct or normal bounds: full scale scandal explodes when Maggie Tulliver spends the night with Stephen Guest, and when Arthur Donnithorne does more than that with Hetty Sorrel; a scandal as intense as these is concentrated in the parlour where Dorothea Casaubon:

> saw, in the terrible illumination of a certainty which filled up all out-lines, something which made her pause motionless, without self-possession enough to speak. Seated with his back towards her on a sofa which stood against the wall on a line with the door by which she had entered, she saw Will Ladislaw; close by him and turned towards him with a flushed tearfulness which gave a new brilliancy to her face sat Rosamond, her bonnet hanging back, while Will leaning towards her clasped both her hands in his and spoke in a low-toned fervour.[5]

A fear of scenes like this one is present whenever bodies that shouldn't engage in such intercourse are left alone in the Eliot novel. '[T]he terrible illumination of a certainty which filled up all outlines'[6] confirms a suspicion admitted earlier, when Dorothea 'found herself thinking with some wonder that Will Ladislaw was passing his time with Mrs Lydgate in her husband's absence';[7] a suspicion like the one marked by the eyebrows raised when the otherwise impeccable Daniel Deronda spends too much time alone with Mrs Grandcourt: 'After a moment's silence, in which Sir Hugo looked at a letter without reading it, he said, "I hope you are not playing with fire, Dan – you understand me"'.[8]

The rumour of impropriety that Sir Hugo and Dorothea Casaubon detect is not confined to unchaperoned intercourse between unmarried men and women. It attends as well the closeted interviews between men, such as those between Fred Vincy and Peter Featherstone, who 'would not begin the dialogue till the door had been closed'.[9] Mary Garth suspects that such 'loitering' costs Vincy his 'manly independence';[10] a perhaps related suspicion is cast by the 'peculiar twinkle', in the eye of the old man: 'When Fred came in the old man eyed him with a peculiar twinkle, which the younger had often had reason to interpret as pride in the satisfactory details of his appearance'.[11]

And if the strictures governing body contact in Eliot are made visible by their violation, their intensity is made vivid by all the care that she takes to prevent their appearance in the first place. The conduct book she keeps of the private interviews between Will Ladislaw and Dorothea Brooke labours to demonstrate that no such scene as that between Will and Rosamond occurs when *these* bodies gather: 'She gave her hand for a moment, and then they went to sit down near the window, she on one settee and he on another opposite';[12] 'Will sat down opposite her at two yards' distance';[13] 'He was standing two yards from her with his mind full of contradictory desires and resolves';[14] 'She moved automatically towards her uncle's chair ... and Will, after drawing it out a little for her, went a few paces off and stood opposite to her'.[15]

The eccentricity of all this detail widens if we consider that it is delivered to the reader, who is privy to these private interviews, and not, say, to Mrs Cadwallader, who might suspect closer contact between Will and Dorothea from the other side of the closed door. It is as if Eliot worries that our suspicion is sleepless enough to imagine all the things she denies here going on in front of our faces; as if she worries we might speculate, unless we are told otherwise, that Dorothea gave Will her hand for much more than a moment; as if she worries we would surmise, without explicit indication to the contrary, that they stand or sit much less than two yards from one another; as if she worries we would suppose, except for her denial, that after drawing her chair, Will *doesn't* walk 'a few paces off'.

Eliot compulsively lodges such affidavits in the minutia of interviews like these, little logbooks showing that bodies which may get
too close to one another don't. Whatever Grandcourt sees when he
surprises Deronda and his wife alone, Eliot takes pains to show that
it is not what Dorothea sees when she comes across Will and
Rosamond: 'What he saw was Gwendolen's face ... and Deronda
standing three yards off';[16] Grandcourt himself, when he is alone
with Gwendolen prior to their engagement, is 'about two yards
distant';[17] even the somewhat ampler allowance of body contact
allotted to a betrothed couple is carefully measured: before they are
married, '[Lydgate] touched [Rosamond's] ear and a little bit of her
neck under it with his lips'.[18]

Such precise accountings hold themselves accountable to a sense
of propriety always on the lookout for three feet on the floor. If
they sometimes seem to aspire to the condition of choreography,
they are always bending over backward to maintain for the bodies
that inhabit them a good reputation in the eyes of an unblinking
monitor of proper conduct. As with the neurosis which seems to
exaggerate, but actually clarifies the ordeals of civility, Eliot's obsessive documentation of adherence to it reflects an endless demand
that bodies keep their proper distances. That such documentation,
while obsessive, is delivered without apparent thought, without any
sign of conscious intention, makes the conformity of the Victorian
novel to the rules of bodily propriety as automatic as our own. With
as little visible resolve as what is disclosed in the straightening of a
wrist or a walk, the duration of a handshake or the length, location
and depth of a kiss, the body everywhere bends to the rigours of
propriety, the body not more at home in the fiction of the nineteenth century than amongst the ways we live now.

Conducted unconsciously, the task of enforcing the rules of
bodily propriety draws upon the defensive industriousness we have
been trained to associate with what is unconscious. Eliot's text
develops an elaborate network of impediments which assure the
conformity that it elsewhere documents in detail, tying hands that
shouldn't wander, turning into marble forms not allowed to
embrace: 'It was if [Deronda] saw Gwendolen drowning while his
limbs were bound';[19] 'It had seemed to [Will Ladislaw] as if they
were like two creatures slowly turning to marble in each other's
presence, while their hearts were conscious and their eyes were
yearning'.[20]

The measures that Eliot's text takes to prevent illicit intercourse do not merely isolate the proscribed body; they do not merely restrain the hand or the lips that would touch it. Such shapes are not simply fettered and distanced, they are entirely altered or even annulled as the meticulous labours of prohibition are aided by the miracles of metamorphosis. The pressure of propriety has alchemical powers: Eliot substantiates her efforts to deny anything scandalous about the intimacy between Ladislaw and Dorothea and between Gwendolen and Deronda by converting the body forbidden to the grasp into an object that one can see, but not touch. Grandcourt may rest assured that his wife has avoided the extremities of adultery, not only because Deronda is 'three yards off' from her, but also, and more importantly, because she is less a body capable of receiving the licentious grasp than a painting capable of compelling the admiring eye.[21] 'What he saw was Gwendolen's face of anguish framed black like a nun's, and Deronda standing three yards off from her with a look of sorrow.'[22] Dorothea feels 'helpless' to manifest her affection for Will because 'her hands had been tied from making up to him for any unfairness in his lot'.[23] But even if they weren't tied, Dorothea wouldn't lay her hands on Will anyway, since all she wants to do is to look at him: 'her hands had been tied from making up to him for any unfairness in his lot. But her soul thirsted to see him.'[24]

Eliot underwrites the distance she interposes between bodies that shouldn't touch by casting the relation between them as the two dimensional communion of spectacle and audience. Or the body that should not be 'grasped' is evacuated altogether:

> The feeling Deronda endured in these moments he afterward called horrible. Words seemed to have no more rescue in them than if he had been beholding a vessel in peril of wreck – the poor ship with its many-lived anguish beaten by the inescapable storm. How could he grasp the long-growing process of this young creature's wretchedness?[25]

Unchaperoned communion between a married woman and an unmarried man is defined here as a kind of communication which excludes any hands-on contact; as if that isn't enough, what can't actually be grasped anyway is then put at more than arm's length, put at a distance as remote as a vessel on stormy waters seen from the shore.

Eliot's accounts of the conduct of couples who shouldn't touch are sometimes less prolix than this, but seldom less busy abstracting the prohibited body. Casaubon, for example, abandoning his wife during their wedding tour, spends time 'groping after his mouldy futilities' instead.[26] That such precautions are doubled – physical or grammatical ('after') distances are imposed which separate bodies who are in any event incapable of touching or being touched – suggests a now familiar anxiety: when it comes to physical intimacy, a single layer of protection may not be enough.

As we might well know, a prophylactic urge to deform or make disappear a body who appears susceptible to illicit embraces extends beyond the work of George Eliot. Leaving aside for a moment scenes and suppressions closer to home, recall the fate of *David Copperfield*'s Steerforth when the plaintive wish that his 'Daisy' had a sister puts into play a desire that it barely misses mentioning for 'Daisy' himself. The usual means by which homosexual appeal between men is covered over even as it is constituted nearly disappears here; the partition separating sanctioned from unsanctioned male intercourse in the exchange between Copperfield and Steerforth that we are about to encounter is narrowed to paper thinness; the by now well-known female figure through whom a desire between men is routinely routed reduced to a pretence as bare as the 'friend' whose troubles are really our own:[27]

> The greater part of the guests had gone to bed as soon as the eating and drinking were over; and we, who had remained whispering and listening half-undressed, at last betook ourselves to bed, too.
> 'Goodnight, young Copperfield,' said Steerforth. 'I'll take care of you.'
> 'You're very kind,' I gratefully returned. 'I am very much obliged to you.'
> 'You haven't got a sister, have you?' said Steerforth, yawning.
> 'No,' I answered.
> 'That's a pity,' said Steerforth. 'If you had one, I should think she would have been a pretty, timid, little, bright-eyed sort of girl. I should have liked to know her. Good night young Copperfield.'
> 'Good night, sir,' I replied.
> I thought of him very much after I went to bed, and raised myself, I recollected, to look where he lay in the moonlight, with his handsome face turned up, and his head reclining easily on his arm.[28]

And again, just as the possibility of illicit bodily contact gains point, the body vaporises:

He was a person of great power in my eyes; that was, of course, the reason of my mind running on him. No veiled future dimly glanced upon him in the moonbeams. There was no shadowy picture of his footsteps, in the garden that I dreamed of walking in all night.[29]

Where is Steerforth in the moonlit thoughts of the boy who admires 'his handsome face turned up, and his head reclining easily on his arm' with an intensity given everything but a name? While the landscape of David's dreamwork is pervaded by this 'person of great power', his body is nowhere to be found there: 'No veiled future [even] dimly glanced upon him'; 'there was no shadowy picture [even] of his footsteps'.[30]

The line of causalities we have been tracing in the work of Eliot and Dickens extends beyond the limits of the Victorian novel. According to Eve Kosofsky Sedgwick's revisionist history, the inclination to conceal the male body freighted with homoerotic potential takes on the global force of a systematic campaign in the war against figuration waged by several generations of literary modernism; in the urge towards abstraction that marks modernism, the strategy of pre-emptive disappearance through which the likes of Steerforth, Mordecai and Dorian Gray are disembodied expands to become the general form of a comprehensive literary imperative:

> Insofar as there is a case to be made that the modernist impulse toward abstraction in the first place owes an incalculable part of its energy precisely to turn-of-the-century male homo/heterosexual definitional panic – and such a case is certainly there for the making, in at any rate literary history from Wilde to Hopkins to James to Proust to Conrad to Eliot to Pound to Joyce to Hemingway to Faulkner to Stevens – to that extent the 'figuration' that had to be abjected from modernist self-reflexive abstraction was not the figuration of just *any* body, the figuration of figurality itself, but, rather, that represented in a very particular body, the desired male body.[31]

The classic story of an absconded body that Sedgwick updates here exhibits a distinct opposition between power and its victims, a Manichaeanism implicit in any myth, or hypothesis of repression, whether its culprit is a jealous god or the pressure of a homophobic propriety. On one side there is the body; on the other, a conspiracy to conceal the body. Displaced by plants or planets, or by non-figurative literary landscapes on which nobody, and especially not the proscribed physique, can be seen, the censored body is set against the repressive forces that hide it. If the ruses of propriety that we have been assessing so far cast the prohibited body out of sight, they stop short of infecting that body. Thus the Foucauldian formation that Sedgwick elsewhere discovers, a 'gay male rhetoric ... already marked and structured and indeed necessitated by the historical shapes of homophobia',[32] has nothing at all to do with the concealed corpus that she disinters in the passage I quoted before, the body abstracted by a homophobia concerned only to repress, rather than to constitute or contaminate it, the body that thus retains an illicit purity even when it is spirited away.[33]

It would be imprudent, if not simply impossible, to deny the enduring and practically pervasive vitality of the urge to hide this body. The habit of abstraction that stretches beyond the Victorian novel, beyond literary modernism into most contemporary spheres of representation introjects, and thus pre-empts, the efforts of an external censor to expunge the body seemingly ready to offer or to receive the wrong kind of touch. Bodies not transformed by the artful wands of sublimation are subject instead to the simpler interventions of a Mrs Grundy or a Jesse Helms.

But even side by side with the perennial effort to censor the proscribed body, the forces of propriety are conducted as well, and sometimes even better, through other, more invasive operations; when these forces do not dissolve and displace the body that seems capable of inviting or offering the wrong kind of touch, they take up residence there. The forces of propriety infiltrate the physique they decline to erase – as anybody knows, who has escaped the demand for concealment only to feel in its place a sense of unease never quite overcome. It is this deeper collaboration between propriety and the endangered and dangerous body that we turn to now.

III

The boundaries of propriety are felt along the pulse: no less than the novels they inhabit, the body in Eliot appears to absorb the rules governing its conduct. If Eliot's text takes and gives notice of these rules in the spectacle of their violation, or in the immense and minute stratagems it enlists for avoiding this spectacle, the body situated there registers the demands of propriety in the form of sensation and perturbations that arise when they are transgressed, sensations and perturbations as slight and decisive as the usually barely noticeable aches and pangs and tics that mark our own fear

that we have erred from the rigours of the social order. Well before
Adam Bede punishes Arthur Donnithorne for what he does with
Hetty Sorrel, even as '[h]is arm is stealing round her waist',
Donnithorne feels the consequence of this act in the form of a vague
but effective unease: 'already Arthur was uncomfortable. He took
his arm from Hetty's waist'.³⁴ When, during his courtship with
Gwendolen, Grandcourt exceeds even slightly the 'limit of an
amorous homage' ('One day indeed ... he had kissed not her cheek
but her neck a little below her ear'), she suffers distress:
'Gwendolen, taken by surprise, had started up with a marked agitation which made him rise too'.³⁵

Such discomfort and agitation is most visible when it attends the
scene in Eliot that comes closest to asserting an illicit desire between
men, the nervous drama of intimacy between Daniel Deronda and
Mordecai. Just as the rules regarding bodily propriety are observed
in the Eliot novel only when they are violated, or in danger of being
violated, the homosexuality that never quite surfaces as explicit
theme is embodied in a homophobic unease – the aversion inspired
by Mordecai's 'spasmodic grasps', 'eager clasps', his 'thin hand
pressing [Deronda's] arm tightly': 'Deronda coloured deeply, not
liking the grasp'; 'Daniel [rose], with a habitual shrinking which
made him remove his hand from Mordecai's'.³⁶

Deronda's aversion desists only when the hands that Mordecai
lays on him are disembodied; only when the clutch of Mordecai's
fingers gives way to the 'clutch of his thought';³⁷ 'a yearning need
which had acted as a beseeching grasp'; a 'tenacious certainty' that
acts as 'a subduing influence' on Deronda.³⁸ This sublimating tide
reaches its height near the end of the novel when the press of the
flesh that everywhere marks the intercourse between Deronda and
Mordecai is cast as the mere expression of a metaphysical communion, safely routed through a female vessel: 'The two men clasped
hands with a movement that seemed part of the flash from
Mordecai's eyes, and passed through Mirah like an electric shock.'³⁹

The discomfort that such abstraction works to attenuate arises
again in the 'strongly resistant feeling' Deronda experiences when,
at the Synagogue, while he is 'moving away with the rest', the body
next to his unexpectedly breaks ranks:

> he had bowed to his civil neighbour and was moving away with the
> rest – when he felt a hand on his arm, and turning with the rather
> unpleasant sensation which this abrupt sort of claim is apt to bring,
> he saw close to him the white bearded face of that neighbour. ...

> Deronda had a strongly resistant feeling: he was inclined to shake off hastily the touch on his arm.[40]

Deronda's civil neighbour is excessively so: the very remarking of his closeness marks it as too close, just as the abruptness of the hand on the arm betrays its deviation from normality. While we are probably inclined to dismiss Deronda's reaction to this as an instance of his often remarked priggishness, Eliot herself casts the 'strongly resistant feeling' that arises for him in the face of even an apparently slight eccentricity from the conventions of bodily contact as a general response: *everyone* is apt to experience the 'unpleasant sensation which this abrupt sort of claim ... bring[s]'. Eliot's penchant for declaring the situation of particular characters a universal condition is quite superfluous here: Deronda's sensations are merely the socially arranged reflex of the male subject when another man's body gets even a little too close, the male subject, it hardly seems necessary to say, not limited to the literature of the nineteenth century. After all, such responses could not be more familiar; they are common to everybody who is subject to a sense of bodily propriety no less active here and now than in the Victorian novel. The discomfort that Arthur Donnithorne experiences and the agitation that Gwendolen Harleth suffers are well known to anyone for whom sexual guilt or sexual threat has ever taken form as a feeling of unease; the aversion that Deronda senses when others of his own gender get too close is the experience of every man, in and beyond the Victorian novel.

But if these allergic reactions are only too familiar to a culture of unease as much our own as George Eliot's, their precise identity, and the nature of the subject who suffers them, remains mysterious. Eliot's profile of these things is too shapeless to conform to a simple physical or physiological definition; too vague to be solely attributed to the body. ('[A]lready Arthur was uncomfortable'; 'Gwendolen, taken by surprise, had started up with a marked agitation which made him rise too'; 'Deronda [did] not lik[e] the grasp'; 'Daniel [rose], with a habitual shrinking which made him remove his hand from Mordecai's'; 'Deronda had a strongly resistant feeling'.)

It's not exactly or exclusively the body that shrinks habitually from a deviant touch; it's not exactly or exclusively the body that is agitated or uneasy when a hand or a kiss steals past a limit at once informal and excruciatingly precise. Nor is it exactly or exclusively the mind that suffers these things. The amorphous experience marked by Donnithorne's discomfort, or Gwendolen Harleth's agitation, or Deronda's 'strongly resistant feeling' or 'rather unpleasant sensation' is confined neither to the province of the body nor the spirit. To be subject to such ambiguous unease is to be a subject for whom the labours of apprehension and the pains of the body are utterly confused; a subject for whom the disturbances of the mind melt into the diseases of the flesh; a subject for whom the laws of propriety make two kinds of sense; a subject in whom a spirit that knows the laws and a body that feels them are so mingled that they cannot be distinguished. The subject susceptible to the forces of propriety, the subject whom these forces are able not merely to repress but to infiltrate, consists not of a body or a mind; it is instead a hybrid formation where these strains are crossed.

The conflation of abstract consciousness and bodily experience drives to the point of identity terms usually more loosely linked by an atmosphere of analogical suffering especially dense in the Eliot novel. What, for the very fact of its frequency, might pass for the usual, even inevitable analogy between physical and metaphysical disease takes on the consistency of an anagogical system in the world of George Eliot: 'Notions and scruples were like split needles, making one afraid of treading, or sitting down, or even eating';[41] 'Will's reproaches ... were still like a knife-wound within her';[42] 'This man's speech was like a sharp knife-edge drawn across her skin';[43] 'His words had the power of thumbscrews and the cold touch of the rack';[44] 'he's got a tongue like a sharp blade, Bartle has';[45] 'as soon as he took up any antagonism, though only in thought, he seemed to himself, like the Sabine warriors in the memorable story – with nothing to meet his spear but flesh of his flesh'.[46]

The subject of mental duress in Eliot is everywhere haunted by a body in pain, a phantom partner in suffering such as the one that Maggie Tulliver devises to represent all her struggles:

> a large wooden doll ... which once stared with the roundest of eyes above the reddest of cheeks ... was now entirely defaced by a long career of vicarious suffering. Three nails driven into the head commemorated as many crises in Maggie's nine years of earthly struggle.[47]

Such chambers of torture can be found anywhere in an Eliot novel; a parallel universe of physical unease, ranging from medieval extremities of agony, to blander or subtler discomfort, hovers, like the roar on the other side of silence, over the ordinary world of abstract distress. The rhyme between apprehension and sensation, 'knowledge' and 'feeling', praised by two Eliots[48] as the touch of the poet, is not the mark of any single class of consciousness; it is a universal facility in the works of at least one of them. An honour-destroying revelation 'enters like a stab into Bulstrode's soul', and is felt as much by his wife who 'needed time to get used to her maimed consciousness, her poor lopped life'.[49] Less apocalyptic apprehensions are no less linked to bodily trauma; even the normal disappointments of maturity are shadowed by the ruin or amputation of the body: 'life must be taken up on a lower stage of expectation, as it is by men who have lost their limbs'.[50]

What such comparisons offer with one hand they take away with the other. It is of course in the nature of analogies to confirm the difference between the terms they draw together, and the correspondence that Eliot habitually proposes between physical and metaphysical pain is no exception to this rule. Such analogies work like the endlessly newsworthy discovery that psychological stress takes tolls on the body ranging from colds to cancer; like the less positivist intuition that the slings and arrows of outrageous fortune, or the push and shove of daily life have more than figurative force; like any incidental lifting of what one theorist of the body's pains calls 'a Cartesian censorship', a 'rigorously enforced separation in the subject between psyche and soma'.[51] The usual link between abstract and bodily discomfort in the Eliot novel depends upon and reinforces their fundamental distinction.

But in the subject who suffers for even the smallest sins of impropriety, all differences between mind and body are abolished; in this conventional character, the partial unity of psyche and soma accomplished by analogy gives way to the more astonishing achievement of incarnation. If this character calls to mind a supernatural conjunction, a word made flesh, it may be as usefully classed amongst the more mundane annals of social reproduction. The subject whose ambiguous sensations enforce the rules of propriety in the Eliot novel joins ranks with an array of others anatomised by contemporary investigations of the body's social construction; the figure, for example, whom Pierre Bourdieu describes as the embodiment of the metaphysical imperatives of a social order:

> If all societies ... that seek to produce a new man through a process of 'deculturation' and 'reculturation' set such store on the seemingly most insignificant details of *dress, bearing,* physical and verbal *manners,* the reason is that, treating the body as a memory, they

entrust to it in abbreviated and practical, i.e. mnemonic, form the fundamental principles of the arbitrary content of the culture. The principles em-bodied in this way are placed beyond the grasp of consciousness, values given body, *made* body by the transubstantiation achieved by the hidden persuasion of an implicit pedagogy, capable of instilling a whole cosmology, an ethic, a metaphysic, a political philosophy, through injunctions as insignificant as 'stand up straight' or don't hold your knife in your left hand.[52]

The incorporation that Bourdieu describes here, the figure in whom the 'fundamental principles of the arbitrary content of the culture' are 'made body' is like the subject that a range of feminist theory has in mind when it construes the sexed body as the incarnation of an abstract gender system; it is like the subject at the centre of Michel Foucault's investigations of modern power formations, a body who incorporates the discursive marks of the disciplinary procedures and sexual identifications that inhabits the brave new world he charted.[53]

These various subjects of social discipline are too various to admit any effort to lock them into step with one another. The embodiments featured in recent speculations on the social uses of the flesh cannot be neatly collated with the figure who is subject to the rules of bodily propriety in the Eliot novel: the terms of mind and body that are drawn together in these figures are too disparate to allow it. But both the body made to bear the discipline of a social order and the composite subject made to feel it are beings at the same time carnal and abstract. In every case, the subject's capacity to absorb the various definitions and demands of the social order depends upon his capacity to be at once spirit and flesh.

It is this conjunction, the one that characterises the subject of social discipline in and beyond the Eliot novel, that is undone by the miser's passion in *Silas Marner*. We turn now to consider how the miser's commerce eludes both the pattern of abstraction which prevents violations of the rules of proper conduct in the Eliot novel from appearing in the first place, and, more crucially, the subjective aversions which typically arrest them when they do. We turn now to consider how the miser's fondlings, his revelry with the 'bright faces' and 'rounded outlines' of his coins supply both an object and a subject capable of resisting what normally thwarts the illicit embrace: we turn now to consider how a certain love of money serves the interests of perversity by baffling all the forces of propriety.

IV

In *Silas Marner*, the love of money becomes the means of indemnifying the subject and object of improper passion against the sense of aversion that normally attacks it, and the force of abstraction that normally eclipses it. In the miser's love, the hybrid subject who is vulnerable to the demands of propriety in the Eliot novel dissolves, and when it does, the social discipline made solid in such a subject melts into air. In the miser's love, the character capable of sensations at once physical and metaphysical is dismantled, and replaced by a subject entirely corporeal, and therefore immune to the amorphous sensations by which the body's correct conduct is enforced.[54]

To chart the avenue of simplification by which Silas Marner eludes the dictates of propriety, we need first to notice how the miser and his money work to form one another. In a condensed version of the labour theory of value, according to which the commodity's worth reflects the bodily effort reposited there, both *Silas Marner* and Silas Marner cast the miser's money as the reproduction of his own body – either his children, or his clones: 'The crowns and half crowns that were his own earnings' are 'begotten by his labour' (p. 70); 'He ... thought fondly of the guineas that were only half earned ... as if they had been unborn children' (p. 70); 'It was pleasant to feel them in his palm, and look at their bright faces, which were all his own' (p. 65).[55] And, conversely, if the money is the re-embodiment of Silas Marner, he, in turn, is the re-embodiment of the coins: 'like all objects to which a man devotes himself, they had fashioned him into correspondence with themselves' (p. 92).

The body with which Silas Marner comes to correspond is invulnerable to sensation of pain or bitterness or unease for the simple reason that it is invulnerable to any sensation at all. '[H]idden away from the daylight', the gold is 'deaf to the sound of birds' – as well as to every other sound; '[it] starts at no human tones' (p. 184) – nor does it start at any other tones. Like Dolly Winthrop's child who 'looked like a cherubic head untroubled with a body' (p. 139), the coins are untroubled by a body, or, more exactly, untroubled *as* a body, by any sensation – not only those arranged by 'the sound of birds' or 'human tones', but also the more complex ones that cause Silas Marner's fiancée to 'shrink' with aversion from him: 'didn't the gold [just] lie there after all?' (p. 93).

Silas Marner identifies with the coins he adores by assuming a version of their insensibility: 'The gold had asked that he should sit weaving longer and longer deafened and blinded more and more to all things except the monotony of his loom and the repetition of his web' (p. 184). Just as his money is cast in his image, the miser himself is reformed in the shape of his money. This reciprocity replenishes the relation between labourer and artifact whose diminution Elaine Scarry mourns as the cost of 'the capitalist economic system':

> The large all-embracing artifact, the capitalist economic system, is itself generated out of smaller artifacts that continually disappear and reappear in new forms: out of the bodies of women and men, material objects emerge; out of material objects commodities emerge; out of commodities, money emerges; out of money, capital emerges. ... In its final as in its first form, the artifact is a projection of the human body; but in its final form, unlike its first, it does not refer back to the human body because in each subsequent phase it has taken as the thing to which it refers only that form of the artifact immediately preceding its own appearance. ... The overall work of its successive forms is to steadily extend the first consequence (capital is, like the solitary pair of eyeglasses or any other made object, the projected form of bodily labour and needs) and to steadily contract the second: each new phase enables the line of reciprocity to pull back further and further from its human source until the growing space between the artifact and its creator is at last too great to be spanned either in fact or in an act of perception.[56]

All that Elaine Scarry declares lost on the path of abstraction arranged by the 'capitalist economic system' is restored in the miser's world, congested with the full complement of two-way traffic between the labourer and even his most attenuated issue. Not only does the miser's money return to him in an 'act of perception', but 'in fact': no less than the body that wears them is transformed by eyeglasses, Silas Marner is changed by the money he adores.

But there is more than one difference between the eyes given sight by the artifact of labour that Scarry mentions, and the miser made blind by the tokens of his work. While the artifact that Scarry envisions reforms the body, the coins effect the complex character we have noticed before, the character in whom the body and mind are merged. The miser's blindness is not of the eyes: when Silas Marner takes on the insensitivity of the coins, he is stripped not of his senses, but rather his sensibility. Here, the composite character who experiences the aversions that arise when the rules of propriety are violated is reduced to the miser's 'shrunk[en]' frame (p. 69). A distinction that the novel admits in the difference it stages between natural and adopted fathers appears again when the miser's physical senses are parted from metaphysical ones; the doors of perception are cleansed of their abstract dimensions, extricated from the faculties of metaphysical apprehension with which they are usually entangled.

And as the miser falls to sleep in spirit, he awakens to a utopian erotics of pure sensation: 'now when all purpose was gone', the 'habit of looking towards the gold and grasping it with a sense of fulfilled effort made a loam that was deep enough for the seeds of desire' (p. 65). The 'thrill of satisfaction' that the coin provides consists entirely of its 'touch'; the miser's 'phantasm of delight', drawn down from the realm of spirit where phantasms dwell normally, is now no more than the simple matter of 'feeling' (p. 68) and 'handling' (p. 129) the coins. Just as his 'life' 'narrows and hardens into a mere pulsation of desire and satisfaction that has no relation to any other being' (p. 68), his 'revelry' (p. 70) of 'immediate sensation' (p. 68) has no relation to anything other than itself.

The miser, now an entirely sensuous being, is no longer a subject in whom the physical and the metaphysical are merged, the subject who is subject to the rules of propriety in and beyond the Eliot novel. A body-wholly-body, the miser is ready to enjoy the revelry that we noticed earlier, a perverse pleasure that would sicken others, and again, not just in the work of George Eliot. And if the influence that the coins exert on the miser renders him immune to the disciplinary aversions to which subjects are generally susceptible when they cross the borders of propriety, the reciprocal projection, which casts the coins as the issue of his body, renders it such a transgression in the first place. *Silas Marner*'s fairy-tale telling of the labour theory of value reverses the defensive bias by which bodies that should not be touched are abstracted in the Eliot novel. That the 'rounded outlines' the miser handles and feels are those of a body is the outcome of a current countering the general tide in the Eliot novel, a tide which draws the desire to touch back into the safety zone of disembodiment.

All of this perversity is dispelled when the miser's money disappears, and his step-daughter arrives on the scene. The therapy administered by the girl who replaces the coins reattaches the sensibility from which the miser is freed by the ministrations of the gold, 'reawakening his senses with her fresh life': 'as her life unfolded, his soul, long stupefied in a cold narrow prison, was unfolding too, and trembling gradually into full consciousness' (pp. 184, 185). Through his life as a father, Silas Marner's feelings are freighted now with metaphysical capacities; his delight in Eppie consists not simply in sensing her, but also in sensing the need to sense her: 'I'd got to feel the need o' your looks and your voice and the touch o' your little fingers' (p. 226). The abstractions of sensibility are affianced again to the physical senses when Silas Marner leaves off the love of gold, and takes up the love of a girl. While the miser 'feels' the gold in one sense only, the 'senses' that are reawakened under the influence of Eppie are doubled, consisting not only of the capacity to apprehend matters of the senses, 'the old winter-flies that came crawling forth in the early spring sunshine' (p. 184), but also of the capacity to apprehend things metaphysical.

While the miser's revelry accompanies the divorce of his senses from abstract sensations, the weaver's respectability emerges with their remarriage; with this remarriage, the normal, the normalised subject reappears. Silas Marner forsakes the eccentricities that rendered him a stranger in a strange land; 'making himself as clean and tidy as he could' (p. 183) he enrols in a remedial course on familial respectability, entrusting both Eppie and himself to the dictates of chapel and hearth. 'He had no distinct idea about the baptism and the churchgoing, except that Dolly had said it was for the good of the child' (pp. 183–4).

Silas Marner's 'new self' (p. 201) is subject to a restraint quite absent for the old one, a reluctance to lay a hand on the body that he considers his 'own child'. The sense of propriety that slept while the miser fondled 'rounded outlines' 'all his own' returns here with a force sufficient to make even the prospect of wholesome body contact unbearable to him. Silas Marner is compelled to refuse the measures which Dolly Winthrop or George Eliot name, or fail to name, with a compunction matching his own: 'Dolly Winthrop told him that punishment was good for Eppie, and as for rearing a child without making it tingle a little in soft and safe places now and then, it was not to be done' (p. 185). The squeamishness manifested in a circumlocution that avoids even the mention of touching the body appears again when the miser declares that he must avoid any discipline that involves its practice: '"She'd take it all for fun," he observed to Dolly, "if I didn't hurt her, and that I can't do"' (p. 188). After its brief interruption, the regime that enforces the restrictions imposed on touching proceeds now with no end in sight. The laying on of hands that was to 'frighten [Eppie] off touching things', is eschewed for other methods to prevent such contact: Silas

Marner, subject now to the restraint he is charged with imposing, must do what Eliot does with the measures of distance she takes to prevent the illicit touch of bodies, 'must do what [he] can to keep 'em out of her way' (p. 188).

Silas Marner takes decisive steps to seal off the channel which enabled the miser's exemption from propriety, steps to stop the intercourse of gold and bodies that produced both a physique able to avert those sensations, and a physique that would allow them to be incited in the first place. The novel puts an end to the intercourse between gold and bodies that makes Silas Marner a purely sensuous subject, and which casts the money he hoards as a shape susceptible to an illicit touch. At first, the miser's 'blurred vision' confuses the gold with the girl, 'but instead of hard coin with the familiar resisting outline, his fingers encountered soft warm curls' (p. 167). The correction which takes form here as a tactile proof that even the dissolute miser can understand, is expanded as the novel progresses, driving a deeper difference between the gold and the body: not only is the weaver wrong to suppose that the gold is the girl, he is wrong to imagine that the gold becomes the girl. A story of metamorphosis, in which gold is transformed into a body, and thus able to preserve its character in translation, gives way to a story of substitution, in which the body merely replaces the gold. This fading of the rumour of transubstantiation takes place in Silas Marner's mind: at first, 'he could have only said that the child was come instead of the gold – that the gold had turned into the child' (p. 180); finally though, he succumbs to the force of disenchantment, teaching Eppie that he 'had taken her golden curls for his lost guineas' (p. 204). While this account puts both the models of metamorphosis and substitution into play, it consigns the first to the miser's own dubious perceptions – his taking gold curls for lost guineas is almost indistinguishable from mistaking gold curls for lost guineas – while granting the second the irresistible power of fact.

Eliot works overtime to discredit the affiliation between money and bodies; the differences that the miser encounters are the subject of the homily that we have encountered before:

> The gold had kept his thoughts in an ever-repeated circle, leading to nothing beyond itself; but Eppie was an object compacted of changes and hopes that forced his thoughts onward ... to the new things that would come with the coming years, when [she] would have learned to understand how her father Silas cared for her. ... The gold had asked that he should sit weaving longer and longer, deaf-

ened and blinded more and more to all things except the monotony
of his loom and the repetition of his web; but Eppie called him away
from his weaving, and made him think all its pauses a holiday, reawakening his senses with her fresh life.

(p. 184)

With an economy we are entitled to expect from a novelist whose
words, no matter how many, always do as much as they can, Eliot
encourages family values, and discourages the condition that disrupted them. However briefly: others have laboured even more consistently to sustain a familial, a familiar regime of propriety whose
profits and whose losses have only accrued with the passing of time.

From *Victorian Studies*, 36:3 (1993), 273–92.

NOTES

[This extract is one of two explicitly socio-political approaches to *Silas
Marner* reproduced in this volume (see Jim Reilly's discussion of the novel,
which follows). The essay, which first appeared in *Victorian Studies* in 1993,
forms part of Jeff Nunokawa's full-length study, *The Afterlife of Property:
Domestic Security and the Victorian Novel* (1994). In addition to exploring
the ways in which nineteenth-century novelists exploit fears about the instability of property, Nunokawa considers the ways in which the nineteenth-
century novel plot often turns on the domestic consequences of economic
failure. Some inalienable property is needed to offset the idea that anything
can be commodified and as Nunokawa points out, that 'secure state' is
invariably the character of the heroine. Nunokawa foregrounds *Silas
Marner*'s anxieties about the kinds of alienation caused by money and capital
alongside Eliot's stress on the virtues of family values and the role of Eppie
in promoting them. Thus in Nunokawa's reading of the novel, the story is
one of 'metamorphosis', a transformation from solitary hoarder and mastur-
bator to cleansed family man and consumer. It is through Eppie's fortuitous
arrival that the 'normalised subject reappears'. All quotations in the essay are
taken from *The Mill on the Floss* (New York: Penguin, 1985). Eds]

1. George Eliot, *Silas Marner* (New York, 1985), p. 72. All further references contained in the text.

2. On the nineteenth-century construction of homosexuality as a desire
   defined by the similarity, even the identity, between its subject and
   object, as a construction which displaces the older notion of inversion,
   which involved no notion of similarity or sameness between these
   terms, see Jeffrey Weeks, *Coming Out: Homosexual Politics in Britain,
   from the Nineteenth Century to the Present* (New York, 1979), pp.

23–32. See also Eve Kosofsky Sedgwick's assessment of the current hegemony of this construction: '*homosexuality* ... is now almost universally heard as referring to relations of *sexuality* between persons who are, because of their sex, more flatly and globally categorised as *the same*'. Eve Kosofsky Sedgwick, *The Epistemology of the Closet* (Berkeley, CA, 1990), pp. 158–9.

3. While 'the City of Destruction' alludes most immediately to *Pilgrim's Progress*, behind that is Sodom. Louis Crompton, *Byron and Greek Love: Homophobia in 19th-Century England* (Berkely, CA, 1985), surveys the ways in which the Biblical account of Sodom and Gomorrah was invoked in the nineteenth century to define and wage war against homosexual activity (pp. 13–15; 258; 275–6; 278–9; 348). See also Sedgwick, *Epistemology*, 127–8; Robert J. Corber, 'Representing the "Unspeakable": William Godwin and the Politics of Homophobia', *Journal of the History of Sexuality*, 1 (1990), 85–101; A. D. Harvey, 'Prosecutions for Sodomy in England at the Beginning of the Nineteenth Century', *Historical Journal*, 21 (1978), 939–48.

4. Pierre Bourdieu, *Outline of a Theory of Practice*, trans. Richard Nice (London, 1977), p. 94. This is of course not to say that such rules are exclusively implicit; they are grasped as well by the formal mechanisms of social power. For a discussion of nineteenth-century legal prosecution of homosexuality see note 3; for a potent contemporary example of the legal codification of homophobia, see the majority opinion of the Supreme Court in *Bowers* v. *Hardwick* (1986).

5. George Eliot, *Middlemarch* (New York, 1988), p. 355.

6. Ibid., p. 634.

7. Ibid., p. 355.

8. George Eliot, *Daniel Deronda* (New York, 1988), p. 389.

9. Eliot, *Middlemarch*, p. 89.

10. Ibid., p. 213.

11. Ibid., p. 89.

12. Ibid., p. 442.

13. Ibid., p. 298.

14. Ibid., p. 445.

15. Ibid., pp. 514–15.

16. Eliot, *Daniel Deronda*, p. 521.

17. Ibid., p. 255.

18. Eliot, *Middlemarch*, p. 289.

THE MISER'S TWO BODIES *185*

19. Eliot, *Daniel Deronda*, p. 389.

20. Eliot, *Middlemarch*, p. 444.

21. None of this of course denies the erotic investment of the visual that has concerned psychoanalytic theory. See Sigmund Freud's discussion of scopophilia in his 'Instincts and their Vicissitudes', in the *Standard Edition of the Complete Psychological Works of Sigmund Freud*, 24 vols, trans. James Strachley (London, 1957), Vol. 14, 109–40, and Freud, *Three Essays on Sexuality* (London, 1953); and Laura Mulvey, 'Visual Pleasure and Narrative Cinema', *Screen*, 16:3 (1975), 6–18. My concern is to notice that the body's displacement by spectacle in the Eliot novel averts the hazards of impropriety, rather than averting the matter of sexuality altogether.

22. Eliot, *Daniel Deronda*, p. 521.

23. Eliot, *Middlemarch*, p. 440.

24. Ibid.

25. Eliot, *Daniel Deronda*, p. 521.

26. Eliot, *Middlemarch*, p. 168.

27. See Eve Kosofsky Sedgwick, *Between Men: English Literature and Male Homosocial Drive* (New York, 1985).

28. Charles Dickens, *David Copperfield* (New York, 1985), p. 140.

29. Ibid., p. 140.

30. Ibid.

31. Sedgwick, *The Epistemology of the Closet*, p. 167.

32. Ibid., p. 165.

33. For a critique of such accounts, see Michel Foucault, *The History of Sexuality, Volume One: An Introduction*. Trans. Robert Hurley (New York, 1980), pp. 15–49.

34. George Eliot, *Adam Bede* (New York, 1988), p. 183.

35. Eliot, *Daniel Deronda*, p. 275.

36. Ibid., pp. 487, 433, 327, 327, 429.

37. Ibid., p. 411.

38. Ibid., p. 431.

39. Ibid., p. 640.

40. Ibid., p. 311.

41. Eliot, *Middlemarch*, p. 18.

42. Ibid., p. 652.

43. Eliot, *Daniel Deronda*, p. 512.

44. Ibid., p. 582.

45. Eliot, *Adam Bede*, p. 213.

46. Eliot, *Daniel Deronda*, 307.

47. George Eliot, *Mill on the Floss* (New York, 1980), pp. 78–9.

48. 'To be a poet is to have a soul so quick to discern no shade of quality escapes it ... a soul in which knowledge passes instantaneously into feeling, and feeling flashes back as a new organ of knowledge' (Eliot, *Middlemarch*, p. 183); See also T. S. Eliot, 'The Metaphysical Poets', in *The Sacred Wood* (London, 1920).

49. Eliot, *Middlemarch*, pp. 568, 614.

50. Ibid., p. 533.

51. D. A. Miller, *The Novel and the Police* (Berkeley, CA, 1988), pp. 147, 148.

52. Bourdieu, *Outline of a Theory of Practice*, p. 94.

53. For lucid critical accounts of feminist theorisations of sex as the incarnation of gender, see Diana Fuss, *Essentially Speaking: Feminism, Nature and Difference* (New York, 1989), pp. 39–72; Judith Butler, *Gender Trouble: Feminism and the Subversion of Identity* (New York, 1990), and Michel Foucault, *Discipline and Punish: The Birth of the Prison* (New York, 1979) and *History of Sexuality*. Such unifications of body and mind may be noticed at times to work like the analogies we have considered in the Eliot novel to maintain the distinction between these terms even as it remarks the suspension of that distinction. The embodiment of social principles may be read as an event, where what is fundamentally or primordially abstract is made flesh.

54. For other accounts of intercourse between sexuality and capital, see Walter Benn Michaels, *The Gold Standard and the Logic of Naturalism* (Berkeley, CA, 1987), pp. 29–58; 113–36.

55. The various permutations of the labour theory of value all involve complications which, even apart from the obvious reason for doing so, would reject the conception of the miser's money as his biological issue or his reincarnation. But in its deviation from the contemporary literature on the relations between the body and economic value, *Silas Marner* describes an important current within it. The condensation of the labour theory of value, the conception of the coins that the miser earns not as the abstract effect or measure of his work, but rather as 'unborn children', the confusion of the earnings that he 'begets' by his labour as the issue begotten through another kind of labour, enacts a

compulsion to incarnate that appears in a wide range of Victorian thought. Catherine Gallagher notes that the major political economists of the nineteenth century, as well as their critics, not only regarded labour as the source of wealth, but also, when calling for a recognition of the superior value of commodities that serve to replenish the body 'accord a privileged position to the commodities that are most easily turned back to flesh'. See Catherine Gallagher, 'The Bio-Economics of *Our Mutual Friend*', in Michel Feher (ed.), *Fragments for a History of the Human Body, Part Three* (New York, 1989), p. 351. The urge to restore the commodity to the body is, according to Gallagher, manifested as a more radical identification of these terms in *Our Mutual Friend*. Here, Gallagher argues, the commodity and the body are revealed to be the same thing. An analogous identification appears in *Silas Marner* when the miser casts his money in the shape of a body. For a survey of the history of the labour theory of value, see Maurice Dobb, *Theories of Value and Distribution since Adam Smith* (Cambridge, 1973).

56. Elaine Scarry, *The Body in Pain: The Making and Unmaking of the World* (New York, 1985), pp. 256–60. As Scarry herself acknowledges elsewhere in *The Body in Pain*, her reading of the Marxist scenario may be taken to literalise excessively the presence of the body of labour in the object of labour (pp. 245–6). To that extent, *The Body in Pain* participates in, rather than merely describes the bias towards embodiment available in a variety of nineteenth-century considerations of economic value, such as *Silas Marner*.

9

'A report of unknown objects': *Silas Marner*

JIM REILLY

> If men no longer had to equate themselves with things, they would need neither a superstructure of things nor an invariant picture of themselves, after the model of things.
>
> (Adorno, *Negative Dialectics*)

> Thus all physical and intellectual senses have been replaced by the simple alienation of all these senses, the sense of having. Man's essence had to be reduced to this absolute poverty, so that it might bring forth out of itself its own inner riches.
>
> (Marx, *Economic and Philosophical Manuscripts of 1844*)

Describing *Silas Marner* to Blackwood during its composition in 1861 Eliot commented that 'it sets in strong light the remedial influences of pure, natural human relations'.[1] Many natural things set in strong light are merely seen to wither, but let that pass. She could not have addressed a more pertinent issue nor undertaken a more urgent literary task. A great topic in British letters for at least the preceding two decades had been the contemporary extirpation of precisely the 'pure, natural human relations' that *Silas* is, in this statement at least, intended to assert. *Dombey and Son*[2] is a thwarted *Silas Marner* in which the emotionally enervated Mr Dombey, unlike Eliot's protagonist, tragically misses his opportunity for redemption through a relationship with a loving daughter. In line with this crucial negation, the novel poses the issues of 'pure, natural human relations' more sceptically. 'Was Mr Dombey's master-vice, that ruled him so inexorably, an unnatural characteristic? It might be worthwhile, sometimes, to inquire what Nature is, and how men work to change her, and whether, in the enforced distortions so produced, it is not natural to be unnatural.'³ Here is the great question posed by Dickens's oeuvre, and one which could not be more relevant to nineteenth-century experience: whether it is not now 'natural to be unnatural'. *Silas Marner* poses a comparable question on its opening page as the inhabitants of Raveloe ponder 'how was a man to be explained' and the novel constitutes Eliot's answer.

In approaching a novel so evidently engaging with a contemporary construction of identity in its new, bourgeois form it might be well to take soundings from the prevailing discourse, and its critics. In the same year *Dombey and Son* asks whether it is not now natural to be unnatural, Marx and Engels in *The Communist Manifesto* (1848) pour scorn on those twin bourgeois illusions, 'Human Nature' and the 'individual'. The former 'belongs to no class, has no reality, and exists only in the misty realm of philosophical fantasy' and the latter only really means the middle-class owner of property (male, of course, married women owned no property) and even his individuality is, under capitalism, an illusion. 'In bourgeois society capital is independent and has individuality while the living person is dependent and has no individuality.'⁴

As Engels had put it in the chapter of *The Condition of the Working Class in England* (1844) 'The Great Towns', the contemporary social formation is exemplified by crowded urban streets where people hurry past

> as though they had nothing in common, nothing to do with one another ... while it occurs to no man to honour another with so much as a glance. The brutal indifference, the unfeeling isolation of each in his private interest becomes the more repellent and offensive, the more these individuals are crowded together, within a limited space. And, however much one is aware that this isolation of the individual, this narrow self-seeking, is the fundamental principle of our society everywhere, it is nowhere so shamelessly barefaced, so self-conscious as just here in the crowding of the great city. The dissolution of mankind into monads, of which each one has a separate essence, and a separate purpose, the world of atoms, is here carried out to its utmost extreme.⁵

It was the 'shock' of such arbitrary and alienating urban encounters which Benjamin found in Baudelaire and regarded as the exemplary modern experience.⁶ These alienated and alienating conditions are

momentarily glimpsed in *Silas Marner* as an apprehensive Silas and
Eppie return to the 'great industrial town' attempting to locate the
religious community of Silas's youth but encountering only 'the
noise, the movement, and the multitude of strange indifferent
faces'.[7] In *A Tale of Two Cities* (1859) Dickens equates with devastating absoluteness the urban scene, a recessive, monadic individuality and death.

> My friend is dead, my neighbour is dead, my love, the darling of my
> soul, is dead; it is the inexorable consolidation and perpetuation of the
> secret that was always in that individuality, and which I shall carry in
> mine to my life's end. In any of the burial-places of this city through
> which I pass, is there a sleeper more inscrutable than its busy inhabi-
> tants are, in their innermost personality, to me, or than I am to them?[8]

In such nineteenth-century townscapes is formed the individuality
which is a synonym of alienation posited by Adorno: 'The individual owes his crystallisation to the forms of political economy, particularly those of the urban market ... If today the trace of humanity
seems to persist only in the individual in his decline, it admonishes
us to make an end of the fatality which individualises men only to
break them in their isolation.'[9]

The immediate discursive context for *Silas Marner* (1861) is the
particular urgency with which bourgeois writing at the end of the
1850s and beginning of the 1860s sets out to effect this 'crystallisation', to engineer this 'fatality which individualises men'. A number
of key non-fiction texts appear at this juncture. J. S. Mill's *On
Liberty* (1859) is a sacred text of nineteenth-century bourgeois individualism and his intellectually scrupulous project – Hardy called
him 'personified earnestness' – is, in essence, the intellectual big
brother – more reflective, less brazen – of that year's other best-
selling entrepreneurial handbook, Samuel Smiles's *Self-Help*. Given
these works' explicit individualism it is easy to imagine that such a
context made it possible for bourgeois readers to assimilate
Darwin's *The Origin of Species* (1859) to the prevailing competitive
ethic even before the formulation of the inevitable banalisation
'social Darwinism'. Burckhardt's *The Civilisation of the Renaissance
in Italy* (1860, English translation 1878) famously discovers in the
Renaissance the birth of the individual which 'led the individual to
the most zealous and thorough study of himself under all forms and
under all conditions'.[10]

Mill's work is at least honest enough to writhe within its own self-cancelling contradiction as a bourgeois critique of a bourgeois reality. In the famous chapter 'On Individuality as one of the Elements of Well-Being' he calls for a humanising regeneration of a society characterised by individualist competition through increased individualism. 'It is not by wearing down into uniformity all that is individual in themselves, but by cultivating it and calling it forth, within the limits imposed by the rights and interests of others, that human beings become a noble and beautiful object of contemplation.'[11]

A devastating analysis did Mill but know it: human subjects under capitalism are rendered, like Arnold's statuary, impotent, alienated, objectified and are furthermore fooled, by analyses such as Mill's, into an aesthetic appreciation of their own degraded condition as 'a noble and beautiful object of contemplation'. The shift from plural to singular is telling. While arguing for a healthily multiplying plurality of subjects Mill's own prose works grammatically to an opposed end, resolving 'human beings' into the smooth totality of the lone 'object'. One can at least respect Mill's impotent humanist protest at the dehumanising tendency of contemporary labour, however muddled it is in hailing the problem as its own solution. 'Human nature is not a machine to be built after a model, and set to do exactly the work prescribed for it, but a tree, which requires to grow and develop itself on all sides, according to the tendency of the inward forces which make it a living thing.'[12] Hardy's admiration for Mill was immense and he had a complex relation to this key chapter. In the *Life* he tells how, like all students of the 1860s, he knew the piece almost by heart and that he re-read it throughout his life in moments of despondency. But when Sue in *Jude the Obscure* quotes Mill's words to Phillotson, it is in terms of a negation. She would so love to live out its vision of individual free-growth, but cannot. 'Why can't you act upon them? I wish to always.'[13]

There were harsher voices than Mill's. Ruskin had anticipated his concerns over the dehumanising subjection of workers to the processes of industrial labour in *The Stones of Venice* (1851). After extensive complaint on apparently purely aesthetic grounds – mass-produced products are drearily uniform – he finally exposes the self-serving politics behind bourgeois concern over the degrading mechanisation of labour:

> It is verily this degradation of the operative into a machine, which, more than any other evil of the times, is leading the mass of the

nations everywhere into vain, incoherent, destructive struggling ... the foundations of society were never yet shaken as they are at this day. It is not that men are ill fed, but that they have no pleasure in the work by which they make their bread, and therefore look to wealth as the only means of pleasure.[14]

So from a bourgeois perspective the dehumanisation of labour is more urgently a political danger than it is a humanitarian/ethical concern. The revolutionary potential within this alienation was the subject of the period's most penetrating analysis, but one that was to remain long silent. In the *Economic and Philosophical Manuscripts of 1844*, unpublished until 1932, Marx details the ways in which the modern industrial worker's alienated relation to the products of manufacture result in his own objectification. Silas, the misanthropic weaver who becomes a function of his labour rather than vice versa, alienated from his Raveloe community, filled with a strange distrust of the natural world, shrivelled and distorted to the status of an object, is clearly a fellow of the alienated, commodified worker of Marx's analysis. Feuerbach's humanism was still a powerful influence on Marx at this early point in his writings and for those sceptical about this posited congruence between Marx and Eliot one can at least suggest that she too, who in 1854 had translated *Das Wesen des Christenthums*, was working through her own relation to these influences. Their characterisations are really strikingly congruent, as is best illustrated by simply placing passages side by side.

The worker is distorted and devalued in proportion to the form and value he gives to the product:

> **Marx:** the more values he creates the more valueless and worthless he becomes, the more formed the product the more deformed the worker ... [15]

> **Eliot:** His gold, as he hung over it and saw it grow, gathered his power of loving together into a hard isolation like its own. (p. 92)

> **Eliot:** Strangely Marner's face and figure shrank and bent themselves into a constant mechanical relation to the objects of his life, so that he produced the same sort of impression as a handle or a crooked tube, which has no meaning standing apart. (p. 69)

His labour objectifies, commodifies him:

> **Marx:** The depreciation of the human world progresses in direct proportion to the increase in value of the world of things.

> Labour does not only produce commodities; it produces itself and the labourer as a commodity and that to the extent to which it produces commodities in general.[16]

> **Eliot:** The light of his faith quite put out, and his affections made desolate, he had clung with all the force of his nature to his work and his money; and like all objects to which a man devotes himself, they had fashioned him into correspondence with themselves. His loom, as he wrought in it without ceasing, had in its turn wrought on him ... (p. 92)

He is alienated from the natural world:

> **Marx:** The relationship of the worker ... to the sensuous exterior world and to natural objects [is] as to an alien and hostile world opposed to him.[17]

> **Eliot:** his inherited delight to wander through the fields in search of foxgloves and dandelion and coltsfoot, began to wear to him the character of a temptation. (p. 57)

> **Eliot:** his steps never wandered to the hedge-banks and the land-side in search of the once familiar herbs; these too belonged to the past, from which his life had shrunk away ... (p. 70)

He is further alienated from his fellows, and even from himself:

> **Marx:** An immediate consequence of man's alienation from the product of his work, his vital activity and his species-being, is the alienation of man from man. When man is opposed to himself, it is another man that is opposed to him ... one man is alienated from another as each of them is alienated from the human essence.[18]

> **Eliot:** he listened docilely, that he might come to understand better what this life was, from which, for fifteen years, he had stood aloof as from a strange thing, wherewith he could have no communion ... (p. 190)

> **Eliot:** So, year after year, Silas Marner had lived in this solitude, his guineas rising in the iron pot, and his life narrowing and hardening itself more and more into a mere pulsation of desire and satisfaction that had no relation to any other being. (p. 68)

Of course *Silas Marner* effects Silas's disenchantment from alienation, but the socialised alternative the novel offers is not unequivocally appealing. His guide is the spinner of nauseatingly acquiescent homespun wisdom and repressive 'good sense', Dolly Winthrop, whose counsel Silas at first finds incomprehensible. 'Her simple view of life and its comforts, by which she had tried to cheer him, was only like a report of unknown objects which his imagination could not fashion' (p. 68). Dolly's homely philosophy perpetuates the dual forms of tyranny and subservience; she advocates punishing children by locking them in the coal-hole and reveres as 'good words' because she has seen them in church, the letters, IHS, she prints on all her baking but cannot herself read. James Kavanagh applies Jane Gallop's term 'phallic mother' to Nelly Dean in *Wuthering Heights* (1848), 'the [female] figure who wields the phallic tools of the symbolic order, of language and culture ... she becomes an agent of patriarchal law'.[19] Dolly Winthrop would be a less equivocal candidate. Her labour, like Silas's, is inscribed with the uncomprehended signs of authority which not only her baking but her discourse endlessly disseminates and prepares for consumption. Her catch-phrase is 'I wouldn't speak ill o'this world, seeing as them puts us in it knows best' and, like Ladislaw counselling Dorothea into 'a sturdy neutral delight in things as they were', she ushers Silas into the acquiescent conservatism which this culture extracts as the price of admission: 'a humble sort of acquiescence in what was held to be good, had become a strong habit of that new self which had been developed in him ... he had come to appropriate the forms of custom and belief which were the mould of Raveloe life ...' (p. 201)

Objectification is certainly the theme of a novel which is essentially a long permutation on the term 'object': alienated amidst a world of 'unknown objects' Silas at first suffers, in the loss of his gold, 'a bewildering separation from a supremely loved object' to be blessed with a human replacement in the shape of Eppie, 'an object compacted of changes and hopes' (p. 201; p.166). Silas's relations to objects are intense. His beloved water pot, which in an odd incident he accidentally breaks but keeps the reassembled pieces, exemplifies the object which, its use-value and sympathy to human purposes shattered, takes on a purely symbolic, fetishistic status.

> It had been his companion for twelve years ... always lending its handle to him ... its form had an expression of willing helpfulness ... Silas picked up the pieces and carried them home with grief in his heart. The brown pot could never be of use to him any more, but he stuck the bits together and propped the ruin in its old place for a memorial.
>
> (p. 184)

Essentially a funerary artefact, the 'memorial' pot is the mourning sign of a lost intimacy between man and the object. Let us register for future reference the historical resonances of that term 'ruin'. Silas is not alone in Eliot's oeuvre as the anal hoarder of death-tainted, fetishised objects detached from use-value. The Dodson sisters outdo each other in obsessive fussing over the quality of their respective trousseaux – linen, china and furniture which become a source of anxiety to Mrs Tulliver greater than her husband's paralysis. Sister Glegg has an expensive, once-worn bonnet as the particular object of her commodity fetishism which, unswathed from its tissue shroud, is displayed to envious relatives in a scene of 'funereal solemnity'. A more literal death-taint lingers over Nancy Cass's drawer full of baby clothes, 'all unworn and untouched', which she has preserved for fourteen years after a stillbirth. She has been wont to visit the little collection in a poignant reworking of the image of Silas daily poring over his gold but where the hoard represents absence rather than plenitude. Mr Transome in *Felix Holt* tends his collection of 'dried insects' and mineralogical specimens in shallow drawers, occupying himself in continual schemes for their rearrangement. Romola's father Bardo collects antiquities and ancient manuscripts, 'lifeless objects' – most antiquities that survive to be collected are tomb-furnishings – which oppress Romola with a 'sad dreariness', 'the parchment backs, the unchanging mutilated marble, the bits of obsolete bronze and clay' (*Romola*, p. 98). [...] No aspect of reality seems immune from being accumulated into little hoards of death-objects, corpse-collections turned capital. In confirmation of a comment of Macherey's that the nineteenth-century bourgeoisie turn history into their private property or, as Marx puts it, history is currently rendered 'a collection of dead facts', [20] even history is here accumulated as one such death-hoard. In fact the whole of Western culture had appeared to Dorothea under precisely this guise, as a stash of corpse-capital, a 'funeral procession with strange ancestral images and trophies gathered from afar'.

This centrality to the nineteenth century of the notion of collecting of which *Silas Marner* particularly is an analysis and a prophecy is worth pausing over. In a withering attack on Lukács for using his study of nineteenth-century fiction to indulge his own fetishism of the object, Brecht indicates the centrality of such fetishism for the nineteenth century and its determining role in the construction of identity. Lukács had been stating his admiration for Balzac; Brecht points out that Balzac was himself an obsessive collector and that his narratives 'follow possessions (fetishism of objects) through generations of families and their transference from one to the other'. Collecting and competition are primary means of the nineteenth century's construction of identity.

> In the primeval forest of early capitalism individuals fought against individuals, and against groups of individuals; basically they fought against 'the whole of society'. This was precisely what determined their individuality. Now we are advised to go on creating individuals, to recreate them, or rather to create new ones, who will naturally be different but made in the same way. So? 'Balzac's passion for collecting things bordered on monomania'. We find this fetishism of objects in his novels, too, on hundreds and thousands of pages. Admittedly we are supposed to avoid such a thing. Lukács wags his finger at Tretyakov on this account. But this fetishism is what makes Balzac's characters individuals. It is ridiculous to see in them a simple exchange of the social passions and functions which constitute the individual. Does the production of consumer goods for a collective today construct individuals in the same way as 'collecting'? Naturally one can answer 'yes' here too.[21]

It becomes characteristic of the novel in English from the 1860s on to centre on the fascination exerted by desired but functionless objects. It is a commonplace for novels to be named after, and for their plots to revolve around, some supremely desired artefact. In Wilkie Collins's *The Moonstone* (1868) an elaborate sensation-plot of thefts and deceptions is generated by an Indian diamond plundered from a Hindu temple, bearing a curse and pursued around the world by its former Brahmin protectors. Anthony Trollope's *The Eustace Diamonds* (1873) also ponders, in a rather inert and literal-minded way, the status of objects and the legitimacy of ownership. The heroine pretends that the Eustace heirlooms of the title, given her by her husband, have been stolen and thus attempts to keep them from the acquisitive Eustace family. Henry James's *The Golden Bowl* (1904) circles, Balzac-like, the artefact of the title, human desires and destinies twining themselves around, and imaged in, the exquisite yet flawed objet-d'art. One feels James is elaborating hints from *Daniel Deronda*, that most Jamesian of Eliot's novels, where first Gwendolen's pawned turquoise necklace and later the ring Daniel has valued take on developing plot functions Eliot had not previously used objects to generate.

James is perhaps the author of the fetishised art-object par excellence. The milieu he brings for the first time into the purview of fiction is that specific to the last quarter of the nineteenth century, a world of culture-fetishising new wealth populated by connoisseurs, aesthetes, collectors and critics, the haunters of auction-houses, antique-shops, palaces and museums. Here is first registered in the novel the commodification of the artwork Adorno analyses as a defining characteristic of capitalism in its world-monopoly phase, where artworks are shrivelled to the status of commodities and where commodities – through advertising or grandiose World Fairs and exhibitions where they are displayed like, or alongside, works of art – are swathed in an aesthetic allure. Here is an exhibition and museum culture in which Americans travel the European Old World trawling for, as another James novel title has it, 'spoils'. This is what Adam Verver does in *The Golden Bowl*. He is scouring Europe for objects to bring back to American City and install in his Palace of Art, a 'museum of museums which 'was positively civilisation, condensed, concrete, consummate'.[22] We find in James also exactly what Brecht observes in Balzac – an equation between possession and identity so that, in accumulating possessions, James's almost invariably wealthy characters foster a sense of identity inseparable from ownership. There is a provocative exchange in *The Portrait of a Lady* (1881) – yet another novel named after an aesthetic object – between Isabel Archer and Madame Merle on precisely this point. Wearied of her house, wealth and position Isabel asserts that these things do not define her and that nothing that belongs to her is any measure of her. 'I don't know if I succeed in expressing myself but I know that nothing else expresses me.' Madame Merle disagrees. For her there is a precise equation of ownership, status and selfhood and she poses some pertinent questions.

> 'What shall we call our "self"? Where does it begin? Where does it end? It overflows into everything that belongs to us – and then it flows back again. I know a large part of myself is in the clothes I choose to wear. I've a great respect for *things*! One's self – for other people – is one's expression of one's self, and one's house, one's furniture, one's garments, the books one reads, the company one keeps – these things are all expressive.'[23]

The unresolved dialogue brilliantly encapsulates schisms within the fraught identities of James's own characters, torn between the notion of a romantic essentialism and an actual alienating refraction of identity through the signs of class and possession. Isabel and Madame Merle merely voice the opposed aspects of a single impossible position. It is precisely the annihilating perversity of identity under late capitalism that the subject's infatuation with itself and the fetishism of the object find their correlatives in each other. Human beings thus become the 'subjective-objective reality, a divided thing hinged together but not strictly individual' Lawrence analyses as the repulsive but all-too truthful characterisations of Galsworthy – he must have *The Man of Property* (1906) particularly in mind. The Forsytes have 'lost caste as human beings'. Entirely subject to the 'money-sway', they have violated their essential human 'naïveté' and consequently sunk to the level of the 'social being' in whom money 'goes right through the centre and is the controlling principle'.[24]

Adorno analyses the museum culture and its construction of alien-ated identities with repugnance in *Prisms*. He discusses the opposed responses to museums of 'the two most knowledgeable men to have written about art in recent times', Valéry and Proust. Valéry loathes, Proust loves, museums but both reactions stem from a shared obser-vation that museums are the mausoleums of their contents. Adorno cites Valéry's repulsion from the crammed, eclectic Louvre described in 'Le problème des musées' – one that recalls Dorothea's sense of the oppressive disorder of Rome and the 'titanic ... struggling' of its artworks as well as Brecht's profound equation of collection and competition. 'Cold confusion', he says, 'reigns among the sculptures, a tumult of frozen creatures each of which demands the non-exis-tence of the others, disorder strangely organised.' Of course Adorno is quick to find in the struggling chaos of the museum a metaphor for the anarchical production of desirous commodities in a fully devel-oped bourgeois society. Perhaps more strikingly, Valéry himself makes the same equation by comparing the museum to 'the accumu-lation of excessive and therefore unuseable capital'.[25]

The Proust argument is more complex: it is precisely the degree of alienation afforded by the museum which, by prising the artwork from any pre-existent context, makes it available for the individual's appropriation as an element within the transforming fabric of memory. The death-struggle amongst artworks Valéry perceives in the museum is for Proust a source of beauty, as objects submit them-selves to the mingled ravages and affirmations of time.

> Valéry and Proust ... agree even to the point of recognising some-thing of the mortal enmity which exists among works and which accompanies the pleasure of competition. Far from recoiling before

it, however, Proust affirms this enmity as though he were as German as Charlus affects to be. For him competition among works is the test of truth. Schools, he writes at one point in *Sodom and Gomorrah*, devour each other like micro-organisms and ensure through their struggle the survival of life.[26]

These meditations might strike the reader as somewhat untimely in their application to *Silas Marner* [...] *Silas Marner* – bucolic, fabular, homespun, warmly humanist – would seem to belong to another register altogether and to carry no whiff of the coming art-fetishising 'decadence' of a rabid commodity culture. *Silas Marner, Sodom and Gomorrah* and late, exquisite James make, I will admit, a provocative comparison even if Proust's characters are fond of reading and translating Eliot and Isabel Archer has been brought up on her. If *Daniel Deronda* is Eliot's most Jamesian novel, *Silas Marner* would appear to be her least. In fact *Silas* so precisely negates such a world as to be suspiciously disingenuous. To negate precisely a given form – as a sculptor's mould does, or a photographic negative – can be the means of its faithful reproduction. *Silas* is the anticipatory negative of a rabid, commodified, fetishistic, anti-humanist world. Thus Silas's revered broken pot is a humble ancestor of James's also cracked and fetishised golden bowl and the miserly Silas himself has been a (barely) living embodiment of the culture Valéry observes which, in its museums and elsewhere, requires 'the accumulation of excessive and therefore unuseable capital'. Readers will readily agree that *Silas* has mythic qualities, myths being those troublesome, indeterminate entities of *Middlemarch*. But why does one need a humanist myth unless everything it wishes to assert is under threat? If *Silas* is a myth it is so in the terms of Benjamin's dictum that while there is a beggar, there will be a myth. In other words myths are required to mask social tensions and oppressions for which they offer purely illusory resolutions.

The equation of the museum and the mausoleum analysed by Adorno, Valéry and Proust is continuous with the argument of Lukács that the nineteenth century is itself 'a charnel house of long-dead interiorities'. As Lukács describes it – and the Dickens of *Dombey and Son* had anticipated the analysis – the nineteenth century displaces nature by a charnel-house 'second nature' of human manufacture.

> This second nature is not dumb, sensuous and yet senseless like the first: it is a complex of senses – meanings – which has become rigid and strange, and which no longer wakens interiority; it is a charnel-house of long-dead interiorities; this second nature could only be brought to life – if this were possible – by the metaphysical fact of reawakening the souls which, in an early or ideal existence, created or preserved it; it can never be animated by another interiority.[27]

Here, in a somewhat mystified form, are all the Eliot cruces. Silas is in desperate need to be 'brought to life', to experience the wakening of his 'interiority', the 'metaphysical act of awakening'. *Silas Marner* is the Benjaminesque myth of that awakening. The novel offers an image of precisely what Lukács describes as what this period has made unattainable, the rescue from the 'charnel-house of dead interiorities' through the blessed 'act of reawakening' as one is 'animated by another interiority'. Eppie, the golden-haired child who tottering into Silas's cottage after the theft of his gold seems its miraculous human replacement, is that other, animating interiority. 'As the child's mind was growing into knowledge, his mind was growing into memory: as her life unfolded, his soul, long stupefied in a cold narrow prison, was unfolding too, and trembling gradually into full consciousness' (p. 185).

Eppie, in a phrase worth pondering in this context, is described as the antithesis of an object or, more contradictorily, as an object inspired with non-objective qualities: 'an object compacted of changes and hopes'.

> Unlike the gold which needed nothing, and must be worshipped in close-locked solitude – which was hidden away from the daylight, was deaf to the songs of birds, and started to no human tones – Eppie was a creature of endless claims and ever-growing desires, seeking and loving sunshine, and living sounds, and living movements ... Eppie was an object compacted of changes and hopes that forced his thoughts onward, and carried them far away from their old eager pacing towards the same blank limit ...
>
> (p. 184)

Two interdependent indices of growth mark Silas's progress in deserving, and achieving, his disenchantment from alienation; the slow shift in his vocabulary whereby he comes to call Eppie 'her' rather than 'it' and the commensurate erosion of his conception of her as his private property. This latter however is never fully extricated from the narrative's own fabular equation of the daughter with her father's treasure, a motif given emphatic stress also in the contemporaneous *Romola*. These are two novels giving utterly opposed readings of what it means for a daughter to be her father's wealth.

Eppie is an exemplary nineteenth-century heroine in having an essentially domestic function. Herself a human object miraculously disenchanted from her objectification, she revokes the alienation from the natural which has been Silas's burden and re-establishes him in his 'parental home'. 'Estrangement from nature (the first nature), the modern sentimental attitude to nature, is only a projection of man's experience of his self-made environment as a prison instead of as a parental home.'[28] The Lukácsian formulations derive from Hegel as, in some sense, does Marx's own analysis of alienation. For Hegel alienation is a facet of the wider contemporary need to feel at home within our own history, and art has the Eppiesque function of ushering us into this domestic/historical idyll.

> The historical is only then ours ... when we can regard the present in general as a consequence of those events in whose chain the characters or deeds represented constitute an essential link ... For art does not exist for a small, closed circle of the privilegedly cultured few, but for the nation as a whole. What holds good for the work of art in general, however, also has its application for the outer side of the historical reality represented. It, too, must be made clear and accessible to us without extensive learning so that we, who belong to our own time and nation, may find ourselves at home therein, and not be obliged to halt before us, as before some alien and unintelligible world.[29]

A novel both brave and defensive, *Silas Marner* first depicts, then denies the truth of nineteenth-century conditions before which Silas is 'obliged to halt ... as before some alien and unintelligible world' – 'this life ... from which ... he had stood aloof as from a strange thing, wherewith he could have no communion'. Its very last line conjures the opposed possibility Hegel posits as the necessary contemporary message of art, the reassurance that we have a home in history. 'O father,' said Eppie, 'what a pretty home ours is! I think nobody could be happier than we are.'

From Jim Reilly, *Shadowtime: History and Representation in Hardy, Conrad and George Eliot* (London, 1993), pp. 83–97.

NOTES

[This excerpt is taken from Jim Reilly's full-length study, *Shadowtime* (1993), which considers the work of Eliot, Hardy and Conrad in the context of nineteenth- and twentieth-century debates about history and historical representation and includes readings of *Romola* and *Daniel Deronda*, as well as *Silas Marner*. A central part of Reilly's argument is that Victorian historical discourses are caught up in the innovative and repetitious logic of *Vergegenstandlichung* ('objectification', 'commodification'). Characters in works by these novelists all find themselves enmeshed within capitalism so arrogantly monumental as to suffer the existence of no 'outside' and no 'outsider'. Indebted to Marxist and post-Marxist readings of history, Reilly suggests that *Silas Marner* can be seen as an attempt by Eliot to engage with contemporary post-industrial concerns about the nature of greed, acquisition and alienation. He locates *Silas Marner* firmly within its own time, drawing explicit links between Karl Marx and Eliot's modes of thought, and also within literary historiography generally, seeing in Eliot's critique of commodification and the lure of objects the kind of concerns that would be replayed by Wilkie Collins and Henry James amongst others. All quotations in the essay are taken from *The Mill on the Floss* (Harmondsworth: Penguin, 1973). Eds]

1. Gordon S. Haight (ed.), *The George Eliot Letters* (New Haven, CT, 1954–5), Vol. 4, p. 87.

2. Charles Dickens, *Dombey and Son* (Harmondsworth, 1984).

3. Ibid., p. 737.

4. Karl Marx, *Selected Writings*, ed. David McLellan (Oxford, 1977), pp. 241, 233.

5. Friedrich Engels, *The Condition of the Working Class in England* (Harmondsworth, 1987), p. 69.

6. See Walter Benjamin, *Charles Baudelaire: A Lyric Poet in the Era of High Capitalism* (London, 1975).

7. George Eliot, *Silas Marner* (Harmondsworth, 1973), p. 239. All further references are contained in the text.

8. Charles Dickens, *A Tale of Two Cities* (Harmondsworth, 1990), p. 44.

9. Theodor Adorno, *Minima Moralia* (London, 1974), pp. 148, 150.

10. Jacob Burckhardt, *The Civilisation of the Renaissance in Italy* (Harmondsworth, 1990), p. 198.

11. J. S. Mill, *On Liberty* (Harmondsworth, 1987), p. 127.

12. Ibid., p. 123.

13. Thomas Hardy, *Jude the Obscure* (London, 1982), p. 244.

14. John Ruskin, *The Stones of Venice, Works*, ed. E. T. Cook and Alexander Wedderburn (London, 1904), Vol. 10, p. 194.

15. Marx, *Selected Writings*, p. 79.

16. Ibid., p. 78.

17. Ibid., p. 81.

18. Ibid., p. 83.

19. James Kavanagh, *Emily Brontë* (London, 1985), pp. 39–40.

20. Marx, *Selected Writings*, p. 165.

21. Theodor Adorno, Walter Benjamin, Ernst Bloch, Bertolt Brecht, Georg Lukács, *Aesthetics and Politics: The Key Texts of the Classic Debate with German Marxism*, trans. Ronald Taylor (London, 1988), p. 78.

22. Henry James, *The Golden Bowl* (Harmondsworth, 1983), p. 124.

23. Henry James, *The Portrait of a Lady* (Harmondsworth, 1984), p. 253.

24. D. H. Lawrence, *Selected Literary Criticism* (London, 1969), p. 121; p. 120.

25. Theodor Adorno, *Prisms* (Cambridge, MA, 1983), p. 183; p. 176; p. 177.

26. Ibid., p. 179.

27. George Lukács, *The Theory of the Novel* (London, 1978), p. 64.

28. Ibid., p. 64.

29. In Georg Lukács, *The Historical Novel* (London, 1962), pp. 57–8.

10

Silas Marner: A Divided Eden

SALLY SHUTTLEWORTH

In her 'legendary tale', *Silas Marner*, George Eliot again addresses the issue of historical continuity. Like the earlier *Adam Bede*, however, the novel seems to evade the challenge of social change and disruption. Against the flow of history, the plot moves backward in time: the dweller from the industrial city is finally incorporated into the world of 'Merry England', 'never reached by the vibrations of the coach-horn, or of public opinion'.[1] Just as Dinah left the harsh world of Stoniton for Hayslope, so Silas leaves the industrial life of Lantern Yard for the rural village of Raveloe which, like Hayslope, stands 'aloof from the currents of industrial energy and Puritan earnestness' (p. 33). In *Adam Bede* George Eliot emphasised the continuity of this process of change: Dinah seemed to evolve, without undue stress, into her natural form of matron. In *Silas Marner*, however, following the pattern of *The Mill on the Floss*, she dramatises the conflict and discontinuity of the historical process. Maggie experienced the 'clash of opposing elements' and was forced into temporary exile; Silas is abruptly cast out from his friends, work, and home.

George Eliot explores the same themes in *Silas Marner* and *The Mill*, but this time she reverses the structural pattern of the earlier novel. Opening with an evocation of the Eden of Maggie's childhood, *The Mill on the Floss* plots the growing division between Maggie's past and present life, which only the concluding catastrophe of the flood resolves. *Silas Marner*, by contrast, opens with a catastrophe which establishes an absolute and immediate break between Silas' past and future existence. Through his later relationship with Eppie, however, we trace the gradual restoration of historical continuity to his life, until he attains the final plenitude in which both the past and the realm of historical change seem to be erased. The conclusion of *Silas Marner*, like that of *Adam Bede*, confirms historical stasis. The fenced-in garden of Silas' cottage, to which the 'four united people' return, symbolises, as in Medieval iconography, their Eden, a world where history and change are excluded. Surrounded by the flowers which 'shone with answering gladness', they have in fact attained the 'daisied fields' of Maggie's heaven.

The structural pattern of *Silas Marner* suggests that George Eliot adopted, in this novel, a more positive attitude towards ideas of historical development than in her previous work; yet, as the plot's movement backward in time reveals, she did not fully resolve her ambivalent responses. In *Silas Marner*, as in *The Mill on the Floss*, she interrogates theories of organic continuity in history, and, to this end, she explores, in each work, the relations between theories of social and psychological formation. The *Mill on the Floss* offered two models of history, based on two different patterns of psychology: the linear development of consciousness, and the atemporal unconscious. The two determining moments in Maggie's life both belonged to this latter model. When she drifted away with Stephen, and when she attempted to rescue Tom from the flood, Maggie relinquished conscious control of her actions, lapsing into the realm of the unconscious. In both cases her behaviour violated the psychological pattern associated, in contemporary theory, with linear theories of social progress; that of a rational actor, responsibly directing her actions in light of her knowledge of the 'law of consequences'.[2] This break from a linear model of psychology is accentuated in *Silas Marner*.[3] During the two determining moments of Silas' life he is in a state akin to death, suffering from a cataleptic fit. On each occasion, when he is framed by William Dane, and when Eppie enters his life, he is entirely without responsibility for his actions. As Eppie wanders into his cottage Silas stands by the door 'arrested ... by the invisible wand of catalepsy' (p. 169). The reference to the magic wand highlights the disruptive function of Silas' disease. Despite the increased interest in abnormal states of consciousness in the mid-nineteenth century, catalepsy still remained a mystery to psychologists.[4] Inexplicable, and uncontrollable, catalepsy seemed to suggest the eruption of chance, rather than the operation of uniform law. George Eliot's treatment of Silas' malady confirms this reading.

Once Silas' senses return, after one of his fits, he remains 'unaware of the chasm in his consciousness' (p. 169). The term chasm, which recalls the 'sudden chasm' (p. 117) created in Silas' life by the loss of his gold, suggests an image of history based on the premises of catastrophism, rather than on uniformitarian theory. Both Silas' social and psychological life conform to these premises: the breaks in his consciousness parallel the discontinuity of his social history. Powerless to control either the workings of his own mind, or the machinations of others, he is abruptly thrust out of Lantern Yard, forced to start an entirely new life. His cataleptic fits function, indeed, as one symptom of a more inclusive powerlessness. Like Maggie's lapses into the unconscious, and *The Mill*'s concluding flood, Silas' catalepsy suggests George Eliot's uncertain allegiance to ideas of uniformitarian development.

George Eliot's contemporaries were quick to note the internal conflicts within her work. Thus E. S. Dallas objected to Silas' trances since they 'render[ed] him a singularly unaccountable being'.[5] The pleasure of fiction, Dallas argued, 'depends mainly on our being able to count upon the elements of human character and to calculate results'. Thus, if an 'imbecile' is brought forward, 'it involves the introduction of chance and uncertainty into a tissue of events the interest of which depends on their antecedent probability'.[6] Dallas' theory of narrative progression and psychological development is based upon uniformitarian principles. The enjoyment of narrative, he believed, is founded on the comforting rehearsal of rational history in which continuous order can always be discerned. Predictability is thus the key to social and psychological order. Unconscious trances clearly constitute a threat since they introduce elements not subject to control.

Dallas jibbed at Silas' fits because they seemed inconsistent with the dominant moral of the tale:

> As in one fit of unconsciousness he lost his all, so in another fit of unconsciousness he obtained a recompense. In either case he was helpless, had nothing to do with his own fate, and was a mere feather in the wind of chance. From this point forward in the tale, however, there is no more chance – all is work and reward, cause and effect, the intelligent mind shaping its own destiny. The honest man bestows kindness upon the child, and reaps the benefit of it in his own increasing happiness, quickened intelligence, and social position.[7]

Chance and the unconscious are balanced against continuity and control, values which Dallas associates with the smooth functioning of economic and social life. Coopting the authority of science to support his arguments, he presents work and reward as synonymous with the principles of cause and effect. His model of society is that of the capitalist economy; each individual in control of his own destiny, freely pursuing his own interest. In personal life, as in the market place, honest investment will reap a merited reward. The idea of orderly sequence within individual life stands as a model for the larger movement of social history.

Despite the fact that Silas' life is dominated more by chance than by rational order and control, George Eliot does, as Dallas correctly observes, draw the moral framework of her novel from these latter values. In accordance with her practice in *Adam Bede* (and, indeed, in all her later novels) she condemns those who subscribe to a belief in chance. Thus the inadequacies of Lantern Yard as a social and religious community are revealed by its members' superstitious trust in the drawing of lots. The novel's two greatest villains, William Dane and Dunsey Cass, are distinguished by their faith in their own luck and the workings of chance; both, as Joseph Wiesenfarth has argued, 'believe in their election to fortune'.[8] Godfrey Cass is similarly tainted by this belief. He is roundly castigated by the narrator for clinging to the hope that chance might release him from the consequences of his unfortunate marriage. 'Favourable Chance,' the narrator gravely observes, 'is the god of all men who follow their own devices instead of obeying a law they believe in' (p. 112).

In adhering to a model of history which permits the intrusion of chance and randomness, Godfrey violates the moral, social and economic assumptions underpinning the Victorians' faith in uniformitarian law. Godfrey's beliefs are quickly linked to the realm of economic activity: to the self-deluding dreams of those who live outside their income, or 'shirk the resolute honest work that brings wages', or, in an even more explicitly directed social commentary, attempt to move up the social ladder. Thus the narrator observes, 'Let him forsake a decent craft that he may pursue the gentilities of a profession to which nature never called him, and his religion will infallibly be the worship of blessed Chance, which he will believe in as the mighty creator of success' (pp. 112–13). Social mobility, like the worship of chance, poses a threat to a 'naturally' ordained social order. Referring to this mode of worship the narrator concludes, 'The evil principle deprecated in that religion, is the orderly sequence by which the seed brings forth a crop after its kind' (p. 113). Ideas of economic and social order are here firmly grounded in a theory of natural, organic, historical growth. Yet, the narrator's declared allegiance to theories of orderly sequence and moral responsibility in action is clearly undercut by the determining role played within the novel by chance and the loss of rational control. Like its predecessor, *The Mill on the Floss*, *Silas Marner* actually offers two conflicting models of history, one based on ideas of continuity, moral order, individual responsibility and control, and another which stresses gaps and jumps in historical development, chance, individual powerlessness, and self-division.

Although *Silas Marner* is cast within an apparently simple mould, George Eliot brings to her analysis of the issues of organic development in this work all the complexity of her previous fiction. Through its legendary form she examines in concrete detail Strauss' and Feuerbach's theories of the mythic imagination, and Comte's theory of the three stages of human evolution, from the fetishism of the polytheistic stage through to the rational thought of positivism.[9] The fictional mode of the work actually functions as a commentary upon the stage of development attained by the Raveloe villagers. George Eliot's treatment of the villagers' initial reactions to Silas, and their discussions in the Rainbow and responses to the 'evidence' surrounding the robbery, reveals her interest in the processes of mythological thought, and the forms of rationality current in man's various developmental stages. Like Comte, she brings to her work a profound respect for the processes of history, a firm belief that each stage is directly linked to its predecessors.[10] Thus Silas' love of his brick hearth is treated tenderly and sympathetically: 'The gods of the hearth exist for us still; and let all new faith be tolerant of that fetishism, lest it bruise its own roots' (p. 212). In *Silas Marner* George Eliot explores the various historical roots of man's behaviour, examining the development of an individual life within the perspective of a larger evolutionary framework. Her aim in returning to the primitive life of Lantern Yard and Raveloe is 'to enter into that simple, untaught state of mind in which the form and the feeling have never been severed by an act of reflection' (p. 18), and to offer, in accordance with Comtean theory, a full account of the ways in which the characters evolved through interaction with their surrounding social medium.[11] As a Victorian reviewer observed, 'It is impossible to dissociate any of the characters from the village in which they were born and bred – they form an organic whole with Raveloe.'[12]

In translating this theory of social organicism into its full psycho-logical consequences, however, George Eliot encounters problems similar to those that emerged in *The Mill on the Floss*. Her analysis of the psychological effects of Silas' sudden displacement recalls nar-rative discussions of the devastating personal impact of the Tullivers' bankruptcy:[13]

> Even people whose lives have been made various by learning, some-times find it hard to keep a fast hold on their habitual views of life, on their faith in the Invisible, nay, on the sense that their past joys and sorrows are a real experience, when they are suddenly trans-ported to a new land, where the beings around them know nothing of their history, and share none of their ideas – where their mother earth shows another lap, and human life has other forms than those on which their souls have been nourished.

> (p. 20)

Silas, like Mr and Mrs Tulliver, loses his sense of identity once his familiar surrounding medium is transformed. He can neither orient himself within the strange world of Raveloe, nor relate to his own past history. He retains no sense of self distinct from his relationship to his environment. As in *The Mill on the Floss*, the theory of psy-chology drawn from notions of organic development and historical continuity actually subverts the idea of a unified, rational actor.

Once displaced from Lantern Yard, Silas undergoes the 'Lethean influence of exile, in which the past becomes dreamy because its symbols have all vanished, and the present too is dreamy because it is linked with no memories' (p. 20). As in his cataleptic fits he enters into a trance-like state, becoming incapable of ordering or imposing continuity on his life. His experience contradicts the accepted psychological pattern outlined here by Alexander Bain in his obser-vation that 'The unbroken continuity of our mental life holds together the past and the present in a sequence that we term Order in Time'. For Bain, this mental continuity was both a measure and a guarantee of social order; he relates the linear sequence of the mind directly to 'the sequences of nature, or the order of the world'.[14] George Eliot's analysis of Silas' loss of personal identity effectively challenges such dominant assumptions of social and psychological continuity. Silas' faith in a benign, God-given order was shattered when the drawing of lots declared him guilty. George Eliot's explo-ration of his ensuing experience suggests that ideas of essential order in the social and psychological realms are also open to doubt.

The portrait of Silas follows the psychological theory of Lewes who differed pre-eminently from Bain and other contemporaries in his belief that the mind had no controlling ego, no 'unity of the executive'.[15] Mind, he argued, like organic life, comprised the processes of interaction between the organism and medium, thus 'psychical Life has no one special centre, any more than the physical Life has one special centre: it belongs to the whole, and animates the whole'.[16] The operations of the mind were not unified and directed by a rational ego, there was no essential self to impose order on incoming sensations, thus mental history need not constitute a linear continuum. In pursuing the psychological implications of Comte's theory of dynamic interaction Lewes and George Eliot undercut Comte's determining social and moral assumptions. Eliot's image of the relationship between the individual and surrounding society is not one of simple reflection, where psychological continuity reflects social continuity. Neither the individual nor society possess intrinsic coherence. In *Silas Marner* George Eliot develops the psychological insights of The *Mill on the Floss* to create a masterly study of the growing disjunction between Silas and his surrounding world. Far from reinforcing an idealistic picture of social life, the novel actually anticipates, in its opening sections, the later *Daniel Deronda*, with its pessimistic vision of the conflict, and lack of communication that can actually characterise social interdependence.

Following the premises of Lewes' psychological theory, George Eliot traces the internal effects of Silas' alienation. She reveals how, within the rural world of Raveloe, he is reduced from human status to a 'spinning insect', until he finally takes on the qualities of an object:

> he had clung with all the force of his nature to his work and his money; and like all objects to which a man devotes himself, they had fashioned him into correspondence with themselves. His loom, as he wrought in it without ceasing, had in its turn wrought on him, and confirmed more and more the monotonous craving for its monotonous response. His gold, as he hung over it and saw it grow, gathered his power of loving together into a hard isolation like its own.
>
> (p. 63)

As his own creativity is drawn from him in his increasing subjection to his loom and his gold, Silas endows these alienated self-images with his own active powers. Clearly he is no rational actor in charge of his sensual steed; indeed, he is unable to establish any hierarchical differentiation between human, animal or even object life. The pattern of his life conforms not to the Comtean theory of evolution from fetishism to rationality, but rather to the 'fetishism of commodities' described by that other great nineteenth-century historian, Marx. In the monetary system, Marx observes, 'gold and silver, when serving as money, did not represent a social relation between producers, but were natural objects with strange social properties'.[17] Gold, for Silas, takes on these strange social properties. His relations with his fellow villagers become for him a mere function through which he can acquire more coins. Reduced into a 'constant mechanical relation to the objects of his life' (p. 29) he looks, for the last vestiges of human contact, towards his gold. Whilst lavishing his loving attention on his piles of coins he 'thought fondly of the guineas that were only half earned by the work in his loom, as if they had been unborn children' (p. 31). He comes, indeed, to believe that his coins are 'conscious of him' (p. 27). Social relations for Silas are displaced entirely into the realm of objects.

This powerful analysis of Silas' growing alienation inverts organicist theories of historical development. Comte believed that the evolution of society from homogeneity to heterogeneity would necessarily bring greater social solidarity. As the division of labour increased, and social interdependence developed, feelings of sympathy would arise, and altruism would supplant the more primitive emotions of egoism. Silas' presence in Raveloe signals a new increase in the division of labour, but he does not create a growing solidarity within the community. He evokes hostility, not altruism, from his neighbours, whilst he himself is precipitated into isolation and egoism, and an ever-narrowing range of response.

George Eliot's critical vision of Raveloe society is not sustained, however. Halfway through the novel the pattern of Silas' life is reversed with the arrival of Eppie. Unlike Maggie, Silas is permitted to grow, in the midst of life, into organic community with his neighbours. The change appears little short of miraculous. Like the concluding flood of *The Mill on the Floss* it suggests a disruption of uniform law. As Strauss argued in *The Life of Jesus*, 'no just notion of the true nature of history is possible without a perception of the inviolability of the chain of finite causes, and of the impossibility of miracles'.[18] Yet, although Eppie is compared to the angels who led men away from the city of destruction (p. 201) there are in fact no miracles involved in Silas' restoration; George Eliot takes care to ensure that the natural chain of causation is not broken. In accordance with her design, the novel reveals 'the remedial influences of pure, natural human relations'.[19] To achieve this end she turns, perhaps surprisingly, to the principles of physiological psychology which had sustained the analysis of Silas' growing alienation. Although Lewes' theories, in their ultimate implications, undercut ideas of ordered social or psychological development, the original impetus behind his work was to affirm the reign of order throughout the physical and social realms. George Eliot's fiction is characterised by a similar duality; she employs the principles of physiological psychology initially to challenge, and ultimately to affirm conceptions of organic unity and continuity.

In accordance with physiological principles George Eliot makes Silas' first response to Eppie one of memory:

> Could this be his little sister come back to him in a dream ...?
> ... It was very much like his little sister. Silas sank into his chair powerless, under the double presence of an inexplicable surprise and a hurrying influx of memories.
>
> (p. 170)

Eppie does not disrupt the continuity of Silas' life but rather stimulates the dormant channels of his mind. George Eliot's analysis in this crucial passage conforms to Lewes' conception of the mind as an 'aggregate of forces' and to his theories of unconscious association. Thus the sight of the child stimulates within Silas a whole chain of associated memories: 'a vision of the old home and the old streets leading to Lantern Yard – and within that vision another, of the thoughts which had been present with him in those far-off scenes' (p. 170). Silas' sequence of memory illustrates the 'law of attractions' defined here by Spencer: 'that when any two psychical states occur in immediate succession, an effect is produced such that if the first subsequently recurs there is a certain tendency for the second to follow.'[20] The physical processes of unconscious association establish continuity in personal life, a continuity which, Spencer believed, was then passed on to future generations through the physiological inheritance of 'modified nervous tendencies'.[21] Physiological structure seemed, to Spencer, to guarantee progressive social evolution.[22]

Although George Eliot did not entirely share Spencer's ebullient social optimism, she did attribute a key role to physiology in Silas' recovery. The physiological unity of mind, represented by his unconscious association of ideas, allows him to heal the breach in his social experience. Through his relationship with Eppie he grows once more into union with his neighbours, and into a sense of continuity with his past. Eppie's progressive development is mirrored in Silas as the underlying continuity of his history is gradually revealed: 'As the child's mind was growing into knowledge, his mind was growing into memory: as her life unfolded, his soul, long stupefied in a cold narrow prison, was unfolding too, and trembling gradually into full consciousness' (pp. 193–4). The term 'full consciousness' is here replete with meaning: it implies not only an integrated sense of self based on continuous memory, but also an open, accepting awareness of surrounding social life. Under the influence of Eppie Silas moves beyond the 'ever-repeated circle' of thought established by his gold to look for links and ties with his neighbours. He learns to channel his previously inert feelings into 'the forms of custom and belief which were the mould of Raveloe life; and as, with reawakening sensibilities, memory also reawakened, he had begun to ponder over the elements of his old faith, and blend them with his new impressions, till he recovered a consciousness of unity between his past and present' (p. 213). Silas grows simultaneously into organic unity within his social and psychological life; isolation and personal disruption are replaced by integration.

Silas' change appears, on the surface, to be a dramatic transformation; but, in charting its course, George Eliot employs the same theoretical premises that lay behind her earlier analysis. Throughout the novel she examines both social and psychological life in the light of Lewes' and Spencer's theories of channelled energy. The great attraction of physiological psychology for these thinkers lay in the fact that it allowed them to extend to the mind the principles they saw operating in the social and physiological organism. They employed in their work a single vocabulary of channelled energy to describe the three different spheres of physiological, mental, and social life. George Eliot readily adopted these theories, since they allowed her to integrate her analysis of the different levels of organic life.

In her study of the effects of the Lantern Yard religion on Silas' mind George Eliot draws together the concepts of external cultural channels, and internal pathways of the mind. Thus Silas accepted the religious explanation of his fits since 'culture had not defined any channels for his sense of mystery, and so it spread itself over the proper pathway of inquiry and knowledge' (p. 11). The image of the force of mystery irresistibly spreading over the 'proper pathway of

inquiry and knowledge' is in accordance with Lewes' Law of
Sensibility that 'No sensation terminates in itself'. Once aroused, a
sensation must necessarily receive issue. The customs of Lantern
Yard formed, for Silas, 'the channel of divine influences' (p. 21).
Following his expulsion from these accustomed channels of expression, his social disruption is replicated internally in the physiological
structure of his mind: 'Thought was arrested by utter bewilderment,
now its old narrow pathway was closed, and affection seemed to
have died under the bruise that had fallen on its keenest nerves'
(p. 23). This sensitive description of Silas' psychological confusion is
based on the physiologically precise idea of energy diverted from its
usual, defined channels of discharge. It conforms to Lewes' theories
concerning the contrast between the ease felt in accustomed action,
and the difficulties of acquiring new patterns of behaviour:

> In learning to speak a new language, to play on a musical instrument,
> or to perform any unaccustomed movements, great difficulty is felt,
> because the channels through which each sensation has to pass have
> not become established; but no sooner has frequent repetition cut a
> pathway, than this difficulty vanishes.[23]

These principles lie behind George Eliot's analysis of Silas' alienation. His growing subjection to the numbing activity of weaving
and the counting of gold is explained in terms of the ease felt in a
habitual action for 'Do we not wile away moments of inanity or
fatigued waiting by repeating some trivial movement or sound, until
the repetition has bred a want, which is incipient habit?' (p. 27).
This suggestion conforms to Lewes' theory that once frequent repetition has cut a pathway actions become so automatic that 'if once
commenced, they must continue'.[24] In hoarding his gold, marking
the periods of his existence only by the acquisition of his guineas,
Silas' life was 'narrowing and hardening itself more and more into a
mere pulsation of desire and satisfaction that had no relation to any
other being' (p. 28). While the physical image of pulsation accu-
rately portrays the nature of Silas' life it also suggests, in moral
terms, its inadequacies: Silas' reduction from a social to a purely
physical being. The physical description in fact reinforces the moral
analysis.

George Eliot did not employ physiological theory solely for the
sake of descriptive accuracy. Its integrated vocabulary allowed her
to shift easily between different levels of analysis, combining intricate psychological analysis with wider social and moral conclusions.

Thus throughout the novel she transposed physiological concepts into vivid metaphorical images to highlight their social and psychological implications.[25] Silas' lack of interest in the hedgerows he had once loved is expressed in the following poetic terms:

> these too belonged to the past, from which his life had shrunk away, like a rivulet that has sunk far down from the grassy fringe of its old breadth into a little shivering thread, that cuts a groove for itself in the barren sand.

(p. 31)

The description is extraordinarily rich and evocative. From the hedgerow banks, which offer both a literal and symbolic image of the changes in Silas' life, it moves to the idea of river banks, and to the contrast between the lush fertility of a full river, and the stark, desert-like conditions of a drought. The passage, with its shift from an historical to a physiological definition of life, captures brilliantly the qualitative changes in the nature of Silas' existence. Reduced to a 'shivering thread', Silas clearly possesses no control over the conditions of his life. Behind these striking natural images lies the physiological premise that streams of sensation, once displaced from their accustomed channels, only carve a new pathway with great difficulty. It is the 'peculiar characteristic of vigorous intellects', Lewes notes, 'that their thoughts are ever finding new pathways instead of moving amid old associations'.[26] Silas, however, has not the vitality to affect this change. Thus, in a variation on the earlier image 'his soul was still the shrunken rivulet, with only this difference, that its little groove of sand was blocked up, and it wandered confusedly against dark obstruction' (p. 132). The 'fountains of human love and faith' in his mind are locked up, unable to find a channel of release. The terms are still those of physiological psychology, but with the relatively simple addition of the word 'soul', the physical description takes on extensive moral and social implications.

Eppie, of course, functions as the catalyst for the release of Silas' energy. Her appearance does not mark, however, the first time that Silas' memories have been awakened. George Eliot charts both the shrinking current of Silas' life, and the movements within his unconscious which lead to his later change. Early in his residence in Raveloe, the sight of Sally Oates suffering from dropsy had recalled memories of his mother and stimulated him to aid her: 'In this office of charity, Silas felt, for the first time since he had come to Raveloe, a sense of unity between his past and present life.' But suspicion and

misunderstanding prevented its growth. Indeed, in precise physiological terms, the incident 'heightened the repulsion between him
and his neighbours, and made his isolation more complete' (pp. 25,
26). But the precedent for his response to Eppie has been set. In
telling the story of his robbery in the Rainbow, and in coming to
terms with his false accusation of Jem, Silas also experienced awakened memories of his past though, as the narrator observes, 'Our
consciousness rarely registers the beginning of a growth within us
any more than without us: there have been many circulations of the
sap before we detect the smallest sign of the bud' (p. 86). The
passage, with its vivid organic images, prepares the reader for Silas'
future development. By establishing a differential time scale between
apparent social history and the hidden life of the unconscious, it
suggests how Silas' fragmentary existence will once more be brought
into union. The appearance of a figure who could release his
blocked emotion and reopen the channels of his mind leads
inevitably to the restoration of social and psychological unity. The
apparent discontinuity of his life is discounted by the stable physiological structure of his mind. History, as the moral critique of
Godfrey implied, is cumulative.

Analysis of the physiological underpinnings of George Eliot's
figurative language reveals the extraordinary complexity of her
work. Each word and phrase was related to her larger purpose as
she attempted to resolve, in concrete terms, the social issues raised
by organicism.[27] The satisfying conclusion of Silas' life, however,
was only possible because the shared vocabulary of organic social
and psychological theory allowed George Eliot to elide these two
distinct levels of analysis. Spencer and Lewes turned to physiological
psychology for scientific validation of their belief in the hidden
order of the world, and George Eliot, in this novel, follows their
example: she employs physiology to reinforce the moral structure of
her tale. In focusing on Silas' physiological growth into unity,
however, she excludes reference both to his disruptive fits, and to
the wider social context of his life. Ultimately, his isolation therefore appears as less a product of the social relations in Raveloe than
an accident of personal circumstance, to be resolved on an individual level. This perspective is at odds, however, with the wider social
analysis offered in the rest of the novel, notably in the history of
Godfrey which runs in direct counterpoint to that of Silas.

After the arrival of Eppie the novel appears to move swiftly
towards a happy ending. The wedding, set in the season of eternal

renewal 'when the great lilacs and laburnums in the old-fashioned gardens showed their golden and purple wealth above the lichen-tinted walls' (p. 270) and confirmed by the, for once, unanimous approval of the Raveloe chorus, certainly seems to validate the organic social ideal. The social harmony is marred, however, by the absence of Godfrey Cass; whilst forward movement of the plot is balanced by the less positive model of history suggested by the destruction of Lantern Yard. Following his 'resurrection' by Eppie, Silas had turned once more to a belief in the providential govern-ment of history. Inspired by her to a sense of 'presiding goodness' (p. 213) he came to believe that his earlier expulsion from Lantern Yard must have been due to some error. He returned, therefore, with Eppie to Lantern Yard to see Mr Paston 'a man with a deal o' light', in the hope that the minister would be able to illuminate the historical process: why the 'drawing o' the lots' did not vindicate Silas' belief in an ordered universe but rather seemed to endorse the rule of chance. In place of the light and order he expected to find, however, he discovered only darkness and destruction: 'Here and there a sallow, begrimed face looked out from a gloomy doorway at the strangers' (p. 268). Into this gloom, so reminiscent of Eppie's origin, Lantern Yard had vanished, to be replaced by a factory, symbol of the industrial changes which, like Molly's dark history, had no discernible impact on Raveloe life. Silas failed to find order or meaning in history. Lacking historical illumination he was left in darkness: 'It's dark to me Mrs Winthrop, that is; I doubt it'll be dark to the last' (p. 269). Through Eppie he found 'light enough to trusten by', but not the light of historical reason he had sought.

Silas' failure highlights the internal conflicts in the novel. The tale is no simple endorsement of organicist theories of social develop-ment. As the stress on moral responsibility is balanced by the seem-ingly uncontrollable nature of Silas' fits, so Silas' growth into psychological continuity is offset by the seeming recalcitrance of social history; its refusal to conform to a pattern of ordered devel-opment. The dark vision of the 'great manufacturing town' where the jail hides the sky suggests that the novel's Edenic conclusion can only be achieved by moving backwards in history to the pre-industrial landscape of Raveloe. Yet even here, it is questionable whether the life of a rural idyll could be attained. George Eliot's portrayal of Raveloe is marked by the same duality that charac-terises the rest of the tale. On the one hand it appears a land of Edenic bounty, with 'orchards looking lazy with neglected plenty'

(p. 21). Protected, like Hayslope, by nature 'it was nestled in a snug well-wooded hollow', and centred round a 'fine old church' (p. 7). These images of a natural, harmonious existence are, on the other hand, offset by descriptions of the peasantry's lives as 'pressed close by primitive wants ... To them pain and mishap present a far wider range of possibilities than gladness and enjoyment: their imagination is almost barren of the images that feed desire and hope, but is all overgrown by recollections that are a perpetual pasture to fear' (p. 6). The image is a grim one indeed, but, throughout the novel, George Eliot offers no direct representation of this poverty and fear. This reluctance to portray the darker side of Raveloe experience suggests George Eliot's own ambivalent response.

The bald references to the poverty and misery of Raveloe life are balanced by the detailed celebration of the organic community of the feudal order. Thus the loving attention lavished on Miss Nancy's arrival at Squire Cass', the feast and the New Year's Eve dance seems to confirm for the reader, as for the assembled community of villages, the 'fitness of things': 'That was as it should be – that was what everybody had been used to – and the charter of Raveloe seemed to be renewed by the ceremony' (pp. l56–7). This ritual of renewal is disrupted, however, by the arrival of Silas with Eppie in his arms. For Godfrey, Silas seemed 'an apparition from that hidden life which lies, like a dark by-street, behind the goodly ornamented facade that meets the sunlight and the gaze of respectable admirers' (p. 174). The dark by-streets are not confined to the manufacturing town of Silas' past, but intrude even upon the gay procession in the White Parlour 'where the mistletoe-bough was hung, and multitudinous tallow candles made rather a brilliant effect, gleaming from among the berried holly-boughs, and reflected in the old-fashioned oval mirrors fastened in the panels of the white wainscot' (p. 156). The villagers' own belief in a harmonious natural order, celebrated here in these images of brilliant festivities, is shown to be founded on an illusion. In place of the villagers' affectionate respect for the gaiety of their superiors' lives, we should perhaps substitute the narrator's vision of our rural forefathers, 'men whose only work was to ride round their land, getting heavier and heavier in their saddles, and who passed the rest of their days in the half-listless gratification of senses dulled by monotony' (p. 44). George Eliot no longer endorses the social vision of *Adam Bede*. Although the earlier novel had condemned Arthur's abuse of his social position and responsibilities it had not questioned the fundamental desirability of the hierarchical social system. *Silas Marner*, however, portrays the life of the squirearchy as intrinsically negative and unproductive. Even the 'order and purity' of a Nancy Lammeter cannot, it seems, bring fertility to a form of life which is essentially barren.

The significant absence of Godfrey Cass from the concluding scene suggests that the final harmony is attained only by excluding the murkier side of Raveloe life. Godfrey's history reveals the petty and even sordid nature of experience within this rural community. In *Adam Bede* George Eliot had portrayed seduction and even murder, but had not even hinted at the form of life she now reveals through Godfrey's backstairs marriage, Molly's death from opium addiction and Dunsey's blackmail and theft. Silas and Godfrey, as critics have pointed out, undergo a similar pattern of experience; both are victims of a scheming brother who plots their overthrow.[28] There is a crucial difference, however, in the mode of presentation. Whilst William Dane is only sketchily presented, we see Dunsey Cass in all his taunting, menacing glory. George Eliot offers the facts of Dane's treachery without exploring fully its causes or motivations, but in dealing with Dunsey she reveals, in careful detail, how the social conditions of the Casses' lives contribute to his behaviour. His malignancy is not an individual aberration but a direct product of his social environment. Even more clearly than in Lantern Yard, evil seems to be endemic to the structure of Raveloe life.

Throughout the novel George Eliot brings to her representation of Godfrey this same clear-eyed vision. In the parallel structure of the plot, Silas' 15 barren years are re-enacted in Godfrey's barren marriage, and Godfrey's loss of Eppie becomes, as U. C. Knoepflmacher has observed, Silas' strange gain'.[29] There exists, however, a disturbing disparity between the two stories. Whilst Silas' fall and later redemption are originally brought about by chance, Godfrey's life is rigorously governed by the operation of uniform law. Though Godfrey, like Dunsey, cares initially, 'more for immediate annoyances than for remote consequences' (p. 52), he comes to learn that an individual must bear responsibility for all his deeds. He becomes, indeed, a living exemplum of George Eliot's doctrine of the 'inexorable law of consequences'. Like Arthur Donnithorne, Godfrey takes comfort initially in casuistry. As Arthur had hoped that good could come out of evil, so Godfrey trusts that, if events turn out better than a man expects 'is it not a proof that his conduct has been less foolish and blameworthy than it might otherwise have appeared?' (p. 183). The narrative decisively rejects such moral relativism. Godfrey's childless marriage, and the recovery of Dunsey's body, function as moral symbols of the workings of inexorable law.

Whilst Silas receives the unexpected gift of Eppie, Godfrey is treated with all the harshness of 'unrecompensing law'. Arthur, despite his crimes, had been welcomed back at the close of *Adam Bede* into the community of Hayslope. Godfrey, however, learns that there are some debts that cannot be paid: 'While I've been putting off and putting off, the trees have been growing – it's too late now' (p. 262). The implicit moral recalls the concluding observation in *The Mill on the Floss*: 'Nature repairs her ravages – but not all.' In both novels this image of historical attrition stands in direct contrast to a more optimistic social vision. *Silas Marner* ends with Eppie's joyful exclamation 'I think nobody could be happier than we are.' But, as in *The Mill*, this joy is only to be attained at a certain cost. Maggie lost her life; Silas and Eppie lose part of their past. Silas no longer looks to integrate Lantern Yard within his present life, whilst Eppie, in an ideologically significant gesture, denies Godfrey's paternal claims, thus violating the natural chain of biological continuity.

Although strong arguments have been made for the satisfying nature of *Silas Marner*'s conclusion, its symmetry seems marred.[30] Godfrey fails to take account of the unity of the historical process and is duly punished; Silas is unaccountably blessed by chance and learns, in consequence, to relinquish his quest for order and meaning in history. He learns, instead, to trust; but, such a position implies a passivity directly at odds with the ideal of active, far-sighted responsibility for action, inculcated elsewhere in the novel. Trust, indeed, is a viable stance only within a harmonious order, a society without conflict; it would not have resolved the dilemmas of Maggie's life. Silas, unlike Maggie, is spared the conflict of irreconcilable claims, but the dual representation of Raveloe life puts into question the quality of his Eden.

The celebration of plenitude which concludes *Silas Marner* is based, like the flood in *The Mill on the Floss*, on an evasion of the preceding attempt to find within history an ordered process of growth. Like the earlier novel, *Silas Marner* offers two models of history. Order, continuity and control are set against chance, disruption and powerlessness: the fairy tale elements are balanced by the darker history of Molly or Dunsey, and the stress on moral responsibility is offset by the seemingly uncontrollable nature of

Silas' fits. These divisions within the novel reveal George Eliot's ambivalent responses to theories of organic development. Clearly, it was no longer possible for her to resolve the issues raised by organicism by turning to the life of 'Merry England'. Thus in her next novel she abandoned her accustomed English setting, choosing to dramatise these questions in the idealised form made possible by the temporal and cultural distance of Renaissance Italy.

From Sally Shuttleworth, *George Eliot and Nineteenth-Century Science: The Make-Believe of a Beginning* (Cambridge, 1984), pp. 79–95.

NOTES

[This essay is taken from Sally Shuttleworth's book *George Eliot and Nineteenth-Century Science: The Make-Believe of a Beginning* (1984), which explores the interaction between the discourse of science and literature. New Historicism is well suited to such a project since it aims to situate the novel in its historical context and investigate the ways in which the ideological divisions and tensions of a period are manifest in the inconsistencies of the text. Shuttleworth argues that Eliot is firmly anchored in the theoretical thought of the period and tries to show how 'scientific ideas and theories of method affected not only the social vision but also the narrative structure and fictional methodology'. Shuttleworth also records the developments in Eliot's scientific thought from *Adam Bede* to *Daniel Deronda*. Thus in her highly original account of *The Mill on the Floss* she stresses the narrator's 'Proust-like submergence into the world of unconscious memory'. In the excerpt produced here, a close reading of *Silas Marner* shows Eliot employing 'physiological theory' articulated by G. H. Lewes and others. Eds]

1. George Eliot, *'The Lifted Veil', Silas Marner and 'Brother Jacob'*, Cabinet Edition (Edinburgh, 1878–80), Ch. 1, p. 7. All references to this edition of the tale will be cited hereafter in the text.

2. Thus Lecky, Mackay, Comte and Spencer all associated social progress with the increasing growth of rational control. Spencer, indeed, placing these evolutionary beliefs on a physiological basis, argued that the 'ever advancing *consensus*' of the mind exemplified the universal Law of Progress governing all natural and social development (Herbert Spencer, *The Principles of Psychology* [London, 1955], p. 485).

3. Knoepflmacher similarly links Maggie's passivity in Stephen's boat to Silas's paralysis which leads to his victimisation by William Dane. Although my conclusions concerning the symmetry of *Silas Marner*

differ from those of Knoepflmacher, I am indebted to his discriminating analysis of the ways in which this tale 'is a reaction to, as well as a continuation of, *The Mill on the Floss*'. Knoepflmacher, *George Eliot's Early Novels: The Limits of Realism* (Berkeley, CA, 1968) pp. 229, 227.

4. Catalepsy, as Oswei Temkin has shown in *The Falling of Sickness* (Baltimore, MD, 1971), was confused with forms of epilepsy from ancient times onwards, and the Victorians seemed no nearer than their predecessors to finding an explanation for its occurrence. Although catalepsy was a common term in mid-century psychological discussions (occurring, for example, in the works of Carpenter and Spencer), it was usually introduced as an inexplicable phenomenon. I have been unable to trace any detailed discussion of its causes. Its inexplicable nature seems, indeed, to persist to this day. Thus Robert Simon concludes his technical discussion of Silas's malady with the observation that 'Narcolepsy is a baffling illness that defies elucidation by the disciplines of neurology and psychiatry. The precise etiology of this malady remains a mystery today as during the lifetime of Eliot, Melville and Poe.' See Robert Simon, 'Narcolepsy and the Strange Malady of Silas Marner', *American Journal of Psychiatry*, 123 (November, 1966), 601–2.

5. Unsigned review in *The Times*, 29 April 1861 in David R. Carroll (ed.), *The Critical Heritage* (London, 1971), p. 182.

6. Carroll (ed.), *The Critical Heritage*, p. 182.

7. Ibid., pp. 183–4.

8. Joseph Wiesenfarth, 'Demythologizing *Silas Marner*', *English Literary History*, 37 (1970), 236.

9. Carroll's formative study reveals how profoundly George Eliot was influenced by the doctrines of Feuerbach in her writing of *Silas Marner*. James McLaverty traces the impact of Comte on the novel in 'Comtean Fetishism in *Silas Marner*', *Nineteenth-Century Fiction*, 36 (1981), 318–36.

10. Comte distinguished his theory from that of earlier historians according to the respect with which he treated the past stages of history: 'For that spirit consists in the sense of human continuity, which had hitherto been felt by no one, not even my illustrious and unfortunate predecessor Condorcet.' See Auguste Comte, *System of Positive Polity or Treatise on Sociology Instituting the Religion of Humanity*, trans. J. H. Bridges, Frederic Harrison, E. S. Beesly, Richard Congreave (London, 1875–7), vol. I, p. 50.

11. See Haight (ed.), *The George Eliot Letters* (New Haven, CT, 1954–78) IV, pp. 96–7 for George Eliot's description of her aims.

12. Unsigned review, *Westminster Review*, 76 (July 1861), 280–2, reprinted in Carroll (ed.), *The Critical Heritage*, pp. 186–8.

13. See the discussion of 'our instructed vagrancy' (Bk VI, ch. 9, I, p. 414).

14. Alexander Bain, *The Emotions and the Will* (New York, 1876), p. 534, p. 537.

15. Summarising his objections to Lewes's theories Bain concluded: 'It seems to me, therefore, that what determines the unity of consciousness, as showing which local currents have found means to activate the collective currents, is the unity of the *executive*.' Ibid., p. 591.

16. George Henry Lewes, *The Physiology of Common Life* (London, 1859–60),Vol. II, p. 5.

17. Karl Marx, *Selected Writings*, ed. David McLellan (Oxford, 1977), p. 442.

18. David Friedrich Strauss, *The Life of Jesus, Critically Examined*, trans. Marian Evans (London, 1846), Vol. I, p. 64.

19. Haight (ed.), *The George Eliot Letters*, III, p. 382. To John Blackwood, 24 February 1861.

20. Spencer, *The Principles of Psychology*, p. 532.

21. Ibid., p. 526.

22. Spencer's theories of progressive social evolution were founded on the premise that unconscious association formed the basis of the individual's adaptation to the environment, and thence of the race's progressive development as these 'forms of thought' were transmitted to offspring. Since relations to the environment once established are, he argues, 'uniform, invariable, incapable of being absent, or reversed, or abolished, they must be represented by irreversible, indestructible connections of ideas' (ibid., p. 580). The physiological unity of mind is taken as a guarantee of essential social continuity and development. George Eliot also believed, in a more moderate way, that physiology played a role in social evolution. Thus she was vehemently opposed to Buckle's theories in *History of Civilization in England* for he held that 'there is no such thing as race or hereditary transmission of qualities'. Haight (ed.), *The George Eliot Letters*, II, p. 415. Without this physiological transmission of experience, she believed, there could be no intrinsic moral advance in history.

23. Lewes, *The Physiology of Common Life*, II, p. 58.

24. Ibid., p. 58.

25. Her procedure in this matter does not represent a departure from scientific precision, but rather an extension of the principles of linguistic analogy that lay behind the development of physiological psychology. In founding their science, physiological psychologists did not create an entirely new vocabulary but rather drew on existing terms like current, channel, or groove, that often carried with them concealed assumptions concerning the formation of the natural and social worlds.

26. Lewes, *The Physiology of Common Life*, II, p. 59.

27. In her letter to R. H. Hutton concerning the writing of *Romola*, George Eliot observed, 'I believe there is scarcely a phrase, an incident, an allusion, that did not gather its value to me from its supposed subservience to my main artistic objects'. Haight (ed.), *The George Eliot Letters*, IV, pp. 96–7.

28. For detailed analysis of the parallels between the lives of Godfrey and Silas see David R. Carroll, '*Silas Marner*: Reversing the Oracles of Religion', *Literary Monographs*, 1 (1967), 165–200, Knoepflmacher, *George Eliot's Early Novels: The Limits of Realism*, Joseph Wiesenfarth, 'Demythologizing *Silas Marner*', *English Literary History*, 37 (1970), 226–44, and Bruce K. Martin, 'Similarity within Dissimilarity: The Dual Structure of *Silas Marner*', *Texas Studies in Language and Literature*, 14 (1973), 479–89.

29. Knoepflmacher, *George Eliot's Early Novels: The Limits of Realism*, p. 250.

30. Thus Knoepflmacher sees in *Silas Marner* a 'reconciliation through fable'. He concludes that 'In *Silas Marner* it is the "glue" of George Eliot's artistry which resolves the conflicts that had divided her previously', Knoepflmacher, *George Eliot's Early Novels: The Limits of Realism*, p. 254. Although the two disparate perspectives are finely balanced within the structure of the novel, I would argue they are not ultimately resolved. *George Eliot's Early Novels: The Limits of Realism*, p. 160–1.

Further Reading

George Eliot recorded her experiences of writing fiction in her letters and journals. Both provide evidence of ambitions for her novels, her dealings with publishers, her anxieties about public criticism, her strengths and weaknesses as a writer and the influence of G. H. Lewes. Students might start their survey of Eliot criticism with the following works:

Gordon S. Haight (ed.), *The George Eliot Letters*, 9 Vols (New Haven, CT: Yale University Press, 1954–5, 1978).

Margaret Harris and Judith Johnston (eds), *The Journals of George Eliot* (Cambridge: Cambridge University Press, 1999).

Joseph Wisenfarth (ed.), *George Eliot: A Writer's Notebook, 1854–79* (Virginia: Virginia University Press, 1985).

A perspective on the history of George Eliot criticism is of particular interest to students concerned with the realist fictional tradition, with the anti-Victorian reaction of the early twentieth century and also with the implication of gender in literary studies. There are several collections, which provide useful information, and the first chapter of Kirsten Brady's study is particularly striking:

Kirsten Brady, *George Eliot* (London: Macmillan Press – now Palgrave, 1992).

David Carroll (ed.), *George Eliot: The Critical Heritage* (London: Routledge & Kegan Paul, 1971).

Ronald Draper (ed.), *The Mill on the Floss and Silas Marner*, Casebook Series (London: Macmillan Press – now Palgrave, 1977).

Stuart Hutchinson, *George Eliot: Critical Assessments*, 4 Vols (London: Croom Helm, 1996).

Karen L. Pangallo, *Critical Responses to George Eliot* (London: Greenwood Press, 1994).

J. Russell Perkin, *A Reception History of George Eliot's Fiction* (London: AMI Press, 1990).

BIOGRAPHY

There are many biographies on Eliot. Among the most useful are:

Rosemary Ashton, *George Eliot: A Life* (London: Hamish Hamilton, 1996).

J.W. Cross, *George Eliot's Life as related in her Letters and Journals*, 3 Vols (Edinburgh: William Blackwood, 1885).

Gordon S. Haight, *George Eliot: A Biography* (Oxford: Clarendon Press, 1968).

Kathryn Hughes, *George Eliot: The Last Victorian* (London: Fourth Estate, 1998).

Ruby Redinger, *George Eliot: The Emergent Self* (London: Random House, 1975).

Jenny Uglow, *George Eliot* (London: Virago, 1987).

CRITICAL WORKS

Several critical studies place George Eliot's fiction in its historical context. Many of the works listed below are written from a feminist perspective.

Gillian Beer, *Darwin's Plots: Evolutionary Narratives in Darwin, George Eliot and Nineteenth Century Fiction* (London: Routledge & Kegan Paul, 1983).

Rosemarie Bodenheimer, *The Real Life of Mary Ann Evans: George Eliot, Her Letters and Fiction* (Ithaca, NY: Cornell University Press, 1994).

David Carroll, *George Eliot and the Conflict of Interpretation* (Cambridge: Cambridge University Press, 1992).

Simon Dentith, *George Eliot* (Brighton: Harvester, 1982).

Elizabeth Deedes Ermath, *George Eliot* (Boston: Twayne, 1985).

Suzanne Graver, *George Eliot and Community: A Study in Social Theory and Fictional Form* (Berkeley, CA: University of California Press, 1984).

Josephine McDonagh, *George Eliot* (Plymouth: Northcote, 1997).

Diana Postlewaite, *Making It Whole: A Victorian Circle and the Shape of their World* (Columbia: Ohio State University Press, 1984).

Bernard Semmel, *George Eliot and the Politics of National Inheritance* (New York: Oxford University Press, 1994).

Alexander Welsh, *George Eliot and Blackmail* (Cambridge, MA: Harvard University Press, 1985).

The contextual study can be expanded through the examination of the relation of George Eliot's work to various literary and artistic conventions and traditions:

Felicia Bonaparte, 'Carrying the word of the Lord to the Gentiles: *Silas Marner* and the translation of scripture into secular text', *Religion and Literature*, 23:2 (1991), 39–60.

Mary Ann Doody, 'George Eliot and the Eighteenth Century Novel', *Nineteenth-Century Fiction*, 35 (1980), 260–91.

Beryl Gray, *George Eliot and Music* (London: Macmillan Press – now Palgrave, 1989).

Joseph Wiesenfarth, *George Eliot's Myth Making Publisher* (Heidelberg: Carl Winter, 1977).
Judith Wilt, *Ghosts of the Gothic: Austen Eliot and Lawrence* (Princeton NJ: Princeton University Press, 1980).

George Eliot's life and novels have always proved of interest for psychological examination. Recently the speculations of nineteenth-century critics have been superseded by more complex readings:

Carolyn Dever, *Death and the Mother from Dickens to Freud* (Cambridge: Cambridge University Press, 1998).
Mary Jacobus, 'Hysterics Suffer Mainly from Reminiscences', *in Reading Women: Essays in Feminist Criticism* (New York: Columbia University Press, 1986), pp. 246–74.
Dianne Sadoff, *Monsters of Affection, Dickens, Eliot and Brontë on Fatherhood* (Baltimore: Johns Hopkins University Press, 1994).

The rise of feminist criticism has been one of the most important factors in the re-evaluation of George Eliot's work in the last thirty years. Eliot is a controversial figure with critics divided over her status as a feminist heroine, her attitude to the 'woman question' and whether her heroines are exemplars of female assertion:

Nina Auerbach, 'The Power of Hunger: Demonism and Maggie Tulliver', *Nineteenth-Century Fiction* , 30 (1975), 150–71.
Gillian Beer, *George Eliot* (Brighton: Harvester Press, 1986).
Sandra Gilbert and Susan Gubar, *The Madwoman in the Attic: the Woman Writer and the Nineteenth Century Literary Imagination* (New Haven, CT: Yale University Press, 1979).
Nancy K. Miller, 'Emphasis Added: Plots and Plausibilities in Women's Fiction', *PMLA* , 96:1 (1981), 36–48.
Diana Postlewaite, 'Of Maggie, Mothers, Monsters and Madonnas: Diving deep in *The Mill on the Floss*', *Women's Studies* , 20:3–4 (1992), 303–19.
Elaine Showalter, *A Literature of their Own* (Princeton, NJ: Princeton University Press, 1977).
Virginia Woolf, *The Common Reader* (London: Hogarth Press, 1925)

Finally, three recent essays draw heavily on historicist approaches:

Jules Law, 'Water Rights and the "'Crossing o' Breeds'": Chiastic Exchange in *The Mill on the Floss*', in Linda Shires (ed.), *Rewriting the Victorians: Theory, History and the Politics of Gender* (London: Routledge, 1992).
Margaret Homans, 'Dinah's Blush, Maggie's Arm: Class, Gender and Sexuality in George Eliot's Early novels', *Victorian Studies* , 36:2 (1995), 155–78.
K. M. Newton, 'Victorian Values and *Silas Marner*', in Gary Day (ed.), *Varieties of Victorianism* (London: Macmillan Press – now Palgrave, 1998), pp. 110–25.

Notes on Contributors

Terence Dawson lectures at the University of Singapore. He has published articles in journals such as *Modern Language Review, George Eliot Fellowship Review, New Comparsion* and *Seventeenth-Century French Studies*.

Joshua D. Esty is Assistant Professor at the University of Illinois (Urbana-Champaign). He has published essays on T. S. Eliot, James Joyce, Virginia Woolf and Samuel Beckett and is completing a book entitled *A Shrinking Island: Modernism and National Culture in England*.

Susan Fraiman teaches English at the University of Virginia. She is the author of *Unbecoming Women: British Women Writers and the Novel of Development* (1993) and has published in *Critical Inquiry, PMLA, Feminist Studies* and *ALH*. She is currently working on *Cool Men and the Second Sex: Reading Left Intellectuals*.

Mary Jacobus is Professor of English at the University of Cambridge (previously Anderson Professor of English and Women's Studies at Cornell University). Her books include *Romanticism, Writing and Sexual Difference* (1989), *First Thing: Essays on Literature, Art and Psychoanalysis* (1986), and *Psychoanalysis and the Scene of Reading* (1999).

Peggy R. F. Johnstone has published a number of articles on George Eliot's fiction in journals such as *Literature and Psychology, Mosaic* and *University of Hartford Studies in Literature*.

José Angel García Landa has published articles in journals such as *Papers in Language and Literature*.

J. Hillis Miller is Professor of English and Comparative Literature at the University of California, Irvine. His books include *The Form of Victorian Fiction* (1968), *Thomas Hardy* (1970), *Fiction and Repetition* (1982) and *The Ethics of Reading* (1987).

Jeff Nunokawa teaches English at Princeton University. He is currently finishing a book about the fantasy of manageable desire in the work of Oscar Wilde.

Jim Reilly lectured at Queen Mary and Westfield College, University of London. His publications include *Shadowtime: History and*

Representation in Hardy, Conrad and George Eliot (1993) as well as contributions to *Joseph Conrad* (1996), *Literature and Culture in Britain, 1: 1900–1929* (1993).

Sally Shuttleworth is Professor of Modern Literature at the University of Sheffield. She is the author of *George Eliot and Nineteenth-Century Science: The Make-Believe of a Beginning* (1984) and *Charlotte Brontë and Victorian Psychology* (1996), and editor of numerous volumes including *Embodied Selves: An Anthology of Psychological Texts* (1998) with Jenny Bourne Taylor.

Index